Also By P. F. Kluge

The Day That I Die

Eddie and the Cruisers

Season for War

MacArthur's Ghost

THE EDGE OF
PARADISE

THE EDGE OF
PARADISE

America in Micronesia

P. F. KLUGE

RANDOM HOUSE NEW YORK

Library of Congress Cataloging-in-Publication Data
Kluge, P.F. (Paul Frederick)
The edge of paradise : America in Micronesia / by P. F. Kluge.
p.   cm.
ISBN 0-394-58178-4
1. Micronesia—Relations—United States.   2. United States—
—Relations—Micronesia. 3. Micronesia—Social life and customs.
4. Micronesia—Social conditions. 5. Micronesia—Economic
conditions.   I. Title.
DU500.K58—1991   996.5—dc20   90-53145

Manufactured in the United States of America
98765432
First Edition

Book design by J. K. Lambert

The ends of the earth, the depths of
the sea, the darkness of time,
you have chosen all three.

E. M. Forster
"A Letter to Madan Blanchard"

I

PROLOGUE: THE DAY THAT HE DIED

fter he died—and dying the way he did—people in the islands agreed that Lazarus Salii was a moody fellow. Sometimes he sought people out but more often, especially toward the end, he avoided them, though they were his constituents and he their president. He worked mornings, napped afternoons, prowled and brooded into the night. He stayed up late, well into the wee hours, on the phone to Washington, or reading books on World War II, or watching tapes of Muhammad Ali's great fights. When nothing else could please him, he turned to Ali, the taunting dancing champion, in whose flash and wit, and triumphs over strong men, he surely saw something of himself. Toward morning, he'd catch some sleep, curling up on a living-room couch. Then, at sunrise, he'd emerge for a solitary car ride through the streets of Koror, the main settlement of the Republic of Palau, a flotilla of Pacific islands south of Guam, east of the Philippines; small, beautiful, troubled places, escapes for outsiders coming in, traps for those who stay too long.

If you dream of islands, dream of them at dawn, on the border between night and day, sleep and waking; dream of them when they are cool and hushed, before heat and light chase the dream away. Like all tropical places, Palau is best at dawn, a beguiling hour of returns and departures, with dogs and roosters stirring, old women—*mechases*—headed to taro patches, men tinkering with nets, spears, outboards. This shaded nuanced time is precious, for the sun comes up at full glare, poaching what it does not fry; the humidity rolls in as regularly, and almost as wetly, as the tide. Cherish the edges of the day, survive the middle. Lazarus Salii's appearance at dawn was nothing to be remarked upon, no more than that of a small town mayor cruising a main street—there are only fourteen thousand Palauans in Palau, after all—the president of the Republic, driving slowly around his bailiwick, Saturday morning, August 20, 1988.

Friday had been busy for Salii, and Sunday promised more of the same. A political season was just opening, and this in a place where politics was preoccupying, an obsessive blend of war, sport, and possibly religion, the ultimate and, sadly, the only game in town. Salii was a willing player. He was the president of the Republic, an office he'd fought hard to win and wanted to keep. Or so it seemed. Sitting at lunch with a visitor from Guam—an admiral—a few weeks before, he'd sounded like an incumbent, poised to run and be reelected. He'd spoken with an urgency that, later, seemed ominous. "You must realize," he said, "that I cannot *not* be president." On Friday, Salii had met with his brother Carlos, a local lawyer, whom he planned to send in search of crucial expatriate votes from Palauans living in the Mariana Islands, on Saipan and Guam, and in Honolulu. That same day, he'd talked with Polycarp Basilius, a powerful local businessman whose support he was anxious to confirm, and spoken by phone to John Ngiraked, the tiny republic's minister of foreign affairs and Salii's nominal campaign manager, whose loyalty was reported to be wavering. On Sunday, he was scheduled to announce his candidacy for reelection to supporters at a one o'clock meeting at the Ombaul Restaurant in the basement of the Koror Hotel. Already his backers were killing pigs, catching fish, preparing taro, tapioca, rice.

Meanwhile, there was Saturday, an island Saturday, with no place to go and not much to do and barely enough road to make an aimless ride worth taking. Salii's morning drive first took him through Koror, a place he'd seen change utterly since his boyhood. In pre–World War II days, when the Japanese had ruled the islands, Koror had been a handsome tropical city, with well-built concrete homes and temples, shrines and arches, busy shops, neatly laid-out streets and gardens. The Americans had bombed and razed most of that. Among the ruins of Koror, its mossy steps, bullet-pocked foundations, run-over gardens, the American-era town had arisen: Quonset huts and prefab schoolrooms, weathered wood and rusted tin. The place felt like a ruined estate, abandoned by owners and overseers, inherited by local workers, newly liberated and somewhat at a loss. In recent years, with money coming in, Palauans built solid, concrete houses. Air conditioners, sewers, paved roads, and shopping malls upgraded the place without changing its essential nature, ramshackle and nondescript, a disappointment to visitors who expected thatch roofs, breezy porches, and raffish charm.

Lazarus Salii had seen Koror go from a Japanese colonial capital to district center of the U.S. Trust Territory of Pacific Islands to provisional capital of the Republic of Palau. And he was president. But of what, really? A crowded contentious settlement in the middle of what everyone had told him was one of the most beautiful places on earth. Unspoiled. Never change it. They said it and they left. They did not live in Koror. He did.

Driving down the main road, through a ridge-top area known as "topside" since navy days, Salii gradually left Koror behind. He crossed the bridge that connects Koror with Palau's largest island, Babelthuap. Here, the road lifts out of mangrove swamps and winds up into the hills of Airai, red-clay grass and pandanus highlands surrounding the airport that links Palau with Guam and Manila. This is where you have your best view of the islands, immediate confirmation that the trip was worth taking, that there are lagoons this blue, hillsides this green, air this hot and greenhouse smelling, a horizon of sea and islands on all sides. You have not come too late, it is still here, not gone, not yet, the islands say. But do they say this to their sons and daughters, to the ones who watch the planes arrive from Guam and Manila? Tourists take pleasure in a sign outside a local hotel that informs them that they are 1,065 miles from Manila, 1,900 miles from Tokyo, 2,500 miles from Bangkok, 2,700 miles from Sydney, 4,750 miles from Honolulu, 6,300 miles from Moscow, and 10,600 miles from New York. But what pleasure—what frustration—in such distances for someone like Lazarus Salii? What solace is there in this landscape? What prospects for deliverance? Another damn enchanted evening: punch line to an old joke about living on islands.

North of the airport, the green flanks of Babelthuap roll on for more than twenty miles, coming to a point that gestures across Kossol Reef toward Kayangel Atoll. South, beyond the rooftops and causeways of Koror, are the beginnings of Palau's Rock Islands—"floating garden islands," in the tourist brochures—two hundred emerald islets, a realm of coves and channels, hidden beaches, and marine lakes. Farther south, out of sight, is Peleliu, island of Bloody Nose Ridge, rusted landing craft and war-littered caves, famed for the savagery of the battle fought between Japanese and Americans during World War II and, more recently, for the high quality of its marijuana, grown in sawed-off oil barrels, smuggled to Guam in Styrofoam coolers, in hollowed-out baseball bats, in the bellies of frozen fish. Further still, outside the main reef, lies Angaur, pancake flat and pitted by phosphate mining. Salii had been born on Angaur in 1936, in time to be given a Japanese middle name, Eitaro—shortened to Eta—and to see Japanese and American planes skirmishing in the skies above his home island. In a week, he'd be back there.

By midmorning, President Salii had returned home, but not for long. He received a call from Haruo Willter, an aide who'd spent the last eight months in Washington and had arrived in Palau late the preceeding night. They could meet at any time, Willter said, implying no urgency. "Come over now," Salii said, "and we'll go someplace."

Willter's job was to report on the latest episode in a drama, or melodrama, that had dragged on for twenty years. In 1969 Salii, a senator in the Congress of Micronesia, had initiated future political status negotiations intended to end the U.S. administration of the Trust Territory of Pacific Islands. By now, the other Trust Territory islands had settled their fates, made their deals with the Americans. The Northern Marianas was a U.S. commonwealth. The Marshall Islands was a republic. Ponape, Truk, Yap, and Kusaie were bundled together as the Federated States of Micronesia. But Salii's own home islands of Palau remained in turmoil. Six times a majority of Palauans had endorsed the Compact of Free Association, which would grant Palau self-government, assign defense rights to the United States for fifty years, and bring in about $1 billion of U.S. funds over fifteen years. But a majority of Palauans—73 percent in one vote—wasn't enough. Palau's constitution contained a clause banning nuclear materials from the islands. The constitution clashed with the compact. To be adopted, the compact needed a 75 percent vote; that would give it the same force as a constitutional amendment. And, close as he came, that 75 percent eluded Salii, just as it had eluded his predecessor, Palau's first president, Haruo Remeliik.

Salii welcomed Willter that Saturday morning. He smiled, shook Willter's hand, and the two went for a drive in Willter's new Subaru. As they drove through Koror, across the Babelthuap Bridge, into the hills around Airai, they discussed Washington politics. Willter had nothing new to report: the Compact of Free Association was still bogged down, buffeted by criticism of the document itself and of Salii's management of increasingly bitter campaigns to secure its approval. They then turned to Palau politics, the upcoming campaign, candidates declared and undeclared. They discussed people, not issues, though there were serious matters at hand: future relations with the United States, government budgets, possible military bases. They were Palauans and they both knew that what an island election turned on wasn't what you believed but who you were. Island politics were especially personal. Salii knew this. He'd been through it before.

The two men headed back to town, stopping only once, at a gas station owned by a Salii supporter, Hokkons Baules.

"What's the news?" Baules asked, stepping over to the Subaru. Seeing the two men, informally dressed, Baules thought they looked like they were off to play tennis.

"Nothing, we're just talking," Salii replied. "Haruo has a new car and we might as well drive around."

At the end of their ride, Salii reminded Willter of the Sunday campaign rally. "Don't forget to come," he said. "Go and rest. You look tired. Don't forget—tomorrow, around noon."

▲ ▲ ▲

Whatever charm outsiders find in thatch roofs and rattan walls, wide verandas under slowly turning fans, Palauans are practical people who know the value of a place that is air-conditioned and typhoon-proof. At the end of a road in the Koror hamlet of Tiull, bordering a mangrove swamp, President Salii's home was comfortable, roomy, and concrete. Modern. It could almost have been mistaken for the California embassy. Almost, but not quite. Out back stood one of those hammered-together shelters no island home is complete without: a place where people sit and talk and drink, hang laundry, barbecue fish, watch traffic. Salii's wife Christina was sitting there when Haruo Willter dropped her husband off around ten o'clock. A handsome woman, Tina Salii had much to endure in her marriage to the moody, rambunctious Salii. She shared, however, some of her husband's shrewdness and sharpness of tongue, and frustration with Palau. Complimented on being the first lady of Palau, she'd been heard to retort "First lady of *what*?" On this morning, she was feeling a bit lazy, lingering over coffee and cigarettes. Her husband, having quit smoking, forbade others from smoking in the house, so Tina sat outside with her maid, taking her time about getting to the beauty shop she operated. With the president inside, Tina Salii and her Filipina maid cooked a fish on an outdoor grill. A search of local markets had failed to turn up crab, one of the president's favorite foods, so he remained in the house, while the others ate without him.

Salii's driver was helping at the grill. Around one o'clock they heard a sound like a rock hitting the roof of the house.

"Hey, what was that?" Tina Salii asked the driver.

"What?" The driver stood there until she gestured for him to check around the house. He sauntered around the building. He didn't go inside. He returned, fork in hand, with nothing but a shrug. Twenty minutes later, Tina Salii walked into the kitchen, pot in hand. She saw her husband, sitting in his chair, head forward, "like he fell asleep watching TV." Approaching, she saw blood coming from his nose.

"Your nose is bleeding again," she said. But he was motionless. She nudged him and saw the gun, the .357 magnum, at his feet. Then it began: the rush of phone calls, the wail of sirens, and the rush of cars to the hospital. Rumors: the president has had an accident, a stroke, a heart attack, been shot, shot himself maybe, maybe badly, maybe dead. People lined up to donate blood while doctors pounded Salii's chest in vain. And then: a Korean pathologist, brought down from Guam to do the autopsy; the long-distance phone calls, the obituary announcements; the story on an inside page of *The New York Times,* and a tiny follow-up in *USA Today.* The arrival of dignitaries from Washington, resolutions and solemn mourning mingling with poolside quarrels about what happened and who was to blame. A formal ceremony at the legislature, his enemies' stronghold, where Christina Salii was barely able to contain her anger. And then: the viewing of his remains, puffy under coffin glass, a divot replacing the hair that a bullet transplanted onto his office wall. Finally, the burial on Angaur. His funeral, and mine.

II

GAMBIER, OHIO: THE REPROACH OF SUNSET

hen word came of my old friend's death—first pronounced a murder, then a suicide—I was on my way to an island quite different from the one where he died, but an island nonetheless. I was returning to Kenyon College, the same place I'd graduated from in 1964, to teach fiction writing. And it occurred to me, while I was mourning someone who had died half the world away, it occurred to me among the orchards and corn fields, dirt roads and trestle bridges of Knox County, Ohio, there on that green and pleasant hillside campus, that the place where I taught and the place where Salii had died had island qualities in common: isolation, intensity, passionate attachments, politics to the point of exhaustion. They were both places where everything that happened, no matter what the stated issue, whether a debate on the curriculum, say, or on the Compact of Free Association, everything that happened could be, had to be, taken personally. That was the good news about them, and the bad news too. There was another thing about islands, whether in the central Pacific or middle America. As a matter

of pride and faith, the people who lived on islands constructed seawalls against despair: the belief that their island was the center of the world, the center of the universe, the most important place. Why else would they be on it?

There was a time when I thought Lazarus Salii would do great things in the islands. I would be there too, working with him, for him, whatever. I just wanted to be around, because Lazarus Salii had magic. He could take conquered, colonized misadministered places and make them proud. He could transform remote, welfarish backwaters and turn them into lively, prosperous communities. He could make small islands, dots on the map of the Pacific, feel like the center of the world. Or so I thought. He was my friend—my friend in paradise—and nothing else I did counted as much as what I did with him. No other job was as important, no matter what it paid or where it led; no other friendship, no love of a woman could stand in the way of our matchless alliance. So I thought.

And now he was dead, in murky circumstances, and I sat in Ohio, dear, complacent Ohio, red-pencilling my students' work (how many ways can you slice a *B*?), jogging cidery lanes, cobbling away at my own stubborn, vulnerable novel, which suddenly felt irrelevant. Distracted and divided, I sat on one island and wondered about the other. Suicide comes as a reproach to those who remain behind. I felt that now. I resisted the impulse to throw over my Kenyon appointment and fly off to Salii's funeral. A funeral was a funeral, after all, a round-trip ticket was two thousand dollars, and I was not an official mourner. I talked tough to myself. What was I going to do? Raise Lazarus? Before the investigation was finished, in that odd time when suicide and murder both were contemplated, I asked myself which I hoped it would be. A gunman coming in off the road, or out of the mangrove swamp? Or a last moment, alone in his study, his wife and maid and driver eating outside, raising a gun to his head?

Copies of his obituary arrived in my mailbox outside the English department office, an autopsy report tucked in among sample text-books, class lists, campus announcements: Newt Gingrich coming to town, Ladysmith Black Mambazo in concert. President Reagan noted the passing of "a Palauan patriot." Secretary of State George Shultz remembered "a leader of great vision." Less flatteringly, a magazine suggested that those who live by the sword die by the sword. It all found its way to me, piece by piece. Letters from Saipan and Honolulu, clippings from Washington, tangled with announcements from the Gay/Straight Alliance, rides-wanted-to-NYC at Christmas break, items of L. L. Bean clothing lost and found. In Palau, I left a piece of myself behind, which was either too little or too much. I'm not good as I ought to be at making clean breaks. I sat in my office, late afternoons in the latitudes of liberal arts, and thought of Salii, buried now on Angaur. It bothered me, knowing that he wasn't out there anymore, waiting, pacing, scheming: that his island restlessness was ended. I wondered how he'd died and why, surrounded by enemies. I wondered if his worst enemy hadn't been himself. I wondered if things might have been different, if I'd been there; wondered about a late night phone call from him, a few months before. Morbidly, I pictured the settling of the grave, the decomposition, the fast working of the heat. Being buried in the tropics had always terrified me, moldering in that dark, primal greenhouse warmth. Shuddering, I forced myself to put things in order, first things first, the way I told my students to lay out their stories and, in that way, go back to the beginning.

◄ II ►

I felt uncomfortable about joining the Peace Corps. Sometimes, I still do. A children's crusade, I thought, an act of missionary arrogance, a naïve parade of newly minted liberal arts graduates. But I had no choice. It was 1967. I was twenty-five, I was a Ph.D., I was 1A—a prime candidate for Vietnam. I'd applied for Ethiopia and Turkey, where I thought the women would be interesting. I was assigned to a clutch of islands I'd never heard of. Micronesia. No one I knew had heard of Micronesia. It was only after I'd received the offer that I noticed the recruiting ads in newspapers and on campus bulletin boards: a shipwreck-cartoon of an island, a patch of sand and palm, a headline that proclaimed: THE PEACE CORPS IS GOING TO PARADISE.

Micronesia! I can still picture my friends' reactions, stares, shrugs, hugs that seemed to say: *Remember him as he was.* It wasn't Ethiopia or Turkey, not by a long shot. Polynesia? Now that was something people could get behind, Gauguin, Robert Louis Stevenson, James Michener. The South Pacific! Or even Melanesia, dark, mean, aboriginal, anthropological places like the Solomons and New Guinea. Headhunters and cannibals. But Micronesia? It was barely on the map. Go try to find it. A swatch of dots that might be islands, or a printer's errors, out west of Hawaii. If your finger landed there, in a game of spin-the-globe, you'd spin the globe again. Micronesia? A bit much. Sure, small is beautiful but . . . this was out of sight. Maybe I should rethink my misgivings about Vietnam, my relatives implied.

Even the names were a tangle. Micronesia, i.e., small islands, was a sort of geographical umbrella, roughly congruent with the area's current political title, the Trust Territory of Pacific Islands, a United Nations trusteeship administered by the United States. We'd captured the place from the Japanese who'd run it under a League of Nations mandate. There were three main groups of islands—the Marshalls, the Marianas, the Carolines—over two thousand islands in all, half the land mass of Rhode Island, scattered over an area the size of the continental United States. A population of less than one hundred thousand that could be comfortably seated in the Pasadena Rose Bowl. Nine mutually unintelligible local languages, plus smatterings of German, Japanese, English, the conquerors' tongues. A shaky, artificial, lopsided economy based on scrap metal (declining), copra (stagnant), fish (caught by foreigners), and government (U.S. subsidized) . . . an archipelago of Lilliputs.

At first it bothered me, that I wasn't headed to a more important place, a major culture, some place people had heard of. Micronesia felt perverse. So far, so small. Off the edge of the earth. But after a while, the idea of going there appealed to me. I did some homework.

"The Spanish came for God, the Germans came for glory, the Japanese came for gold, the Americans came for good." That was the islands' history in brief. While genuflecting in the direction of eventual self-government, the United States had not lost sight of the area's military importance. Sure, most of Micronesia's islands were obscure, but there was "blood on the reef" at places like Kwajalein, Truk, Saipan,

Tinian, Peleliu, and Angaur. What we had conquered, we didn't want to reconquer. We wanted to keep other nations out and we had the power to do just that. Though there were eleven postwar U.N. trusteeships, the Trust Territory of Pacific Islands was in a class by itself, a "strategic trusteeship," the only one. The other places were run by the General Assembly, through the Trusteeship Council. But the Trust Territory of Pacific Islands, though it reported to the Trusteeship Council, was ultimately subject to the Security Council, where the United States had the right to veto any change that conflicted with its war-won prerogatives. There'd been a time, right after the war, when the Pentagon pushed for outright annexation of the islands but then we decided to play by U.N. rules, pledging to promote independence or self-government . . . someday . . . Meanwhile, we kept a tight grip on the place.

For its first twenty years, the Americans had run a torpid, caretaker operation, headed by a politically appointed high commissioner and staffed by a mixed bag of ex-marines, cashiered politicos, exiled bureaucrats, research anthropologists, miscellaneous island lovers, and—from the middle levels on down—by elite Micronesians. Much of the budget—$5 million in 1960—was absorbed by expatriate salaries and staff housing. But then, in the mid-sixties, things had started to change. Embarrassed by critical reports from U.N. visiting missions, by journalistic descriptions of the "rust territory," the Kennedy administration started rolling up shirtsleeves and raising budgets, replacing derelicts with can-do guys. If the United States wanted to retain control of this part of the Pacific, it would need more than invocations of blood on the reef. The locals would have to go along with . . . well . . . whatever kind of relationship felt right to us. It was hearts-and-minds time in the Pacific and that is how the Peace Corps came to paradise, with a saturation program designed to show what the Peace Corps could do when the host-country government was basically American. "The Peace Corps intends to alter substantially in a relatively short period of time, say three to five years, the twenty-year record of neglect and dismal achievement," one memo crowed. That, it turned out, was a mistake. The Peace Corps oversold itself enormously, with a Stalingrad of good intentions, over nine hundred volunteers at one point. If the same ratio went to India, someone joked, there would be no young people left in the United States. What the arithmetic really worked out to, I learned later, was that if the same ratio went to India, there'd be five million Peace Corps volunteers there. In its nonaligned wisdom, India satisfied itself with sixty-five of America's finest.

The groups of volunteers who came to Micronesia were numbered, something like military historians number the days around an invasion, D-Day Plus One, and so forth. I was part of Micronesia Five, but there were still some Micronesia One volunteers around when I completed training and arrived on the island of Saipan, in the Northern Marianas. Finishing up their stints, they regaled us with tales of what it was like, having been the first to hit the island beaches: weeks of receptions, invitations, parties. Everyone knew their names. "A new kind of American" was arriving. That was the impression. Just as the Spanish had yielded to the Germans, the Germans to the Japanese, the Japanese to the Americans, now the American period itself was mutating: from naval administration to Department of the Interior control and now . . . Kennedy's children, who spoke a little of the local language, shunned automobiles, moved into beat-up village houses, enthusiastically sampled local foods. Oh, they'd had a good war all right, the men and women in Micronesia One, but by the time I arrived the honeymoon was over.

People were wising up. Many of the career administrators in the Trust Territory government felt that the Peace Corps made them look bad. Some of them were ex-marines, blood-on-the-reef irredentists, quick to resent the long-haired, pot-smoking, draft dodging hippies who now cluttered what used to be a simple, neo-colonial landscape. Peace Corps volunteers hassled them. The architects didn't order building supplies through government channels, the lawyers encouraged local clients to sue the government. Down in Yap, some guys showed up with island tattoos, chewed betelnut. A girl or two went topless. What the Peace Corps brought wasn't a new era or a new regime so much as another level of American presence, a stratum of cut-rate Americans, cheaper by the dozen, a buffer state between the Trust Territory government and the locals.

The Saipanese—all of the Micronesians—were less impressed as well. Game and likable as the volunteers might be, they were youngsters in a place that valued seniority, innocent and unarmed in a place that respected clout and—surprise!—they were poor in a society that esteemed wealth. That was the crushing lesson: *Voluntary poverty did not impress.* "Living on the level of the people" came off as naïve, as downright wacky, when it was from that level people were trying to escape. We learned local languages while locals learned English. We hitchhiked while they shot by us in brand new cars. We wore zoris— rubber thonged sandals—while they aspired to white Bally loafers. The conflict was basic, classic, poignant. The Peace Corps worried about American military bases while the islands' brightest kids rushed off to Guam to enlist in the very war many of us had come to Micronesia to avoid. We worried about identity—theirs, not ours—culture, ecology, the life-giving reefs, the unspoiled islands, dying handicrafts, and clean lagoons, while locals pondered fast roads, new cars, big hotels, and a ticket to Honolulu.

It didn't take long for the Peace Corps staff to figure out that volunteers did best outside of district centers—modern settlements—like Saipan or Koror. The farther away, the better. Thus, most Peace Corps stints combined the charms of spearfishing on outlying atolls with long, lonely battles on behalf of sanitary waterseal toilets, and hours of teaching English in a baking classroom right out of *The Bridge on the River Kwai.* I, thank God, escaped all that.

My billet was in the Northern Marianas on Saipan, headquarters of the Trust Territory government, an office right down the hall from the high commissioner. Capitol Hill, the place was called, although it was Mount Tagpochau on maps and "Mount Olympus" to the locals. It commanded a view of the island, the invasion beaches on the west side, Japanese bunkers, spiked and gutted, pointing out toward rusting American tanks and landing craft. On the south were airstrips, Kobler and Isley, and, across the three-mile strait, Tinian Island, and the airstrips that the *Enola Gay* took off from, Hiroshima-bound. Saipan's west side was rocky, a moonscape of limestone cliffs that climbed toward the north end of the island, Marpi District. That's where the World War II fighting ended, with mass-suicides off Suicide and Banzai cliffs. It was still an eerie, death-haunted place. At night, Saipanese crept through fences, risking arms and hands to strip bronze and copper casings off of live shells that had been stockpiled a quarter century before for the invasion of Japan. In Marpi, you could crawl into caves, forage for bullets and mess kits, sake bottles and skulls.

I was a "high-caste" volunteer, editing a quarterly magazine, the *Micronesian Reporter,* traveling at will—and on per diem—through a swath of islands that were going to be my personal Yoknapatawpha. I saw the Marshall Islands, palm-fringed atolls traumatized by nuclear testing at Bikini and Eniwetok. I hiked the rain forests of Ponape, drank in the famously squalid bar of the Truk Trading Company. When Lee Marvin came, scouting locations for something that was later called *Hell in the Pacific,* I accompanied him on a beery tour of Saipan, searching out the place where he'd been wounded, shot in the ass he claimed, twenty-five years before. On Tinian, I could find my way down baking empty runways to the bomb pits where they'd loaded the *Enola Gay.* On Yap, I visited the village of Rull, where topless locals had been known to throw stones at Japanese tourists. And then there was Palau, where an air of conspiracy, ambition, and sensuality hit you the minute you stepped off the plane. A steamy, movie set of a place, cameras ready, actors clamoring, everything in place, and its script still waiting to be written.

Palauans had a reputation. Other Micronesians found them pushy, cocky, arrogant, and opportunistic. Americans said they were the Jews of the Pacific: hustling, entrepreneurial—or the Irish: talky, charming, political—or the Chinese: hustling and entrepreneurial again. They led the other districts in athletics, in scholarships, in government appointments; also, in barmaids, conmen, litigants, and lawyers. There were plenty of them on Saipan—too many, the Saipanese said. They attended schools, poured drinks. They pushed papers on Capitol Hill, which is where I met Lazarus Salii.

The best part of the *Micronesian Reporter*—and the only way of getting some island voices in the magazine—was a long front-of-book interview section, much like *Playboy*'s. Lots of head shots. I was looking for a lively Micronesian voice. So many of them said little, or clowned, or catered to their questioner, or kept their best words for closing time in bars, with Jim Reeves on the jukebox and bottles breaking out in the parking lot. Someone recommended Salii, a young Palauan who'd graduated from the University of Hawaii, spent some time back in Palau, and was now doing something or other in the Trust Territory personnel office. ("They had him grading job examinations," someone later told me. "I'll never forget the look on his face.")

Salii was a dark man of medium height with the sort of chunky body you could tell was going to bother him someday. His voice, low and hoarse, had some of the Brooklynisms he'd picked up from Jesuit priests; he'd talk about how things were "gonna" be. His face was what you watched. No inscrutability, no island coyness here. His frown was the essence of worry, his glare was all-out contempt, and his smile, when it broke through, was every good joke.

The interview was no barn-burner. He offered sensible, temperate criticism of a government that wasn't used to hearing it, at least not in print and not from Micronesians who, by god, worked at headquarters! What people noticed was Salii's assumption—not insistence, but assumption—that Micronesians had the right to decide what became of this trusteeship, whose days were numbered. The islands belonged to them, not to the U.S. or the U.N., and so would the government. It wasn't a radical argument, it wasn't made in anger. Sovereignty, self-determination, self-government: surely there was nothing dangerous in all this, nothing that Americans could fail to understand. No? Then let's get on with it! Sooner or later, Americans were going to have to talk about the future of these islands. They were going to have to acknowledge that the people they administered—their wards—had the right to say yes or no: to independence, to territorial status, to military bases and missile test sites. That was what Salii insisted upon, a role for the islanders. A role for himself. When the game started, he was going to be there.

Salii was brisk and businesslike. So was I. It wasn't until later I realized that we were destined to be friends. Just as my Peace Corps stint was ending, Salii called me to the Congress of Micronesia, where he'd become a senator from Palau. I hadn't seen much of him since the interview appeared, though I was aware he'd gotten some copies for use in a political campaign back home. He wasn't much for easy socializing. You heard from him when he wanted something. Maybe this was Palauan opportunism. Or some combination of arrogance and shyness. An awkwardness with friendship. I suspected this, because I sensed the same thing in myself.

The old Congress of Micronesia—which was torched a few years later, when the Trust Territory was splitting up—was a couple of military-surplus buildings perched on a limestone crag above the upper-crust housing area on Capitol Hill. Low on money, low on power, high on noise-making, it drew most of its members from the Micronesians who worked for the Trust Territory government. What pleasure they took in calling their bosses into hearings, grilling them about pay-scales, promotions, waste! This gave Congress the air of one of those youth-takes-over-days in which bright-eyed students play at being mayors and city councilmen. Still, something was up and Salii was right in the middle of it. He headed the Future Political Status Commission. Everybody granted that the U.S. trusteeship would have to end someday, but no one knew when, or how, or what would follow it. Annexation by the United States, a territory like Guam, just to the south, or like American Samoa? Commonwealth, like Puerto Rico? Statehood? Independence?

Salii and the other members had traveled from Samoa to the Virgin Islands, taking notes which he halfheartedly suggested I might want to read sometime. But what was needed now, he said, was a short statement, sexy and eloquent, a way of capturing the United States' attention. A statement of what?

He laid it out for me, in about five minutes, and then he walked away, leaving me with a naked yellow legal pad. He liked doing that, I later learned. Wham, bam, thank you ma'am, the destiny of Micronesia. Take all the time you need, he indicated. He made it sound like a challenge. Stay with me if you can, I'll be moving fast on this one, he implied. I stayed with him for the next twenty years, in a relationship that exhilarated me at times, depressed me at others. I wondered about it. In everything else I wrote—books, scripts, magazine articles—I worked in a measured, disciplined way, three pages a day or five, pacing myself, planning for the long haul, realizing that each day's increment was a fraction of the total manuscript I aimed for. Discipline, not inspiration, were what counted. Stamina. I watched my writing the way I watched my drinking, not wanting to wake up in a strange place, hung over, wondering what happened the night before. Salii was the one exception. Something clicked between us. For him I went all out, drained the bottle, closed the bar, finished the document he wanted in one sitting, service ace, never worrying about the number of words, or pages, or hours.

In fact, it took about an hour, words and music, and it was his doing as much as mine, the Statement of Intent, which later was compared to the Declaration of Independence and Africa's Lusaka Manifesto. There was a dash of history, conquest upon conquest, war after war. The early colonizing powers. Then a glance at the U.S. record in Micronesia, with some pointed references to the U.N. trusteeship agreement, which obliged the United States to offer "self-government or independence." Then, the assertion that the islands belonged to Micronesians, after all, and so did the responsibility for governing them. The choice was theirs. And what they chose was . . . tricky. The Micronesians said they'd like to negotiate a relationship of "free association" with the United States. The islanders would write their constitution, control their lands, run their government, and have the right to end their relationship with America, the right—you could almost see the Pentagon swallowing hard—to secede. The United States would be granted defense rights in exchange for an unspecified amount of money. And, if free association didn't work out, the Micronesians would go for the only other worthy alternative: outright independence.

Never before, never since, have I seen anything I'd written so please a reader. A secret weapon, a manifesto! But it wasn't what the Statement of Intent said. Salii had left lots of crucial questions undecided. The free association he talked about was a compromise between heart and head; between the desire for independence and the realities of a tiny, sluggish, neo-colonial economy. There was no way of knowing what free association would amount to or where it would lead. Was it an end in itself? Or was it a temporary status, something that might lead toward eventual independence? Or gravitate, instead, toward closer ties with the United States? Free association was vague, open-ended, subject to later change. It wasn't the end of the game, just a beginning. And the whole issue of U.S. military rights was undecided. How much was the United States willing to pay for the so-called "right of denial": the promise that no other powers would be permitted in the islands? What about existing U.S. facilities, like the Kwajalein Missile Range in the Marshalls? What about possible new installations, naval bases in Palau, airbases on Tinian? How much money? How many years?

Salii seemed to feel that the negotiations would be brisk, straightforward, quid pro quo. Smart men could always reach an agreement and he was smart. I had my doubts. But the important thing was that the islanders were taking the initiative. They weren't going to let the decision be made in Washington. Here they were, taking on the Americans. That was the drama of it. And I was coming along. Salii asked me to stick around a few months, past the end of my Peace Corps service, to join him and some other congressmen on a tour of the districts, holding village meetings, trumpeting the Statement of Intent. Starting, he said, in Palau. I could sense the excitement in him; we were building a nation, or something.

The boat rides, the village arrivals, the feasts and meetings, the nights in men's houses and municipal dispensaries, joking and bullshitting and dreaming: those next weeks stayed with me for years. Looking back on them, I think they were what Peace Corps service should have been like. For that matter, they were what writing, politics, life itself should be: the close-up knowledge, the behind-the-scenes struggles, the passionate campaign, a little place taking on a giant, going against the longest possible odds.

It wasn't all fun. The village meetings were difficult. People pleaded ignorance, prayed for caution, asked for time. They wanted independence. They worried about money. They feared change. The Trust Territory government wasn't great but it was bearable. Getting closer to the Americans was scary; moving farther away from them was scarier still.

Sometimes the meetings went way off track. One man held forth at length, insisting on restitution for a breadfruit tree that had been bombed a quarter century before. Sometimes my friends contradicted themselves. In one village, they'd proclaim the need for a strong central government that could work to keep the islands unified. In the next village, they'd prescribe a loose federation, reserving maximum power at the local level. They were improvising, feeling their way, yawning, stumbling. But every now and then, I found myself in the middle of a special moment. Often, Salii provided it. There was an afternoon in Truk, on the island of Tol. Sweaty and tired, Salii got up to wrangle with a question that had no answer: the prospect of military presence in the islands. Would his proposed free association change things?

"If the United States wants to pull out of Okinawa tomorrow and come to Tol, we have no choice," he began. "I'm old enough to remember the last war and I know what war means and I have spoken out against their coming. This proposal of ours doesn't necessarily mean they can't come in. It gives us a voice in the matter. Now, we can't say *anything* about it. Do you want to continue under the current system or change it?"

While he paused to have his words turned into Trukese, I glanced around the room: a hundred men inside a meeting house, dirt floored, thatch roofed, open at the sides. Outside, dozens more were underneath the eaves, in the shade. On a nearby hillside, some old men and women sat underneath a mango tree. Farther uphill, a woman knelt by a stream, pounding wash against a slab of rock. Salii resumed.

"We have seen how the military worked in Kwajalein and Eniwetok and Bikini. They used their legal power to acquire land with nominal payment. If we continue the trusteeship system as it is today, this is the kind of situation we will have to face. Now, under our proposal, we are saying that if the United States wants to use some land, they will come to the government of Micronesia and ask where they can put bases and airstrips. And the government will designate islands and areas that can be used and arrange for compensation. We would do this under the proposed free association. We cannot do this today."

Another pause for translation. Why hadn't he given a simpler answer, I wondered, something less hedged. *Now the United States can do what it wants. We want to limit their power. But we can't get rid of it com-*

pletely. The other guys often clowned and joked when they spoke. Salii soliloquized. He wasn't speaking to the crowd, I realized. He was talking to himself, thinking out loud.

"This is a very important and difficult question and I'm sure we're not giving very satisfactory answers. But we have agonized over these questions for the past two years. As we look over our history, wars have always been a part of us. We are situated between two huge masses of land, and great powers cross through us on their way to fight. Knowing human nature, we will have to accept the military in our lives and learn to live with them."

I don't know if what he said pleased Salii. I don't know whether he believed it, or half-believed it, or believed half of it, then or later. I doubt that more than a handful of his listeners grasped the balances and compromises he set out for them. I was his best audience, I guess. And what startled me was hearing him, there, then, weighing the hardest of questions in a village meeting house, with a sunken Japanese fleet in the lagoon and rusted artillery pieces still pointing out of hillside caves. That, I thought, was something.

I never cared as much about politics in Los Angeles or New York as I did there, at the end of the world, and never met a more congenial bunch of leaders. Splendid fellows, I thought, the first generation of American-educated politicians, returning home determined to hold the United States to its word. No military garrison state here, no Indian reservation either. These were nation builders, San Martíns and Bolívars, Paines and Washingtons, and my pleasure, as I got to know them, was to wonder who was who. The burly Yapese, John Mangefel, chewing betelnut and citing Chaucer, what role would he play? Or Luke Tman, a Palauan-Japanese, raised in Yap, mixing the nearly scholastic mind of a chess player and parliamentarian with the looks of a matinee idol? And Amata Kabua, courtly mandarin boss of the Marshall Islands, Bailey Olter, loud and buoyant, a connoisseur of dredges and backhoes, an earth-moving, shit-kicking man. From Truk there came Tosiwo Nakayama, already an advocate of independence, a quiet man whom I suspected didn't quite trust me, or maybe it was that he didn't know me, which made his occasional confidences feel like medals. But Salii was at the heart of it all.

I had a better sense of him now. I saw how strengths could shade into weaknesses. Drive and urgency, for instance, imploded into plain restlessness, never more evident than when he was in Palau. He lacked patience, what the Germans call *Sitzfleish*. He was anxious to take off, go somewhere, confront and flurry, when he'd have been better off letting things ripen, letting others come to him. There was more. As impressed as I was by Salii's drive, I sometimes wondered what his ends were, whether he looked beyond the negotiations that were just starting. Did he have an idea what victory was? Could he enjoy it? How did he want things to be really? I saw that he was moody and impulsive, I wondered if he were a stayer, a ten-round fighter. Still, he was my pick for George Washington. Once, just before I left, he thanked me for what I'd done, the statements and speeches and newspaper accounts.

"We won't forget you," Salii said, while we drove around Koror one morning. "Hell," I responded, prematurely cynical. "Who remembers the name of Paul Revere's horse?"

"Paul Revere did," he replied.

◄ III ►

It was hard, living in Los Angeles in 1969, covering annual meetings for *The Wall Street Journal,* running footraces to telephones against Reuters' guys, racing to tell a waiting world that Standard Brand Paints was going to be up a couple cents per share, it was hard not to think that leaving the islands was the worst mistake I'd ever made. That's when I started thinking of Micronesia as the life not lived, the cause abandoned. That's when I began dividing my life into two categories of time: time in the islands, which was maximum life, and time away from the islands, which was exile. Politics and romance were in the islands and writing was what I did there: I was Edgar Snow in the caves of Hunan; William Shirer covering a Nazi rally at the Berlin Sportspalast; Lowell Thomas out riding with Lawrence of Arabia. In Los Angeles, though, I was a journalist among journalists, another sweaty-palmed sprinter, part of the reporting pack. And all the time, while I was filing stories on annual meetings and quarterly earnings, while I was composing features on casino gambling and endangered mustangs, Mexican boxers, the future of the urban neighborhood bar, all the time I was doing this Kuralt-ish stuff, this miscellany, out there, west of Santa Monica, through the offshore fumes, out there, damn it, the fate of paradise was being decided.

I heard from the place just often enough to keep memories alive. There were letters from Salii, long letters detailing negotiations with Americans, intramural squabbles among Micronesians, fevered politics at home in Palau. He'd meant to hire me, as soon as he could. I'd left the islands thinking I'd soon be back. The job hadn't panned out though. Things were moving slowly. Still, his letters suggested he had things in mind for us to do together, some ultimate campaign even he wasn't sure about, but he would need me for it and I would go. I would get a long-distance phone call, late at night, at the worst possible time in my career, and I would go. I would get some vague offer on short notice and I would go. No matter what, I'd go.

And I went. In 1970, on vacation from *The Wall Street Journal,* I was back to help Micronesians prepare to meet the U.S., and that summer my speech-writing services were in great demand. The United States had led with its chin. Its first offer was that the Trust Territory become a territory of the United States, then—second offer—a commonwealth. Members of the Congress of Micronesia lined up for speeches denouncing the callous superpower's bid at annexation. It was a heady time alright, oratory in season, gestures, and postures. But there was one huge question. Were they roughing up the United States in order to escape it . . . or to fit themselves more comfortably under its wing? Cutting ties or cutting deals? Were my speech-writing clients patriots or realtors?

In 1972 I was back again, sitting in on meetings between Salii and company and a U.S. interagency task force that included an ambassador, F. Haydn Williams, and a future head of the Joint Chiefs of Staff, William Crowe. That beat what I was up to in New York, writing celebrity profiles—Ann-Margret, John Wayne, Flip Wilson—for *LIFE* magazine. Those days, whenever I flew from New York to Los Angeles on assignments, I felt that the flight stopped five thousand miles short of its true destination, hijacked by circumstance. When *LIFE* folded in 1972, the novel I turned to was set in Palau, *The Day That I Die,* all full of barmaids, Japanese bonehunters, Pentagon spooks, island politicians. By the time the novel appeared, in 1975, I was back in the islands on a year long job I suspect Salii got for me, though I never asked him, as a director of the Micronesian Constitutional Convention.

After that, the island fever subsided. It died down, but it didn't die out. There was a trip in the late seventies, another in the early eighties. But how many articles could you write on Micronesia? I'd written pieces for *The Wall Street Journal* op-ed page, for *Reader's Digest, Geo, Quest.* Salii and I started on a book together. *Micronesia: The Unending Struggle,* he called it, a title that characterized our collaboration, alternating chapters by mail. It also described what had happened in the islands. The status negotiations had bogged down, comically, boringly, end- lessly. There were problems with the Americans about money, about land, about military rights, about spying. (I suspect the Micronesians loved to think that someone was spying on them, tracing their move- ments, eavesdropping on their conversations, building up dossiers in Washington.) But the biggest issues were between the Micronesians themselves. What had kept the various islands together—the Marshalls, Ponape, Truk, Yap, Palau, the Northern Marianas—was the same thing that had brought them together: the United States. Wealthy, clumsy, easily distracted, the United States played an all purpose role, savior and villain, financier and flak-catcher. Now that the U.S. was pulling back a little, this old unity-of-opposition fractured.

The Salii I saw at the Micronesian Constitutional Convention was a changed man. Once an advocate of unity, the leader of the pack, he now seemed tired, bored, equivocal. He knew the future was going to be played out back in Palau, and big deals were in the works down there. A troika of Americans, Japanese, and Iranians had proposed a "Super- port" for Palau, a costly, lucrative, potentially ruinous installation, which involved the storage, refining, and trans-shipment of Iranian oil to Japan. The Superport was a controversial issue, and Salii was one of the Palauans linked to the proposal.

Salii and I never talked about the Superport. Later, he backed away from the project somewhat, said it was up to the people of Palau to decide what to do. They never had the chance. The project fell apart, wounded by environmental protest, killed by the fall of the shah. Still, it was ominous. Other proposals would surely follow; the parade of outside idea-men, hustlers, agents—carpetbaggers—was only beginning. Those of us who had rooted for the islanders now confronted the ambivalent prospect of our patriots using their newfound powers to trash the place we loved. What had been a simple confrontation between the U.S. and Micronesia was getting tricky and double-edged. At the Constitutional Convention—charmingly shortened to "Con-Con"— I'd written dozens of speeches on behalf of Micronesian unity. That should have told me that the place was falling apart. Money was the culprit. The "haves" were the Marshalls, Palau, and the Northern Marianas, where the United States had an active military interest. Truk, Yap, and Ponape were the have-nots, huddling together as the Federated States of Micronesia. Everybody was trying to cut the best possible deal with Washington and nobody was looking very good.

So I left Micronesia and went about my life, traveling between New York and Hollywood, working at novel-writing and teaching, journalism and movies, a life that seemed less exotic than what I'd had, out in the Pacific. The islands stayed with me. Sometimes it pleased me, sometimes it hurt, knowing I had friends out there, and a life I'd never lived. Far off as they were—or because they were far off, small as they were— or because they were small, the islands stayed with me. New York was where I ought to be, I supposed, the Big Apple, the big leagues. It had always been that way. Like so many other kids from New Jersey, I first saw New York as a kind of Oz, a magic city. In high school, I explored the city, staking it out, like a ballplayer testing a field before a game, measuring base paths where I expected to run, slide, and score. I went to off-Broadway plays I read about in *The New Yorker.* I took high school dates on hansoms in Central Park, got lost with them in Brooklyn, bought them Ferlinghetti's *A Coney Island of the Mind* in the Sheridan Square Bookstore. There was music at Gerde's Folk City or the Half Note Club, Zoot Sims and Al Cohn blowing saxophones while I sat at a window table watching cabs cruise chilly, cobblestone streets where the very steam blowing out of manhole covers, white and wispy, seemed romantic and promising as the life I hoped to live, once I made it to New York.

Later, though, I'd had a half-dozen addresses in the city and I had come to see the place through a prism of compromise, a stressed mix of success and failure I couldn't control, like a phone that would, or wouldn't, ring. And it was only once in a while, in a taxi, slightly drunk, watching traffic lights turn green in front of me or maybe in Central Park, first thing in the morning, seeing the buildings on Fifty-ninth Street turn pink, only now and then, at the edge of the day or the turn of a season, that I caught a glimpse of what I used to love, a glance so quick, so passing, so almost completely gone that, while it reminded me of why I came, it equally asked me why I stayed. And that's when I thought of Palau, and Lazarus Salii.

I could still picture myself out there, campaigning, writing. Given half a chance, I still yearned to chuck it all—the jobs I should have taken more seriously—and make my stand in the islands. I had fewer illusions than before, but I was still waiting for a call from Lazarus.

◄ IV ►

I am at my best in the morning. I come into the English department offices at Kenyon College early. I sit on a porch outside my office, a handsome porch on what used to be a handsome house, some tenured professor's roost, before the college turned it into a warren of offices where faculty nest among coffee cups and lecture notes, texts and bluebooks. The sunrise takes its time arriving, for we are at the far edge of the eastern time zone. I hear crows cawing over fields of Knox County corn stubble, I picture pigs rutting in plots of not quite frozen mud, I watch my colleagues fill up parking spaces with sensible, scruffy, mid-sized cars, black and brown and gray. Our students do not admire us for the cars we drive or the clothes we wear, do not covet the houses we live in, yet for a short time they are in our power. We preside over their four-year rite of passage into the upper-middle class and, if that should fail, we equip them with many definitions of irony. Sometimes we leave marks upon them. I have opinions about landscape and sense of place, about narration in the first person and the third, about dialogue and character. But this morning thoughts go west, out of American Lit's range.

I enter the zone of last things, a zone we cross in ignorance, map in retrospect. The only guide is memory, and memory could use some warming up. Okay. Warm up on my parents. The last time I saw my mother she lay in bed, too thin, while a car waited in a snowy driveway to take me off to college. Her teary partings were tradition, almost clichés. Now she choked them back. "You see," she said, "I've finally learned how to say goodbye." She was a thoughtful and measured woman; an apple, a piece of bittersweet chocolate, and a *Reader's Digest* article each night before sleep. I guessed she would outlive my father, a hard-working hectic machinist. Wild-card cancer faked me out. My last sight of my father: up from Florida, getting onto a New York City 104 bus in front of Sloan's Supermarket at 100th and Broadway, headed to the too-expensive hotel room we'd gotten him on 59th Street, so he could sight north across Central Park and pick out the Harlem apartment building where he'd worked as a janitor the afternoon of the day he'd come through Ellis Island fifty years before. Five months later he was dead of cancer too.

The last time I saw Lazarus Salii in Palau was in February 1986. Though Palau's political status was unsettled, Salii was its president, relaxed and decisive. "I always liked calling the shots," he said, grinning, when I dropped by. The deal with the Americans—the Compact of Free Association—was finally about to be approved, he felt. Though negotiations and plebiscites had dragged on for years, he thought that everything had turned out for the best.

"There was not much of a hurry to settle for less than the best that we could get," he reflected. "People weren't starving. Life was going on acceptably. There was education. Standards of living were slowly improving. There were no catastrophes, no disasters. The Trust Territory high commissioner wasn't a dictator. We had the luxury of waiting it out, and it speaks well of the United States that they let things happen that way. If we had settled earlier, we wouldn't have gotten such a good deal."

As I sat there taking notes on what must have been my two-dozenth article involving Lazarus Salii, I felt some disappointment that the old, heady issues—independence, identity, culture sovereignty—were passé and that what his long campaign had come to was the best possible deal with the Americans, that Palau was about to take its place as one of a group of American client states, a funny little armada of Pacific-stans, floating out west of Hawaii, not quite assimilated, not quite independent. A new game would begin. America and Palau. Salii—President Salii—was looking forward to it.

"The United States is our positive outlet," he said. "People will be traveling to the U.S. That's where the excitement comes from. Meanwhile we can create a paradise in Palau: no pollution, enough tourism to maintain things. At the same time, our kids go to the U.S. for adventure and education and when they have their fill, they come home."

I watched my old friend closely and wondered if what he said was going to happen—the best possible deal with the Americans—and if it happened, whether that would match the hopes I'd had for him. I watched Salii deliver a speech on a sweltering hillside near the Palau Museum, dedicating a statue of his late predecessor, Palau's first president, Haruo Remeliik. Later, I caught him in a genial mood, presiding over a beauty contest—"Miss Palau"—at a lavish resort hotel the Japanese had built. And I joined him on a picnic to the Rock Islands where old staples, beer, fish, and lobster, now were complemented by new choices, wine and fresh-brewed coffee. And, hell yes, it was fun for an ex-Peace Corps volunteer to claim friendship with a head of state.

Still, though his welcome was warm, I felt less close to him than before. I was a writer but now he was dealing with lawyers, lots of lawyers, all kinds of lawyers; he didn't need me, I guessed, and he never would again, because the game had passed me by. I was yesterday's speech writer. But there was more. Sometimes I thought my appearance in Palau was mildly discomfiting; that I reminded him of another time and an earlier, more idealistic self. So we had our picnic, bantered about boxing, and went our separate ways. I had been a part of his starting-out, "the Ph.D. PCV from the P.I.O. (Public Information Office)." But it worked both ways. He was part of my past. And what I remembered was a winning, tough, driven man who'd come home to dismantle the American trusteeship and put something better in its place; a dark, haunting thinker who seemed to have all the answers, the ones he shared with me and others he was saving and some answers he hadn't come up with yet but, count on it, he would. Now the answers seemed less interesting, the questions less pressing. His magic had turned into power all right, but not magical power. In a fast boat, speeding through the Rock Islands in late afternoon, whipping around cliff faces, dancing over coral heads, pounding through a maze of shaded channels, that was the last time I saw him in Palau. Is that all? I wondered. Is that it? Not quite.

In the summer of 1986, again in the summer of 1987, Lazarus Salii came to New York to appear before the United Nations Trusteeship Council. It was a tired ritual by now, representatives of the last trusteeship dragging into town to deliver speeches no journalists cared about, addressing nearly empty galleries. Still, it was a little like the old days, Salii calling ahead from Washington or Honolulu, warning that he'd be needing a speech, always assuming—correctly—that I would be there to write it.

Most islanders in town for the U.N. were awkward. They sat in hotel rooms, ate deli sandwiches, watched television. "Dancing bears," one American called them: slow, ponderous red-eyed creatures, hung over and overweight, just going through their lawyer-trainer's motions. But Salii was different, this time, autumn 1987. I walked him through galleries in Soho, we ate paella at El Faro, stopped for coffee along Bleecker Street. We were both wrapped up in boxing, probably for the same reasons—a need for honest combat, one on one, no fussing with gear, no coddling of teammates, no nonsense about representing a college or a town. In short: no politics. He bet fifty dollars that Michael Olajide, a flashy, too-cute middleweight would never be a champion. He advised me that my novels were too serious, too intellectual. I should loosen up some, write something he could find at an airport book rack, something like Ludlum and Sheldon. He was always telling me to loosen up. Stop jogging, he told me, and learn golf, a real sport. He thought I could be good at golf, he said.

That last time, Salii wanted to visit Father Hugh Costigan, a legendary Jesuit with years of missionary service in Ponape, who lay dying in the Bronx, at a hospice near Fordham University. I suggested the subway. He insisted on a cab, which he kept nearby, meter running, while we talked to Costigan, shook his hand, winced at the pregnancy-sized tumor that poked lopsidedly under the sheets. On the way back to Manhattan, we got caught in traffic on the West Side Highway. Junked cars, rusted bridges, graffiti overpasses. We moved so slowly you could count the smashed cans and blown out tires that fetched up against the divider strip. Somewhere along there, with the meter ticking toward forty dollars, Salii abruptly suggested that we build houses next to each other in Palau. He knew just the place, he said, a bluff that overlooked the Rock Islands, faced west across the Philippine Sea. And that was when I realized, way late, that it wasn't just politics and public relations, ghost-writing and speech-writing, Salii wanted me for. This was about friendship, about having me around; about helping him solve problems he had, maybe, but also helping him escape from problems that were insoluble. Fatal problems, it turned out. I pictured those houses, side by side. But then he was gone, and that was the last time I saw him, in New York or Palau or anywhere.

Now, the last of the last. In 1988, I spent a long wintry time in a bleak neighborhood at the edge of Interstate 71 in Columbus, Ohio. I was a writer-in-residence, living in an apartment in the attic of James Thurber's boyhood home, now a museum and bookstore. Out the window, I could see a highway sign, white letters on green, pointing motorists the way to Wheeling, West Virginia. Then the phone rang. Salii was calling from across the world, sounding troubled, back in paradise. He talked of boxing, of a trip upcoming to Washington, and maybe he would visit me in Columbus, drive up to this Kenyon College place I talked about. Or maybe we'd go to Las Vegas for one of the big fights; he'd send me the ticket. Then: "I want you to come to Palau." A pause. "As a writer . . . you could do some writing for us." He sensed my hesitation: how does a government hire a writer, how does a friend hire a friend? "In any way that's comfortable for you," he added. "I'm surrounded by people here, but they tell me what they think I want to hear. I want you to come to Palau."

That was it. The call I'd been waiting for—the summons—had finally arrived. But I didn't drop everything and fly off to Palau. Maybe Palau had changed, maybe Salii had changed some too. Then, maybe I had changed as well. I wasn't the same person I had been when I waited in Los Angeles and New York to hear from him. I was older, more guarded and skeptical. I'd lost my faith that islands could be the center of the world. Too often, the wisdom of editors and agents had been impressed upon me. Grow up. Get smart. Those places are too small, too far away for people to care about. You're a good writer, pick a better subject. The islands that mattered to me didn't matter to others. So, in the end, they mattered less to me. Six months later he was dead. And six months after that, I was on a plane, headed west, chasing a sunset that now reproached me because I had waited too long to follow it. That didn't stop me from going.

III

MAJURO: THE FIRST PLACE WEST

I like leaving some things open about a trip. I like relying on the books I find along the way, for the same reason that I take my chances on the songs that come over car radios, though others travel with cassettes beside them. My way, I tell myself, the books I read and the music I hear become part of the trip rather than part of the baggage. The Honolulu airport is discouraging, though; lots of Ludlum and Sheldon, the authors that the late Salii counseled me to emulate. My attention is drawn to a line of pornographic double novels published by Beeline Books. One of their authors is named Willie Makeit. I am torn between Willie Makeit and Paul Theroux, unsure which will be better company across the dateline.

In Honolulu, I stayed at a friend's home in Makiki Heights, a high-up place that once commanded a view of the shoreline from Diamond Head, through Waikiki and Ala Moana, all the way downtown. A view of the Pacific, it once had been; now the Pacific was fenced off by a wall of high-rise offices and condominiums that the sunset happened behind. At night, that twinkling skyline marked enemy territory; the Japanese were back and buying Waikiki. I sat on a plumeria-scented hillside, the Punchbowl Cemetery behind me, Ernie Pyle and thousands of other World War II dead buried in the volcanic crater, the tourist gaggle of Waikiki below. I thought about the waves of empire that sweep across the Pacific, splashing and roiling as they meet, whirlpools and eddies all around. Hawaii absorbs them, transforms them. It has the weight and substance of a destination attraction, a thing and an end in itself. But the islands west of here are small, fragile places, more easily swept over, more casually conquered or bypassed, less solidly anchored in the sea itself, small islands where lives turn strange, circling, spiraling, and crashing, as though the islands' very dimensions forbid orderly progress, linear thinking.

Before long, almost every conversation I had in Hawaii turned to Lazarus Salii, his meteoric career and violent end. The tone would change then, perhaps because people knew I was an old friend, or maybe because I was an old friend with a few lessons left to learn, so they wanted to break it to me gently, the bad news about what happened, while I was away. An ex-Peace Corps volunteer who now works for the governor of Hawaii remembered writing home that Salii was Micronesia's Patrick Henry. He shook his head, chagrined. A newspaper man commiserated about Salii's death but warned of rumors that he was about to be indicted. Finally, I checked in with an old friend, someone I met twenty years before, one of the ones who used to think that proud, cocky Palau was the center of the world. We sat in a Greek restaurant near the university, talked about life in New York, life in Honolulu. We were friendly acquaintances, talking about other places. But when we turned to Palau, we were close again. We were Micronesia heads, part of a tiny freemasonry that could indulge itself, pig out on talk about places hardly anyone else knew. But here again was another warning for me, a warning about opportunity turning into opportunism, a syllable's change, but heart breaking if you ever hoped that, though the rest of the world might turn to shit in your lifetime, these few scraps might be spared, this handful of people, coming into the game late and from far away, with everyone's mistakes to learn from and the benefit of our counsel besides! You hoped they'd get things right.

"In Palau the people we know went bad," my friend complained. "The ones you could respect, you can't respect anymore. You go out there now, you'll see the wreck of what could have been. It used to feel like a special place, but it went sour."

My partner paused, denunciation slowing, an adjustment of tone. "I always blamed you for Lazarus. The way you wrote him up. Before that, he couldn't have been elected anything. You did a lot of work for him, writing him up in the papers, casting him as a leader. . . ."

I shake my head, try to wave it off. Salii was his own man, I tell myself, but I cannot leave it at that, because he was my friend at the gallant David-and-Goliath beginning of his career and he called out to me when he was near the end. Should I blame myself for my presence at the start? Or my absence at the finish? Or both? I should have been there, I tell myself, so often that my very conviction becomes suspect. My presence wouldn't have made a damn bit of difference and I should stop kidding myself. I presume too much. But that last call from Lazarus keeps coming to mind. "I want you to come to Palau."

On my way, now.

◄ II ►

My plane is called. Air Micronesia, a Continental Airlines operation. There's no one I recognize in the waiting room—that's a disappointment—but still there's a sense of returning to an old neighborhood. A whiff of pomade comes off a guy's slicked black hair. Trukese, I bet. Some heavy-bodied matrons wear the bright, flowery prints I associate with the islands. Their high cheekbones give them away: Marshallese. I spot some wised-up, casually dressed *haoles.* Skin divers, I bet. And the luggage I see is islands luggage, taped-up boxes with names written in Magic Marker, cheap whale-sized suitcases crammed with stuff from the Ala Moana Sears and Woolworth's. It's odd seeing islanders—real islanders, not some aloha-shirted bozo who plays at being Hawaiian—wearing leis made out of chewing gum, Tootsie Rolls, and lemon balls. Brace yourself, I say. Now it begins.

I resisted the temptation to fly directly to Palau. Instead I'm doing the islands the old way, hopping through what used to be the Trust Territory, now divided into a gaggle of post-territorial states, all linked to the United States. First Majuro, capital of the Republic of the Marshall Islands, then Ponape and Truk, parts of the Federated States of Micronesia, then—through Guam, a U.S. territory—to Saipan, capital of the U.S. Commonwealth of the Northern Marianas, then back through Guam to Yap, which will return me to the Federated States of Micronesia. Then at last, I will come to the Republic of Palau.

The names have changed, as Micronesians shed colonial pronunciations and spellings. They're changing still, Ponape turning into Pohnpei, Kusaie into Kosrae, Truk into Chuuk. Palau is sometimes called Belau. New flags and stamps besides, all the trappings of semi-independence. I wonder what else has changed. It feels odd, it makes me nervous as though after years of happy marriage in other places, I'm going back to visit an old girlfriend. I expect change and loss, maybe growth, and I wonder—against all warnings—what remains of the old magic. There's more, though. These islands, these girlfriends, have eyes too, and memories of their own, and I wonder how I'll look to them and what faults they'll find. A double jeopardy of blame: blame the young committed writer of twenty-plus years ago or blame the been-around-the-block wised-up novelist who steps off the plane today. Or blame both.

I might be ancient history, part of an idealistic past best left forgotten. We were all younger twenty years ago, and the songs we sang are out of date now. Showing up now could be a little embarrassing, like shouting a request for "You Are My Sunshine" at a Bon Jovi concert. Sit down, please, and shut up! Old songs: colonialism, neo-colonialism. Independence. Pride, culture, unity. Blasts from the past, oldies from the oceanic grooveyard. But lyrics come back to me, fine, eloquent, and possibly mendacious things I wrote myself, so that even thinking of them puts me in mind of some medley-singing lounge lizard pattering obnoxiously between tossed-off tunes. "Thanks very much . . . and then I wrote . . ." They come back. Lyrics from the Statement of Intent, 1969: "The basic ownership of these islands rests with Micronesians and so does the responsibility for governing them." And, for Tosiwo

Nakayama, addressing a Trukese graduating class in 1969: "Like our schools and our clothes, our hopes and dreams have been designed in America according to American models. In the decades to come we may have to sacrifice these things, may have to dream dreams and hope hopes that can be realized in Micronesia. We must hope to become a big Micronesia and not a little America." And, for Salii in 1970, urging rejection of integration into the U.S., a fine fiery tune. "The United States offers us a new name. This Trust Territory would become a commonwealth. But the United States would hold power over our land; the United States would control our future. Micronesia would become a permanent part of the United States' political family—that is the phrase they use. Micronesia would become the newest, the smallest, the remotest nonwhite minority in the United States' political family—as permanent and American, shall we say, as the American Indian."

Old songs. The last that comes to me was the best, the one I'd turned out in 1975 when some Palauans, Salii among them, dropped by my office at the Con-Con with a draft constitution. The preamble needed work, they said; it was flat. Did I think I could . . . you know . . . give it the treatment? I set to work, scribbling, revising, inserting. "To make one nation of many islands, we respect the diversity of our cultures. Our differences enrich us. The seas bring us together, they do not divide us. . . . Micronesia began in the days when men explored seas in rafts and canoes. The Micronesian nation is born in an age when men voyage among stars; our world itself is an island. . . ."

My god, how they loved that preamble! They couldn't agree on lots of other things, but that preamble was a unanimous hit. Throughout the rest of the convention, they read that preamble aloud every day, first thing, like saying grace. In the end, only the Trukese, Yapese, and Kosraeans voted to accept the constitution. The Ponapeans voted against it. The Northern Marianas, Marshalls, and Palau went off to cut separate deals. That was the end of the Trust Territory of Pacific Islands. But everybody, the strayers and the stayers, loved that preamble. It went into schoolrooms, it was printed on T-shirts. It was my work. But was any of it true?

◄ III ►

Landscape, I tell my writing students, is a matter of perspective. It changes with mood and moment, changes as we change, our appetites and nerves and all. It has no objective existence: we create it as we write. So there's no truth down below this plane, no truth in the first appearance of the Marshall atolls, those strands of palms and sand that float below, like shavings off a larger, sculpted continent. Watch out for that first thrilling surge that they are there, that you have found them, startling as that once-a-year-day when you glimpse snow on the mountains around Los Angeles. Remember this first sighting and the high joy of arrival. You'll need it later, for there's a crazy dialectic that buffets you around the islands. You bounce from glory to squalor a dozen times a day, so often that you wonder whether there isn't a linkage between the two, some weird symbiosis between lagoons and diapers, sunsets and beer cans. A couple thousand miles out of Honolulu, like a gull hunting a minnow, the plane picks Majuro out of the sea. Beware of Majuro. Majuro will convince you that people are the worst thing that ever happened to the planet. Paradise ends where people begin.

Majuro is a feast of ironies, a warren of houses and warehouses and shacks that feels like a slovenly picnic in mid-Pacific, like Central Park after one of those Puerto Rican holidays, all trashed and pissed on. There are nearly fifty thousand Marshallese now, about half of them under fifteen. The birth rate's close to 4 percent. And twenty thousand Marshallese are packed into Majuro. That's the number one irony in paradise. The people who are born in a state of grace on outlying islands, rafts of palm and coral in a clear turquoise lagoon, can't wait to rush off to squalid, mean places. They come to Majuro to have babies at the hospital, to attend high school, to drive taxis, to watch videos and drink Budweiser and Mountain Dew, to work for the islands' employer of first and last resort, the government, or to live off relatives who do. They jump at the chance to escape from paradise, so now almost half the Marshalls' population is jammed into three municipalities, Darrit-Uliga-Dalap, collectively DUD, at one end of the atoll.

I'd been warned about Majuro, I grant, back in Hawaii by a professor who described unplanned urbanization, growing aspirations, doubling populations, scant resources, no real economic growth. "Third World problems cropping up all over the place," he'd said. But that was without the smell of rotting wood, the sight of rusty roofs, the mid-day heat, the flies and mosquitos, potholes and puddles, ghetto crowding, and bus-terminal torpor. That was before I saw the ring of rust around the atoll, wrecked fishing boats and landing craft, trucks, public works equipment, pipes and cranes. You could hammer together a 747 out of the aluminum cans tossed along the road. Majuro is bare concrete, naked light bulbs, dripping air conditioners. Now there's a typhoid scare, and people carry blue plastic containers of drinking water out of stores. Imported water. Imported food. Over 90 percent of what Marshallese eat is imported. The island is starting to feel like a lifeboat.

Everybody, almost everybody, could be someplace else. Nothing obliges nearly half the population of the Marshalls to live on 1 percent of the land. They could be out on the islands with heart-tugging names—Jaluit, Ebon, Ailinglaplap, Namorik—out fishing, making copra, carving and chanting, sailing outrigger canoes between islands, navigating by the stars. But they come to an island of flies, coral dust, and tin cans. I walk down an alley toward a car rental place and pass a teenager, standing midway between two dripping air conditioners, pissing against a wall. "Sorry about that, man," he says with an apologetic smile.

I take a ride to blow off my bad mood. After the war, the Americans built bridges and causeways that connected Majuro's separate atoll islands into one long, thirty-mile chain, never more than a few hundred yards wide, often less. This road, all the way from DUD to Laura is the longest drive in Micronesia, and the best. South of the airport, the island narrows drastically. On one side, the ocean rolls in dark blue, on the other, the water is calm and pastel blue and you can look across to the islands on the far side of the lagoon. The breeze is constant along here, and the palm trees lining the road make it feel like a rich man's long, long driveway, with ginger, bougainvillea, and plumeria beneath the palms. The houses are few and far between, tin and wood shacks with carefully swept crushed coral yards, the day's laundry spread out, like a bright carpet, or hung on washlines, like paintings at an outdoor gallery, or thrown over the tops of bushes, like a sheet of flowers. Lots of houses have graves nearby, and the graves are bright with plastic flowers. Odd blend of K mart and Gauguin—plastic buckets in front of tethered pigs, kids walking down the middle of the road, net fishermen walking into tidal pools, husked coconuts and pandanus fruit for sale at roadside stands. Finally I come to Laura, the end of the atoll, shady trees and coral shelf and piles of driftwood impaling plastic bags, stirring in the constant breeze.

This is one of the spots I thought about, while I was away. When people in New York talked about Bermuda or Jamaica, all their beachy getaways, I'd picture Laura. It's much as I recalled it, ocean rolling on one side, lagoon on the other, pockets of sand, tidal pools, currents coming together, a constant breeze riffling through the trees. People sit on benches or just open the doors on both sides of their cars and stretch out for a nap. Why don't people live down here, instead of crowding into that shantytown at the far end of the atoll? Land tenure probably has something to do with it. Power and water. Distance from jobs, from the hospital and airport. Distance from beer and jukeboxes. Never underestimate the power of jukeboxes and beer. You can revel in isolation only so long, before you need a cold one.

Seeing Laura restores me. I return to town in a better mood, and a better town awaits me. It is that certain time of day that comes to me whenever I miss the islands, that redeeming and forgiving hour around sunset. It never lets me down. This is when girls walk down the road, holding hands, and dogs who've been sleeping on sand piles next to construction sites scratch and stretch, and kids play volleyball. And then, as tropical evening rolls in, knots of people converge around mom-and-pop grocery stores, gazing at the convoy of passing taxis, headlamps on. There's a fashion show at the Tide Table Bar, beautiful girls modeling while an emcee calls out the prices of what they have on. The bars get busy. A drunk stops me, asks if I'm a contract worker from the missile test site over on Kwajalein, in town for a little R and R. Would I like him to take me to a disco? Tennis courts are crowded, islands of light till well after midnight. Everywhere there are people out and about in the evening cool, less like residents than voyagers on a ship, leaning against the railing, catching the breeze, watching their passage across the Pacific.

This is how you fall in and out of love with islands. Again and again, every day.

◄ IV ►

"Hey," Joe Murphy asks, "you want to tread water or you want to stand on toxic garbage?"

He is bantering with a nuclear-free Pacific activist out of San Francisco who arrived just ahead of me at Murphy's office at the *Marshall Islands Journal.* I'd considered skipping Majuro altogether. Of all the Micronesian districts, the Marshalls was least familiar to me. But there were some people I wanted to see and Murphy was on the list, which is a list of stayers-on, Peace Corps volunteers who never went home. Just as the Japanese left stragglers behind, soldiers who hid out and lived off the land for years after the war ended, so the Peace Corps deposited volunteers, dozens of them throughout Micronesia. I want to check on some of them, to see if I can find some clue about how my life might have turned out, if I'd stayed.

Fortyish and Philadelphia Irish, Joe Murphy was one of the first volunteers, back in the early sixties. Coming to the end of his service, he faced the same questions I faced and he answered each of them differently. I left, he stayed. He married an island girl, and had seven children. I had an American wife and no children. Now it seems like he's been around Majuro forever, a small-town publisher-editor, a storyteller, schemer, practical joker, poetry quoter, cracker-barrel theorist, and informal historian.

"I came out to fight ignorance," he cracks, "and I lost." Faced with Murphy's assignment, I'd have gone home—"deselected myself" as the Peace Corps put it. They sent him to Ujelang, a remote atoll, three hundred miles from its nearest neighbor, six hundred miles from Majuro. The place had a godawful reputation. Home to a colony of

Eniwetokese displaced by nuclear tests, Ujelang was known for low morale, isolation, and rats. The rats swarmed the island, brought copra production to a standstill, swiped food, gnawed at children's feet. Attempts at poisoning the rats misfired: sixty-five dead pigs. Murphy recalls his first night on Ujelang, competing with his roommate to see who could kill more rats, racking up runaway scores, nineteen to seventeen. Later he brought in a cat. "She killed five the first night, three the second, two the third. And after that there were no rats."

Leaving the nuclear-free guy behind, assuring him that the crack about toxic waste was just a joke—Murphy leads me to a local restaurant. It's the sort of place that would be a dump anywhere but here, where it becomes tangled with your memories of the islands: sticky oilcloth tablecloths, poker machines twinkling on the bar, Marshallese music on the radio, and that certain way waitresses have of not walking but slouch-sliding across the floor, arms swinging, thighs a-swish, but zori-clad feet never leaving the floor. Forward progress is barely measurable, ultimate arrival punctuated by a bored, sighing collapse into an empty chair, followed by a bemused scrutiny of the customer reading the menu. The steak? We don't have. Cheeseburg? We don't have. She doodles on her orders tablet, writes her name, quietly waits for you to find something the restaurant has, never dreaming of volunteering a recommendation, any more than a newsstand owner in New York would think of volunteering numbers to a customer hoping to get lucky in the state lottery. You order coffee.

After years of editing the weekly, bilingual *Marshall Islands Journal,* Murphy has pulled out of the writing, branching into printing, into real estate. A connoisseur of the fly-by-nighters who've washed up here, he nurses a scheme of his own, a mail-order gimmick that would have him sending out credit cards to anyone who pays a small fee. The credit cards would be entitled "Major Credit Card." He savors the confusion that his good-hearted scheme might generate.

A little later, we drive to the far end of the airport, sneak through a hole in the fence, and jog up and down the runway, as we have whenever I've visited Majuro. It's on my list of Majuro pleasures, this illicit gallop on the edge of the sea, breakers splashing onto the runway, air like warm pudding, running half an hour, sweating for an hour and a half, repairing to a bar and talking trash.

Real trash. Lots of it. I'd heard about it in Washington and Honolulu, reports accompanied with nervous laughter and a now-he's-really-gone-and-done-it headshaking. What Amata Kabua, president of the Republic of the Marshall Islands has done is come up with a proposed deal with a stateside firm, Admiralty Pacific, to have up to 10 percent of the West Coast's garbage shipped out to paradise in oceangoing barges. The garbage will then be dumped around Marshallese atolls, low-lying places, never more than a couple yards above water. The United States will be cleaner and greener; the Marshalls, thwarting the rising ocean anticipated from the greenhouse effect, will be high and dry. And everybody makes money—$16 million a year for the Marshalls, $22 million for the Americans.

Does it strike you as shrewd, filling up Pacific lagoons with Pampers and paint cans from Seattle? Does it smell like money to you? There's more. In the late forties and early fifties, in its worst breach of the U.N. trusteeship agreement, the United States commandeered Bikini and Eniwetok atolls for nuclear testing. Now, after years of exile and litigation, some of those islands are being resettled. Others were obliterated. And a third group of islands won't be safe for thousands of years. Thus, the Marshallese suggestion for solving U.S. nuclear waste disposal problems. Bring the stuff on out! Hey, when you're hot, you're hot!

No one knows exactly why things are this way in the Marshalls, why the Marshallese are so . . . well . . . nice. "I don't know why they don't tell us to fuck off," muses one American in Washington. We've taken a whole atoll, Kwajalein, to use as a missile test site. We've blown up and contaminated two others, Bikini and Eniwetok, displaced their populations, while accidentally irradiating two more, Rongelap and Utirik. There've been cancer deaths blamed on us, and malformed infants: "jellyfish babies." And yet, of all the Micronesian districts, the Marshalls is the most genial and welcoming. The charm of the Marshallese people may have something to do with it, or their leader's laissez-faire attitude. Or maybe it's just geography, since whatever shakes loose of Hawaii washes up here first. Anyway, the islands have always attracted operators, con-men, drifters, and visionaries. People who would have been stoned or poisoned in Yap and Truk, burned out of their houses in Palau, roost comfortably, schemes and scams intact. Now into its third year as a freely associated state, the Republic of the Marshall Islands resembles one of those gas stations you come across out West, one of those hard-scrabble, what-the-hell operations that offers the last gas and soda, the last phone booth and rest room for two hundred miles. Need a passport? The Marshalls sells them at $250,000 a throw. Commemorative coins? On sale here. Need to register a ship under the Marshallese flag? Can be arranged. Interested in an island business, your own version of Joseph Conrad's Tropical Belt Coal Company, some joint venture in agriculture, mariculture, underwater mining? Come on down! Money in your pocket, garbage in your trunk, the islands oblige.

Murphy and I watch the Tide Table Bar fill up, beery and congenial Marshallese and American characters mixing amiably, T-shirts and aloha shirts, bullshit and Budweiser, all the deals and secrets of a small town multiplied, Richter scale, because this is a small island, a far-off place, and just lately a sort of republic. Gesturing out the window of the bar, out toward the darkening lagoon, Murphy tells me about a shark they caught last week, caught within sight of where we're drinking. Someone had been dumping spoiled fish. That attracted the shark. Some fishermen got a quick strike and a half-hour-long fight, with hundreds of spectators lining the shore. They brought in an eight-hundred-pound tiger shark, ten feet eight inches long. Amazing, to find it inside the lagoon. More amazing: what was found inside the shark. A bellyful of paper cups, diapers, and plastic garbage bags.

I hear about that shark again and again while I'm in Majuro, and what strikes me is that there's booster's pride in the way they tell it, the same way we used to talk about the fabulously polluted Raritan River back in New Jersey, the same way we admired those pastel-colored chemical ponds, those Kilimanjaros of garbage in the Meadowlands under the Pulaski Skyway, on the way to New York City. Hey, it takes plenty of diapers to feed a shark and, by god, if you had to choose between a place that was just mildly screwy and another place that was well and truly fucked up . . . I mean, come on! Because you're with the tide, you've caught a wave, you're about to make the next discovery, which is—witness Joe Murphy—how happy you can be in such a place. I sense this when he talks about his kids, seven of them, and about kids in general, how wonderful they are, how cheap they are out here, how—well—*everything* they are. I nod agreeably I guess, but that won't do. Murphy persists. I have come eight thousand miles to have my mother-in-law's argument echoing across the Pacific, like those far-off radio stations that people here used to pick up at night, parked out at the airport where reception was good, this before video stores came to the islands and changed everything. The wrong people are having babies. Murphy is vehement. I'm a slacker, I'm a dropout, I'm selfish. When I call it a night, returning to Ajidrik's Hotel, I feel like twice a freak, neither a father nor a philanderer in latitudes where most men are both. I know I will hear this again and again out here, and I dust off the answers I've used before. My shopworn responses to "how many children do you have?" "None . . . is there a shortage?" "None . . . I'm making room for Marshallese." "My books are my children." I need new answers. These aren't convincing. And they aren't funny. I could tell them I have a dog, I guess. Then they'd ask if the dog had puppies and the answer is no.

◄ V ►

"Are you still working for the CIA?" Carl Heine asks. It's an old line, less an accusation or a joke than a kind of affectionate greeting, hearkening back to the times we were both around the Congress of Micronesia. The future of the islands was being negotiated, and everyone was titillated by the prospect of rooms being bugged, secrets stolen. Heine had just returned from the University of Hawaii. He'd written a book, *Micronesia at the Crossroads.* Back in the Marshalls he was a leader of the opposition, which challenged but could never dislodge the longtime leader, Amata Kabua. Twenty years later, Kabua is still in charge and Carl Heine is still in the opposition and there's something a little sad about this. If Micronesia were a larger place, Carl Heine would be a lecturer somewhere, a writer, an area studies professor, solid, scholarly, a little pontifical. He performed well in Hawaii, prospered in the old Trust Territory government on Saipan, but those were American operations. Now returned to the Marshalls, he sounds disconsolate.

"It's getting worse around here," he says. He glances around the patio where we're sitting out an afternoon that, like so many other afternoons out here, passes slowly. You get the feeling that every passing car is familiar, every face inside, every yard of road. Islands get cramped; on hot afternoons, small gets less beautiful. Small confines you. Carl talks about going back to Hawaii, back to graduate school, about sending his son to Kenyon College. Odd, that island-to-island connection. That restlessness. "I want to get out," he says. "The government is getting bigger and bigger and more and more abusive."

Amata Kabua is more and more a dictator, Heine claims, surrounded by sycophants and relatives. A son is minister of foreign affairs, a son-in-law is minister of finance, a daughter is mayor of Majuro. The judiciary is kept on laughable short-term contracts; the thirty-three member legislature, the Nitijela, is a rubber stamp with only Heine and a couple others as naysayers. U.S. aid is being wasted on showy projects and all that anyone can do, it seems, is wait the old man out. Meanwhile, Heine thinks of Hawaii or California, teaching and writing. I ask him about going back to Jaluit, his home atoll.

"One week in Jaluit is enough," he says. "You want to come back and drink some cold beer."

Carl's house is in a compound full of flowers, dogs, and chickens, a pleasant well-kept place, all of it in back of a store that seems mostly shut down, except for some poker machines. It's a nice spot, but seeing him there feels odd. There is something forlorn and tired in his attack on Amata Kabua. No wonder. Islanders know each other forever—not intimately, maybe, but well enough so that their confrontations are predictable, their arguments sound for the record. One wins, one loses, but the very size of the place muffles victory and cushions defeat. Everything has a history and nothing is ever over. How much more exciting, when the Americans were around; missions, task forces, junketeers, fact finders, when Kabua could thunder against "the neocolonial yoke under which we suffer," when Carl Heine could write long, whither-Micronesia pieces, pondering the choice between coconuts and Coca-Cola. The islands have gotten smaller since then.

And dirtier, maybe. Suave and smart, Tony De Brum was Amata Kabua's right-hand man, at his side as he led the Marshalls out of the Trust Territory and negotiated a separate deal with the Americans. De Brum was impressive. A deal maker and a charmer, he was equally at ease discussing tax shelters or country-western music. He could go anywhere, first class and five star. He was Amata Kabua's second in command but, evidently, not his successor. These days De Brum is a member of the opposition, a prodigal turned apostate.

"I still believe Amata was necessary," he concedes. "No one else could have formed this country. If what it took was someone who could command feudal loyalty, come hell or high water, we could not have done it without him. But that was the end of it. He's running the country as if it's his money, his assets."

Cronyism, carpetbaggers, finders' fees, sweetheart deals: this is the Marshalls that De Brum describes, a cunning blend of traditional control and contemporary scams; the commemorative coins, the fishing boats, the passports, milk factories, power plants, airplanes. Notions of self-sufficiency deteriorate into an orgy of self-enrichment, a "papaya republic."

"You're going to see turmoil in the Marshalls," he forecasts. "Things look good on the outside now. There's a lot of construction. But everything is mortgaged. Bills will become due, basic services will decrease. There'll be upheaval in the Marshalls that no one has seen before. It's going to be sad."

Smooth Tony, I always called him, one of the islanders who could make out anywhere. He still does: politics, insurance, who knows what else. A trip coming up to Atlanta that has something to do with cable television and Ted Turner. He's in opposition but still part of the elite. A frequent flier all right, but disheartened at home.

"What's that phrase from the Pharisees?" Tony reflects. "Someone said the hungry are fed and the blind can see? Well, in the Marshalls, the hungry are blind and the blind are deaf."

◄ VI ►

The rains rolled in last night, caught us out on the lagoon, Murphy and me, coming in from an island he bought for one of his kids. "A three-bag island" he called it: just enough coconut palms to produce three, one-hundred-pound bags of copra a year. We stayed till dusk, an engine died, we limped in on a smaller engine, drenched and laughing. The rains kept on, though, and this morning is gray skies and puddles, Majuro at its bleakest, the lagoon and sea hidden by sheets of rain. My wallet is wet, my dollars degrading into mulch. Taxi drivers and politicians linger over coffee, rain dripping down onto restaurant tablecloths. At Murphy's office, I watch a videotaped documentary, *Half Life,* which suggests that the nuclear fallout on the island of Rongelap, always blamed on a freak shift of winds, was a deliberate, cynical experiment in which the Marshallese, some of whom later died of thyroid cancer, were used as guinea pigs. A depressing film, a depressing morning. I browse at Robert Reimers' Store, where an eighty-nine-cent can of Barbasol Shaving Cream goes for $1.80 and paperback books—I choose Anne Tyler's *Celestial Navigation*—are marked up $1.00 over their jacket price. Gaudy Hawaiian-style T-shirts evoke a romantic land of surf and flowers and romance—"if it swells, ride it"—which this place is not. I step out onto the street and jump into a taxi, which takes me south along the main road. We pass the Eastern Gateway Hotel. Surrounded by scaffolding, cement mixers, construction sheds, the place looks abandoned, like the V-2 sites at Peenemunde after the missile scientists took off but before the allies came walking in. The stillborn hotel belongs to the phosphate-rich Republic of Nauru, the Saudi Arabia of the Pacific. So does the *Enna G.,* a freighter, tied up in litigation, rusting to death out in the lagoon, a skeleton crew aboard a skeleton ship. So does a floating bar, a wrecked lopsided hulk down the road from Robert Reimers' Hotel. "Good government," the president of Nauru, Hamer de Roburt is famous for saying, "is no substitute for self-government."

And now I sit in the anteroom of the republic's government, awaiting

Amata Kabua, its president. Tentatively promised an audience at one, I arrive while it is lunch hour and the place is deserted. It's raining outside, frigidly air-conditioned within. The offices of the republic are up and down the hall, left and right—Public Works, Health Services, Justice, Finance, Foreign Affairs, Social Services—as if a whole government had been squeezed into a Motel 6. I wait an hour and a half. Polite, puzzled secretaries wonder about me. Finally, a press aide hops into a government sedan and drives to the president's home. A little before three, Amata Kabua arrives.

Amata Kabua is a round, courtly, bespectacled man. Amata Ka-Buddha, some call him. He has always seemed confident, in control, unintimidated—not above slyly needling outsiders. "We do not know exactly when the first people settled these islands," he has stated, "but we do know that our ancestors were dauntlessly sailing the vastness of the Pacific, in hand-hewn wooden canoes, without instruments, while Europeans were still arguing whether the earth was round or flat." In the manuscript we never finished, Salii described Kabua as the one man who could have kept the old Trust Territory together. But unity was not his goal. In the Congress of Micronesia, he sponsored an eminent domain bill that would have given islanders control of their own land; it was vetoed. He pressed legislation that would have returned to the Marshalls its full share of locally generated revenues. It failed. Protective and proprietary about the Marshalls, wary of unity with poorer, more populous places like Truk, he led the Marshalls into free association with the United States. Ten years down the road this may result in bona fide independence or tumble backward into a U.S. commonwealth. Meanwhile, Amata Kabua runs things. He has always run things. If independence means doing your own thing, it is a status Amata Kabua has long since attained.

"Hello, Doctor," he says, greeting me cheerfully. Micronesia is the only place where my Ph.D. has translated into doctor. Kabua shows me into his office and I realize our session will be courteous and short; already a group of elderly Marshallese are waiting outside for a signing ceremony of some sort. Later, people are surprised I got to see Kabua at all. One of the scandals that wounded Salii—a $200,000 payment allegedly made to him by a power company—touched Kabua as well. He was on the list too, it seems. But Kabua has endured in a way that Salii did not. He had chiefly rank, control of the situation, control of himself. Still, the word is that the old man is careful about the press these days, a little touchy.

We talk garbage. Kabua soft-pedals the proposal to accept municipal wastes. "All I'm asking for is a feasibility study." Then we turn to nuclear wastes and he makes it sound like the Marshalls is doing the world a service, its noble intentions cynically distorted. "Maybe they shouldn't tell me not to accept nuclear waste," Kabua says. "I have it already. The important thing is to put it where we can check it and monitor it. I'd rather see it on my island than dumped in the middle of the sea. The islands are already contaminated. Don't give the Japanese reasons to dump. Oh, they'll bow their heads in international forums—and let drop a few containers from an innocent-looking fishing boat, and no one would know. They're not stupid. They know which way the currents flow."

We talk of other things, in the little time remaining. It's alarming, he grants, how many people have crowded into Majuro, but he's confident that the islands, overall, can sustain a population of one hundred thousand. And those hundred thousand Marshallese may be the citizens of an independent nation, if the economy permits, but then again, the United States is a fine nation to be close to, and after all, the world has become an interdependent place and many supposedly sovereign nations aren't all that free. Meanwhile, life is easy in the Marshalls. "This is the most peaceful country I have ever seen." As for himself, he looks to retirement on the outlying atoll of Wotho. A beautiful place. "A little fishing, a little farming, a little writing."

This is a classic. I knew I would hear it, another old song, a kind of Micronesian pastorale. All Micronesian politicians talk of returning home, to the place and life they left behind. Even Salii sometimes mused about returning to Angaur. He accomplished that, all right. They buried him there.

◄ VII ►

I'm at the airport, waiting for the island hopper to Ponape, nine hundred miles southwest. After less than a week in the Marshalls, I'm feeling at home. In the zone. My beard grows faster here, and my fingernails too. Leather shoes, wallet, belt begin to degrade. Paperback books swell oddly, glue turning to sap, paper pages rotting as my eyes pass over them. I am drawn to the people who have stayed here through the years, not that I love the place, not that the people are extraordinary, but I like the investment of time, the combination of the exotic and domestic you find in these small, gossipy places.

And the women. I stare at these short, formidable high-cheekboned Marshallese women. I wonder what's become of my Marshallese girl-friend, from back in Peace Corps days. Ten years ago, passing through, I spotted her at the airport here, sitting on a rock, a flowered muu-muu tented over her knees. I wonder if I could have been happy here. Married and contented. Or maybe I'd have turned into one of those beery satyrs, hanging around bars, pimpy and familiar, running around on their wives while their wives run around on them, living out the lyrics of a tawdry country-western tune. But the thought of even that stirs me, the chasing and catching. And they keep coming, the island girls. The old flames disappear into the island woodwork, into church groups and gardens, behind walls of children, behind those billowing muu-muus that conceal what childbearing and childrearing do to bod-ies I'd have sold my soul for, not that they cared about my soul. And there are new generations rolling in, saucy and big eyed, a bit more jaded, more selective all the time, especially about Americans. I wonder about Arno, an atoll twenty miles from Majuro, once the site of a school where women were instructed in the erotic arts. Some say the whole thing was a joke, to gull anthropologists and titillate tourists and provide slogans for T-shirts: "Instructor—College of Arno." Yet I've had girl-friends who claimed attendance there. I've heard tales of women float-ing on their backs in the waves, coconuts between their legs, mastering grip and motion or—I heard this just the other night—lowering themselves slowly onto the stems of flowers. I could get in trouble here. Airport thoughts, in an airport restaurant where flies circle around slow-moving overhead fans that slap at cooking odors and there's a towel on the wall with an American eagle on it and the Marshallese radio station is playing "Listen to the rhythm of the falling rain. . . ."

I am one step closer to Salii now and I can feel Palau reeling me in from the other side of Micronesia, tugging at me, taking its time, sport-fishing. Palau knows I won't be able to throw the hook. I've picked up my share of Salii stories and theories in Majuro. I've heard that he was working for the CIA, had been for years. That he'd been murdered. That he was manic-depressive. But what comes to me now is Amata Kabua's reaction, one founding father reflecting on the passage of another. "I still can't believe he did it," Kabua said. "That money they said he took was peanuts." Two hundred thousand dollars isn't worth killing yourself for, Kabua implied, and probably he's right.

Another airport thought: there are lots of politicians out here who've gotten caught doing this or that. Small things like drunk driving, using government labor and material on private homes. Stolen typewriters, stolen pigs, ripped-off petty cash. There've been larger things: renting offices from themselves and to themselves, hiring wives and relatives. And larger conflicts of interest: cutting business deals, leasing land, collecting fees while holding office. And it's remarkable how forgiving the islands are. If you got your money off an outsider, no problem. You were still an islander, playing for the home team, and the crowd was on your side. You sat on the bench for a while, or out in the bull pen, waited for your turn to come around again. There were second and third chances out here. Hearts stopped beating, livers checked out, but no one died of a guilty conscience. And nobody in public life committed suicide, except my friend. What did he think he was doing, anyway? If all the people who were guilty of what he's been accused of put a bullet through their head, it would sound like first day of deer hunting season in New England out here. Oh hell. Any way I look at it, there's something singular about his death.

Disconsolate, I heft my hand-carry baggage and leave the airport café, pay the airport tax, then repair to the bar where Joe Murphy is in his glory, flanked by a Bahamas-based Peruvian who wants to sell metal houses out here and a Japanese who sort of works for private business and sort of works for the Japanese government, it's not entirely clear.

"Look at this place," Murphy exclaims, gesturing around the bar. "A movie set decorator couldn't create it!" He points to the cement block wall, where an exposed electric wire snakes upward through a field of institutional green paint, toward a naked light bulb. "Look how carefully they avoided painting over the wire. And check out the orderly stacking of soft drink cases behind the bar. And the calendar art . . ." A Smokey the Bear poster is peeling off the wall, curling up like a diploma. A Winston Sweepstakes poster hovers overhead. Along the bar, someone has laid a protective strip of masking tape. "That knocks me out!" Murphy says. He moves in his chair, or tries to. "And this must be the only bar stool in the world that's stuck to the floor with chewing gum." He glances out the hallway, which leads into the terminal: a fire alarm and water hose against the wall. "See that alarm? Where it says to break the glass? The glass is already broken? Ready to go!" Everywhere, he finds endearing points of quality, a trove of charm, and you begin to feel there's no place like this in Hawaii, no place in the world. "It's . . . what . . . April?" Murphy says. "We still have our Christmas decorations up!" Finally, he directs our attention to the red-lettered sign above the bar: WELCOM. This is how you fall in love with islands.

IV

PONAPE: RAIN

Into the dim reaches
Beyond cloud haze
I make my way
Toward Ponape

◄ I ►

The Japanese are promiscuous in their regrets about the war.
Never again, never again, their monuments and markers
cry, from the limestone cliffs of Saipan to the blasted ridges
of Peleliu and Angaur, from the beach at Majuro to the
starved, bypassed islands of the Truk Lagoon. No end of regretting.
Surfeited by plaques, arches, bottles, and Buddhas, I want to say,
enough already! But this inscription, set in Japanese characters on a
roadside pillar near a river that plunges down out of the rain forest, out
of the mountains, rings true.

Anyone would miss this place. Ponape is a green, hulking, high island,
with ridge after ridge of rain-forested mountains. Four hundred inches
of rain a year make those peaks among the wettest places on earth, a
wilderness of tropical hardwoods, moss and fern, and mountain deer.
It rains often in Ponape and when the sun comes out, it steams. Ponape
drips; it never dries. Those showers that seemed so wasted in the
Marshalls—such petty targets—have found a worthy landing here,
where forty streams rush down out of the mountains, plunge over

waterfalls, fashion pools and rapids, course into the sixty thousand acres of mangrove swamps that surround the island. No sand beaches here, amen, no Caribbean sparkle, no aloha spirit, in this fecund, empty-feeling place.

I arrive in the rain. Clouds veil the mountains, sheets of brown water flow over the roads, the inside of the hotel van is steaming. And this is the dry season. Along the road, those same junked cars that would be bleached, salted, and rusted in Majuro sprout trees through floor-boards. Vines curl around headlights. A car turns into a tropical planter, overnight. The growth is constant here, and the rot. The rot stays in my mind, especially when I glance up at those socked-in mountain peaks. Handsome they may be, but there's something menacing about them, an air of failure. A mountain ought to soar, not sulk. It should burst out of the sea, off of underwater plains; it should break the timberline and pierce the clouds. Smothered in cloudy shoals, carpeted in rain forest, these are resentful-feeling mountains, wet morbid places where you can lose your grip, slip and fall, and die. And that is another reason I am wary about Ponape. I almost died here once, in these mountains.

In 1976, I was commissioned to prepare a travel guide for the Trust Territory; actually, to update a lively much-plagiarized pamphlet I'd written nine years earlier, while still a Peace Corps volunteer. It was a piece of cake. Ponape hadn't changed much. Kolonia was still a ram-shackle town of red-dirt streets with, as I had written, "fifteen bars serving 3,500 people or should we say 3,500 people serving fifteen bars?" The names and numbers had changed, but not the feeling of the place, a tin-roofed rattletrap of a town, but with history all around. An hour's boat ride away were the ruins of Nan Madol, a medieval stone city sitting in a moldering tidal swamp, a place of basalt rock walls, vaults, canals, pathways, temples. Around town, a ten-minute ride could cover the wall the Spanish left behind, ruins of Fort Alphonso XIII, and the obscure German graveyard, with the names of colonists who'd witnessed the bloody Sokehs rebellion of 1910, and the even more obscure graveyard where the rebels themselves were executed by German-officered troops brought up from Rabaul. "So that's where they're going to put us," one of the about-to-be-executed Ponapeans remarked, gazing into his grave. "There's water in it." The Japanese had left waterworks and rock crushers and a lovely tropical agricultural experiment station, with groves of breadfruit and mangosteen. And then there were the marks of the American period, bars mostly, the Darling Bar and Seaman's Inn, jukebox joints where Jim Reeves's laments carried up and down the street, out into the hot and heavy night. Country music felt oddly right in Kolonia, Ponape. It had the sense of small places stayed in too long, compromise and failure.

Beyond Kolonia, though, there was a Ponape I hadn't seen. Those cloudy, jungled mountains tempted me, and the accounts of waterfalls way up there, Yosemite-like waterfalls. I decided to hike to one such place, on the Awak River, in the municipality of Uh. Two guides, a Ponapean and an American, accompanied me into the rain forest, skirting farms, following the river upward and inland, to where it plunged into a dark, rock-lined pool. I should have stopped there, nodded, noted, and turned: jungle cataracts, cool pools, gleaming black rooks, greenhouse foliage, thank you very much, lunchtime! But I wanted to get to the top of the falls.

The deceptive thing about a rain forest is that it keeps you so busy watching your next move, dealing with a vine that wants to garrote you, or testing a solid looking log that collapses underfoot, you lose your sense of the overall terrain. That's what happened to us. We were led on without knowing where we were going, feeling our way toward the top of the ridge. Edging nervously around a bay window of rock that bucked out before us, we saw we were at a dead end, trapped on a tiny ledge of rock at the edge of what we now realized was a precipice.

When fear comes to me, it comes first to my legs: a trembling, twitching, draining-away of confidence. I felt that now, knowing we'd have to go back around that rock, seeking out handholds and footholds so trivial they seemed like acne scars on a Mount Rushmore face. I didn't want to go back around that rock. I took a deep breath. Whatever happened, I wanted it to be over fast. A sudden fatalism overcame me. No struggle, no cry for help, no interesting thoughts. Just a sudden sense of . . . whatever. Right out of the blue, in the midst of life, in love and on a roll, I couldn't manage to protest or reflect. Was it the same sort of mood that overcame my friend Salii, at the end? No closing monologues, no careful note left behind. Death in the middle of the day, right here in paradise.

That was what surprised my guides, they later said. Not a sound out of me. I clutched the rock, bear-hugged it, arms and legs wide apart and then—like a coconut coming off a tree—I fell, sixty feet through the air, twenty feet rolling over rocks, ass over elbows. They rushed down to where I lay, fearing I was dead. But I was only sleeping, deeply, luxuriously, and when I started to stir, when I heard voices—"Are we ready to move him now?"—it was only to wonder why I'd gone to sleep in this particular spot, which wasn't comfortable, for there were rocks beneath me.

A few weeks later, in a Honolulu hospital, dealing with a left arm that would never straighten again and a wrist that would never entirely turn, I got mail from Patti Arthur in Ponape. She ran a new hotel, the Village, and her husband Bob had helped carry me out of the rain forest on an improvised stretcher. "The Ponapeans didn't want to talk about this," she wrote, "but Bob and I remembered hearing about that place belonging to one of the spirits, so asked. There is a woman here, Nimoadoalang, although I probably misspell it, who years ago suffered an unjust fate at the hands of the Nanmwarki, Ponape's paramount chief, and was subsequently put to death. She haunts this island regularly, usually in the form of a breathtakingly beautiful young girl, dressed in red. She has been known to stand at the side of the road with a basket of food in her hand, offering her morsels to innocents passing by. To accept her proffered gifts is to court disaster. Many who have partaken of her food and/or charms have gone insane. She often changes from a nubile maiden to a wretched hag, feared universally by all Ponapeans, and is by far the most notorious of all—and there are many—of the ghosts here. She has this rather annoying habit of haunting and laying claim to places where fresh water flows . . . I believe this has something to do with the way she died, which had to do with water. Anyway, guess whose waterfall that is that you were trying to reach?"

So I return to the Village, where the Arthurs still preside, even though it is not where most of the island politicians and resident American characters put up. The Village is a collection of thatch bungalows, airy and comfortable, perched on a jungled slope twenty minutes from town. Staying there casts me as something of a tourist, for it's a rare Micronesian who'd *pay* to sleep under a grass roof, to look out a screened window at a hillside of breadfruit and bananas. To hell with it. Happy to be back, I repose in the outdoor dining area, pleased to watch mosquitoes and moths destroy themselves spectacularly, flying up against an electronic bug zapper above the bar. Elsewhere in Ponape they are watching videotaped films on television. Ironic: the old Peace Corps dictum was that we live on the level of the locals, impress them with our intercultural sensitivity, our vows of voluntary poverty. But what happens when people want to live like Americans? What happens is island lovers coming in and California dreaming islanders going out. Maybe everybody is born in the wrong place.

◄ II ►

They have tried rice and cacao in Ponape. They have tried—are still trying—gourmet pepper, trochus shells, fishing. The time will come, everyone says, when they try big-time tourism, resorts and golf courses for the Japanese. What they are mainly trying now is government. Ponape is the national capital of the Federated States of Micronesia, which includes the neighboring state of Truk, populous and troubled, and two smaller places, Yap and Kusaie, now called Kosrae.

The precise status of the Federated States of Micronesia—and the republics of Palau and the Marshalls—is far from clear. Once part of the Trust Territory of Pacific Islands, they all now claim sovereignty while at the same time maintaining close ties with the United States. Count them among the world's not-quite nations, along with Lithuania, Bophu-thatswana, Puerto Rico. Some people claim the Federated States of Micronesia is an independent nation, notwithstanding its relationship of free association with the United States. Critics demur: you can't rely on Washington for money and delegate military rights to the Pentagon and be considered anything but a territory in disguise. Sovereign but not independent, some say. Independent, but not sovereign. Both or neither. The argument goes on. Is the trusteeship over, as the United States claims, unilaterally? Or are the others right, the ones who say the trusteeship continues until the U.N. Security Council says it's over. That's the Russian claim, and they have a veto in the Security Council. As in the Marshalls, arguments about what the place is now shade into disputes about what it will become—an independent nation with close, friendly ties to the United States or a pathetic American client state, dependent and adrift.

Meanwhile, Kolonia is a government town, with offices behind gas stations, above grocery stores and dress shops, along the main street, and down by the docks and in an old hospital across from the Spanish Wall. The place has the hasty, improvised appearance of a government in exile, on the lam after the fall of Washington or Richmond. Soon there will be a new capitol that a Korean construction firm is close to finishing, an $11 million campus that Washington paid for, outside town at a place called Palikir. It's a gorgeous, hopeful site, with rain-forested peaks on one side, hills rolling into mangrove swamps on the other; a great sense of new beginnings, compared to sad, soggy Kolonia. There's only one drawback that I can see, and even it may turn out to the good. Near the new capitol is a conical little hill, a volcanic plug that's known in Ponapean as *pewshin malek*. These days, what with the new capitol so nearby, you have to press before people tell you what it means in English: chicken shit.

I have to watch myself out here, with chicken shit jokes, watch what I say to old friends. They've spent their lives, some of them, wondering what to do about the United States, and this . . . for now . . . is the result. How close did they want to be? How far away could they afford to go? What did they want their kids to be? Who did they see as their neighbors? Were they prepared to compete against Americans and Japanese? Where? Here . . . or there?

If they disliked us, as some of them did, they still had to wonder what they could do about it, without damning themselves to poverty and isolation. If they loved us, if they wanted to go to America, was that the same as allowing America to come here?

Sometimes you could almost see them weighing things. What was good about America: health care, schools, federal programs, scholarships and travel, chicken and steak, cold beer and soda, ice cream and movies. What was bad about America: taxes, regulations, racial problems, federal agencies, auditors and prosecutors who didn't understand "island ways." Good: the chance of escaping to America. Bad: the prospect of Americans escaping here.

You watched them go through all of it. You pointed out some good things, you warned them about the bad. Peace Corps volunteers were full of warnings about America. But it didn't matter—the islands were tied to us. We represented the world to them. Years later, I saw the same thing in the Philippines, saw Marcos fleeing to the same country that Aquino had fled to. We were tied. Like the Philippines, only more so, Micronesia was bound to us. They were one of those places that decolonization orphans as much as liberates.

A likable young man named John Haglelgam recently became the president of the Federated States of Micronesia, and there's a lesson in his rise to power. People come to islands thinking that their lives will be simplified. Leave the world's dissemblings and complexities behind, confine yourself to a small, manageable place, confront directly what is important. Nonsense. Islands are tangled and intricate places, not in spite of their smallness but because of it. If hell is other people—Sartre's line from *No Exit*—if hell is an unchanging cast of characters on a small stage, islands are hell.

The constitution I saw written provides that the president be elected from the national Senate. There are two-year senators and four-year senators. The president comes from among the heavyweights, the four-year men, and the first president was a heavyweight champion. Tosiwo Nakayama was a longtime member of the old Congress of Micronesia, later president of the Constitutional Convention and, thus, one of the founding fathers. He also comes from Truk, the FSM's most populous district. An impressive man, conciliatory with other Micronesians, firm with Americans, he was an obvious first choice. After he completed two terms, things got tricky. The word was that Ponape, the second-largest state, would have the second president. Waiting there was Bailey Olter, another old-timer. He was expected to run for and win the four-year Senate seat and then become president. Then, things went awry. Bethwel Henry, an old-timer as well, joined the race. Henry and Olter were both from the outer islands of the Ponape state. They split enough of their home-island vote to permit Leo Falcam, a main-islander, to capture the four-year seat. And, yes, Falcam was also an old-timer, but the wrong kind. He'd been a special assistant to the high commissioner on Saipan, an appointed district administrator in Ponape, later an elected governor. He'd spent years as a Trust Territory representative in Washington. All his experience was outside the legislature.

When the maneuvering was over, the hallway meetings and long-distance phone calls, Falcam was still in the Senate. Bailey Olter went to work for the Ponape state government. Bethwel Henry was given Falcam's old job, postmaster general of the FSM. Nobody starved, nobody died. And the presidency went to a newcomer, someone from the boondocks of Micronesia, the outer islands of Yap, low lying and low caste, someone from a place called Eauripik. I have been to Eauripik, years ago, near the end of a long voyage through the Yap District, and I have not forgotten it: a scrap of sand and palm, half a mile long, I estimated, and a couple hundred yards wide. A cold rain confined us to a boathouse; there wasn't much copra on Eauripik, and I wondered how the people would pay for the California rice and Taiwan sugar, New Zealand corned beef and Australian flour that the ship's boat was bringing in. Then a dozen men came in out of the rain, carrying handicrafts, spreading them out on an outrigger. It was sad, how few of us there were to buy, for this stuff was finer than any we'd seen. There were carvings, stiff monkey men with unexpected, feline eyes of white shell. There were graceful streamlined fish, breadfruit-wood tackle boxes with turtle shell hooks inside; adzes of wood and shell; carved bowls, hibiscus bark sarongs with intricate designs. And, best of all, the superb turtle shell belts made only on Eauripik, hundreds of individually carved and pierced turtle shell rings strung on strands of coconut rope, four dollars a strand. We sat there in the boathouse, near the fag end of a field trip that had started a week late and lost another week along the way, the men showing their wares and the women, bright faced with yellow paint, sitting at the other end of the boathouse. Then the rain let up and we walked back through the shallows to where the ship's boat would take us out to the field trip vessel, hovering offshore. I remembered one other thing about Eauripik. For some reason, the handshake had caught on, even among the women. Some of them even called us back to shake hands, as if to thank us for coming to the island, and wish us a Merry Christmas.

Now a man from Eauripik is president. I know his island and I know John Haglelgam too; he'd been a delegate at the Constitutional Convention a dozen years before, a quiet, unassuming fellow whom no one would have guessed would be the second president of the place whose constitution we were writing. A 100-to-1 shot from Eauripik, accidental president, accidental island. His office is in the same grungy old hospital building where I lay for three days, shocked and amnesiac after my rain forest dive a dozen years ago. "Ask me anything about American literature," I had pleaded, not sure my brain still worked, "go ahead, anything about American literature," to nurses who wrapped my powdered, comminuted elbow, to barmaids from the Palm Terrace who brought me chicken soup, to my wife. "Go ahead, ask me." I have a different line of questions for President Haglelgam: deficits, boondoggles, partisanship, corruption, division, secession, all the time the clock ticking away on the fifteen years of U.S. funding.

On these subjects, Haglelgam tells me what I expected to hear. Unity is growing, he argues, the nation is coming together, the worst frictions are behind. There are worries, yes, about the economy, about whether the Americans' money is being spent on projects that will lead to self-sufficiency or—a more common view—dissipated on pork barrel projects. A recent audit of government projects showed money spent on outboard motors, private vehicles, nonexistent docks and meeting halls in Truk; in Ponape, public funds were spent on pigs, yams, sakau, private vehicles. In Kosrae, money went for renovation work that was never done and for a nonexistent playground on land bought twice from the same owner.

"I almost threw up when I read that report," Haglelgam confides. He urges revenue-generating projects, canning factories, fishing boats. He

argues for prudence, austerity. "We were spoiled by the Trust Territory," he grants. "People believed the government had an infinite supply of money. You hear people say, so what if the government incurs
a deficit. Uncle Sam will give it to us." I take dutiful notes on all of this.
He's game enough, but it's all for the record, his comments and my
scribbling. Another islander mixing up a batch of good intentions, un-
foreseen difficulties, gallant efforts, bracing for the day when they ask
for more money. But what I want to know about is Eauripik. I ask if he's
returned there, since becoming president. He nods. What was it like, I
ask, and his face lights up. He's enjoying this part of our talk. Eauripik.
We have it in common. For a moment, we're connected, drawing lines
between the smallest possible dots. "Even my mother came up and said,
'Okay if I shake hands with you?' " he says. "And all my aunts—in my
language we call aunts, mothers and mothers, aunts—they wouldn't
even come close."

They don't make copra anymore on Eauripik, he says, and local
canoes, carved out of breadfruit wood, are being challenged by Japanese Yamahas. The handicraft goes on, but the island mainly lives off
remittances from sons and daughters who've moved off the island. "I
just sent six hundred dollars to my father," Haglelgam says. And then
I ask the old question: about going back.

"I can go back and live for a short time," he says. "But I couldn't go
back and stay there for all of my life. I'm a scholarly type. I lack what
my father has. I lack the ability to make canoes. I'm too old to learn the
traditional skills, to live there and enjoy life. My orientation is toward
Western culture. Books. Government. Discussion. I really enjoy the
academic life."

I'm surprised. I'd expected another version of the island pastorale:
home island, return to roots, Pacific way. He doesn't oblige. That may
be the difference between the first generation of island leaders—
Nakayama, Kabua, Salii—and men like Haglelgam, now in his early
forties. The founding fathers thought that they could go back, that they
could choose one way or the other. Even if they postponed the choice
indefinitely, they liked to think it was there for them—and that they
were there for it. So instead of opting for outright independence or for

straightforward assimilation into the United States, they tried to have it both ways. They came up with free association, an open-ended, indeterminate status. They weren't divorcing the United States, and they weren't marrying it either, they were . . . well . . . engaged. Not engaged to be married, just engaged to be engaged. Shacking up. The new guys know better, or know different. They know there's no going back to their personal Eauripiks. Once you leave, you're gone. The older generation was caught between its past and future. These were complicated men. Their children, more ready to adapt, move on and out with ease. It's the difference, I guess, between being torn and being cut.

◄ III ►

Let it be said, up front: people drink an awful lot out here. Blame it on the weather, blame it on boredom and confinement and paucity of choices, lack of art or sport or warfare. They drink beer mostly— Budweiser has the market cornered these days—and a case of beer has the staying power of a six-pack in the United States. There are exceptions. The diet-conscious go for wine, usually too late, and sophisticates drink hard stuff. But beer is the drink of the American tropics. It produces piles of empty cans everywhere and it creates stomachs that are unmatched in the world. You see a man walking down the street, you come up from behind, noticing broad shoulders, brawny arms. His legs are sturdy and muscular and—because this is Micronesia—you know that the feet will be a pedicurist's nightmare, scarred with bites and healed-over infections, toenails chipped and broken, with an abnormal callused gap between the big toe and the next digit, a gulf formed by years of wearing rubber-thonged sandals. So far so good. But then you pass and it comes into view, this bulge, this beer tumor, this lifelong pregnancy from which death alone can bring deliverance. Out here, beer isn't an alcoholic drink. It's liquid protein, it's something you hold in your hand like a key chain, it's a quarter-hour's fun, a pledge of allegiance to America. It is ice breaker and air-conditioning, sport and combat. I remember Payday Fridays.

The Trust Territory government paid its employees every two weeks, on Friday, and what followed was a tropical *Walpurgisnacht*. Islanders were famous for casualness about work schedules but they definitely picked up their checks on time and cashed them fast and drank them up in a hurry, before their endless relatives could touch them up for a loan. Payday Fridays brought together weird mixes: Japanese tourists, government clerks, sardonic barmaids, bickering married couples, politicians on the make. I remember a TT employee, an entomologist howling with joy at the madness of it, and a Jesuit priest who took the mike near closing time and produced a wistful, perfect "Unchained Melody." It was the ultimate party.

Almost ultimate. There was that one time I heard about too late, but I had a friend, a yeoman drinker, raised in sandy taverns along the New Jersey shore, who entered a beer-drinking contest on Saipan. Free beer! What he remembers is forty or fifty competitors seated at a half-dozen picnic tables, out in the hot sun, chugging one can of beer after another. The beer was on the warm side too, and that didn't make it easier, but he hung in there as long as he could. He got to the nineteenth beer before he was tossed out for a rules violation: a wet burp. "I burped and about a quart of beer came out." The winner, a Saipanese guy, came in at about forty beers. He had a trick, shaking the beer vigorously, getting rid of the carbonation, flattening it before he drank it. "He didn't know anything when it was over," my friend says, "but he knew he'd won."

In Ponape these days there's the Ocean View, out toward Bailey Olter's hotel, and there's the Low Gear Bar, at the top of the hill near the new capitol, and Little Micronesia, the Green Bay View and Tiny Bubbles and Blue Magic. There are dozens of sakau bars too, purveying the local brew at twenty-five or thirty cents a cup. But at happy hour, right after the government shrugs off another day of free association, the Palm Terrace is the place to be. There among the sundowners is Gene Ashby, a community college teacher who wrote the definitive guide to Ponape. He inscribes a copy "With best wishes from the outer edge of paradise." Down the bar, hunkered over Budweisers, are a couple of American retirees from Kwajalein, weathered and nicotined truck-stop types, spending twilight years with local women. There's a former Peace Corps director who now sells insurance. There are a court reporter, and a guy who used to raise pigs on Yap and another who used to manage a department store on Saipan, and the local sheriff who talks about exploding some 60-millimeter Japanese mortars found in a cave near the community college. There's banter with barmaids. *Smile, Lulu, aw, come on.* Somebody vomited in the john. The crew of a navy tug comes in and whoops it up. The sundowners give them a middling grade: livelier than an impeccably behaved group of Japanese Navy recruits who visited, tame by comparison to the hulksters who stepped off a Samoan purse seiner and wild bunched it through Kolonia. *Aw, Lulu, smile if you're wearing panties.* Ponape's at war with Truk, you know, ready to secede . . . *Aw, Lulu* . . . now they've got that new capitol they can tell the Trukese to piss off . . . whole place is falling apart, gonna be a commonwealth anyway, look at Saipan, happier than pigs in shit . . . Lulu plays basketball with empty Budweisers, clanking them against the inside of a garbage can . . . hell, these are growing pains, just like the United States during the Articles of Confederation period . . . bullshit, the Japanese are coming back . . . no way, the way these people hold on to land, the place'll never develop . . . heard about that damn golf course for years . . . the nice thing about Joe was you could say Joe, I need a bill signed, here's a cow . . . this place has potential . . . this place is fucked . . . the way those Japs vacuum the ocean with drift nets . . . the thing about these people, see . . . friendly . . . devious . . . do you have any Ponapean friends, really . . . come on . . . the women . . . they'll take you . . . sneak around . . . there's nothing here . . . I love it . . . *Lulu!*

As the evening rolls along, the mix at the Palm Terrace changes. Many—not all—of the Americans depart, weaving their way through parking lot puddles, climbing into pickup trucks, driving home to their second—local—wives. It used to be, these unions seldom lasted because the partners were at cross-purposes. You could see it from the beginning. You'd have a Peace Corps volunteer, excited about being an outcast of the islands, getting in on the ground floor in paradise, opening a business, practicing law, teaching. The most mundane practition-

ers back home—plumbers, mechanics—might become colorful characters out here. Then, the wedding: the tables full of fish and pork and
chicken, rice and taro. In-laws galore, a clan of exotics, wizened old men
and women with betelnut-stained mouths, with tattoos, with legends
and stories that stretched back for generations. Consider, now, the
bride, those dark eyes, that lustrous coconut-oiled skin, that cascade of
black hair—has it ever, ever been cut?—flowing down over her waist.
Could our man have done better anywhere? The dream lives! But
then—sometimes, not always—it changes. The bride didn't have an
island life in mind when she married an off-islander. Living well with an
American is not the best revenge. Escape is the point, the same escape
that brought her husband to the islands. And so they sometimes part.
She takes her best shot, Guam, Hawaii, California. And her husband
stays. He's wised up by now, an island hand, a certain air of knowing
how things work out here, what "these people" are really like. He joins
the gang holding up the bar at a place like the Palm Terrace.

By seven the Ponapeans start coming in, sitting at the corner of the
bar, on the edge of the bullshit, and hanging around the pool tables,
darker and more reticent than the good old boys who rule the roost.
By closing time, I hear, the place is an all-Ponapean bar, and that's when
fights break out. There you have it, the history of the late trusteeship
and the newly born Federated States. You kind of need some Americans
around. They're inviting targets, awkward and self-conscious in colonial
roles, eager to demonstrate that this sort of thing doesn't come natu-
rally. America doesn't fight wars to conquer territory. America doesn't
have colonies, not really, so this whole trusteeship thing was a bit out
of our line, all these Smokey the Bear types from Interior running a slew
of islands nobody outside of the Pentagon ever heard of, not knowing
whether they were there to protect the place or develop it, not knowing
how long they were staying or what they were supposed to leave behind, and now, like the sundowners at the Palm Terrace, America
creeps a safe distance away, leaves a generous tip among the empty
beer cans, and the locals in control of the bar from which, as darkness
falls, you can hear the sound of breaking glass.

A coffee cup, actually. The coffee cup heard 'round Micronesia. In a session of FSM Senate a few months ago, Kalisto Refolopei, a Truk senator with a tough-guy reputation, hurled a coffee cup across the room and stomped out of the session. It wasn't clear what was bothering him that day; some people say he was upset at his failure to obtain government jobs for a couple of constituents. The Ponapeans—all but one, who was subsequently unseated—walked out and the Kosraeans followed. The Yapese flew home. All the old questions about unity arose. And remain. Sometimes the very idea of an islands nation seems oxymoronic, internally contradictory, like jumbo shrimp.

◄ IV ►

Along the roads, on rainy afternoons, you pass dump trucks loaded with coral, headed for construction projects, you pass dogs napping, pigs screwing, and you pass kids, lots of them, coming home from school. You wonder what will keep those kids here and then you wonder how they'll manage to leave. Ways of escape. Zippy's, a Hawaiian fast-food operation, just came through on a hiring trip, and U.S. military recruiters periodically snag the bright ones who can pass the test, and last summer a planeload of Ponapeans spent the season picking fruit in Washington State. Ways of escape. Women along the roads at night, wearing those bright, flower-print dresses. You catch them in your high beams, like deer. You give them a ride and the smell of coconut oil fills up the car. God help those Americans who come here to restore a marriage that's fraying, hoping a term in paradise will patch things up. Dead meat.

The road takes me through Kolonia, which looks more ordinary than usual on a rainy day like this: puddles on red-clay roads, a gaggle of mud-splashed cars outside the post office, two-story concrete stores, crowded schoolyards where kids salute the flag of the Federated States of Micronesia—FSM. "Fissems." I saw the preamble I wrote for the constitution posted on a classroom wall the other day. "The seas do not divide us, they bring us together." How odd it would be, if that were the single piece of writing I'm most remembered for.

I cruise the airport. On plane days, the place gets crowded and a couple times a week, when two Air Micronesia flights show up at the same time, the airport is jammed. The island looks outward, fixed on what comes in off the plane. I wonder how many FSM's would take a one-way ticket to California, if they had the chance. Or to New York. For years, whenever Trust Territory delegations came to town for the U.N. Trusteeship Council, I went out of my way to host them. I did anything to get them out of their hotel rooms. I did escort duty at the Staten Island Ferry, the Top of the Sixes, Times Square, Shea Stadium. That was a hoot, me buying smoked fish at Zabar's, carrying the stuff on the subway so my island buddies wouldn't have to put up with ballpark hot dogs. I ended up eating the fish; they preferred wieners. There are always lessons left to learn. Another lesson: though they appreciated the efforts I made, they'd just as soon I didn't try. They'd rather sit and wait their turn at the U.N. They were out of it, in New York, and it broke my heart. They were like fish on a boat deck, losing their color by the minute. Except Salii. He wanted it all, believed he could hold his own with anyone, go anywhere. Sometimes it seemed he was traveling the world, looking for his match. He wasn't intimidated by professors, advisers, experts. He used lawyers like Kleenex. He was happiest when traveling. London, Paris, Teheran, Taiwan, Tokyo, Hong Kong. The sad part was at home. Home brought him down. What would it take, for someone like him to be happy in the islands? "The end of all ambition," Samuel Johnson wrote, "is to be happy at home." Not here, not yet.

Then again, look at the homes they build. Once they left behind thatch and wood and bamboo, once local materials became something impossible to find outside of tourist hotels, the islands were in trouble. They lived in Quonset huts, in wood-and-tin shacks right out of West Virginia. Then they moved up to concrete houses that the typhoons couldn't take away. Alas. Now you see more elaborate places, with porches, balconies, and balustrades. But it all feels imported, brought in from other places. Like Majuro, Kolonia has a shipped-in feeling.

I leave Kolonia, follow the road past the Palm Terrace, turn right, up onto a wooded ridge, into the village of Porakiet, a different-looking place. Most of the people in Micronesia are Micronesians. But Porakiet is an enclave of people who moved up from Kapingamarangi and Nukuoro, a couple far-south Polynesian atolls that got included in the Trust Territory. The village is odd: open-sided buildings with raised sleeping platforms of wood so smooth, so sensuous it almost begs you to lie down in furniture-less rest. The houses are jammed together, even by district-center standards, but the place is saved from outright squalor by the gardens, groves of breadfruit trees, stands of coconut and bananas. Neat, small gardens are filled with taro and tapioca, and flowers are everywhere: hibiscus, plumeria, orchids, croton. I like the place in the morning, when it's just starting to stir, late sleepers still curled up on platforms, a woman raking a red-gravel yard outside, another working in a garden while it's still cool, one hand on a weed, another covering her breasts, as I pass. Washing and cooking begin and the smoke of coconut husk fires drifts through the village. Men wrapped in bright cloth sarongs sit around the men's house, drinking tea and eating canned Steak 'n' Gravy. Almost every house has its compost pile of Budweiser cans.

"This is Poraklet village," a Micronesian politician once remarked to me from behind sunglasses. "This is where you see big tits." Micronesians are nonchalant about toplessness, so I had to wonder whether his crack wasn't for my benefit, just the way I wondered whether comments on sunsets were for my benefit as well. Were these things an islander really cared about it? Or was he just tossing a line my way, knowing outsiders have a thing about . . . tits and sunsets? Sometimes there's no way of knowing if what matters to us matters to them. When an islander praises his island—the beauty and tranquillity of his village say—does this encomium reflect his values, or is he like a car salesman ticking off the fine points of a clunker he wants to get off the lot as fast as he can?

Salii, again. Years ago, at the end of my Peace Corps service, he drove me to the airport, where I would catch the plane that would take me to Guam and then to Newark. I was in a bubbling upbeat mood, looking forward to the States but also assuming that I'd be back in the islands in no time, working with him. "There were three things I missed while I was out here," I said. "Fresh bread—bread that had a real crust on it. Draft beer. And a daily newspaper." I looked over at him. I was going to be his Boswell, his Lowell Thomas, his Edgar Snow. I asked what it was about the islands that he'd missed, those years he was at the University of Hawaii. He paused a moment, the way most islanders did when they were talking with Americans, but the others were usually struggling with English or trying to figure out what you wanted them to say. Salii was exceptional. He thought. And thought. And then he told me what he'd missed. "Nothing." And I decided I admired him for his honesty.

Just outside Porakiet, I see someone walking outside a solid, Western-style two-story house with an exceptionally neat yard. Though his back is turned, I know him at once: that stocky Prussian carriage, alert and ready. A Protestant missionary, Reverend Edmund Kalau first came to Palau in 1965; three years later, he went to Yap, where I did a *Micronesian Reporter* piece on him. A hard-working bricks-and-mortar missionary, Kalau had trained as a German pilot toward the end of World War II, though the Luftwaffe ran out of gas before he had a chance to do harm to himself or anyone else. He found religion after the war and, when I met him, was using his flying skills to bring medical air service to the outer islands.

Micronesia made me a connoisseur of missionaries. They were the ultimate volunteers, the deep-dish stayers-on. Often, the Catholics had a leg up. While the Protestants had wives and kids to worry about, the Jesuits came alone and stayed forever. They were hugely memorable: the chronically seasick Father Walter, who nonetheless spent a lifetime in the outer islands of Truk and Yap; Father MacManus, who went so far into the Palauan language that he came up with words and expressions Palauans themselves had forgotten; Father Costigan, the Bronx-born legend who founded a trade school in Ponape.

And now, Kalau. He and his wife have stayed, and this pleases me, and his children, far from distracting him, are part of the mission. Norbert runs mission boats, Dieter pilots mission planes, and Esther is a nurse. On a rainy afternoon, Kalau brings me up to date on his activities: mission flights out of Ponape and Yap, a maritime academy in an abandoned Coast Guard Loran station on Yap, a ninety-foot yacht converted into a medical ship that will call at all the outer islands three times a year, a television station that will be "fifty percent educational, fifty percent religious." He plans drug rehabilitation centers in Palau and Ponape. Drugs are much on his mind.

"Everybody credits marijuana to the Peace Corps," he says, casting an apologetic smile my way. "Before that they had betelnut, alcohol, and sakau, and betelnut is habit-forming but not addictive. Then marijuana came in, started by the Americans here. And there are people— both Americans and Micronesians—who use cocaine and heroin. Now grandmothers go around and sell marijuana. I've been stopped and offered a marijuana cigarette for two dollars."

Kalau practices the old-fashioned virtues—discipline, honesty, hard work—German style and this in a place where Western ethics—book-keeping, budgets, schedules—come to grief. Though his success has been substantial, his very accomplishments are suspect. He must really be raking it in, one politician implies and an American, sympathetic, refers to him as "the most abused man on the island."

"They believe I have millions stashed away," Kalau says. "We're audited by agencies in the United States and Germany. All the money we make goes back into operations. Not one penny goes to us privately. But you know how people start . . . whatever you do, people will talk. If I worried about it, I wouldn't produce anything."

The rain drips off Kalau's gutters. Chickens forage in his backyard. The room we sit in has some of the German knickknacks I recognize from my parents' house. There's sheet music on the piano: *"Wie schön leuchtet der Morgenstern."* At one side of the room, a bicycle-type exercise machine. *"Biegen aber nicht brechen,"* the saying goes: bend but don't break. Kalau hasn't broken, and he hasn't bent much either and I suspect he's oblivious to island-sniping. He'll march out as he marched in, unencumbered by doubt: "When people say we should leave Micronesians alone, I say, if so, don't teach them to read and write, because the moment their minds are touched, you cannot stop."

What intrigues me about Kalau is that he is a German in islands Germany once ruled, from the turn of the century until 1914. German names are still all through the island, Bismarck, Weilbacher, and Fritz; German blood as well. The past reaches out from the kaiser's vanished empire, more tenuously, also more gently, than from the Japanese imperium. Out here, colonial periods are like so many layers, which you can peel back one at a time. There were old men who spoke German when I came out in the sixties, a few of them left in every district. One of them, half senile, kissed my hand when I spoke a few words. Another got drunk with me, confiding—one Teuton to another—that these new-comer Americans lacked discipline. It's nice to find a corner of the world where Germans are well remembered. Edmund Kalau replicates some of those strengths and makes me wonder what the place would be like if the Germans had stayed. There are houses still standing in the Marshalls that have a German look. There are government offices in Western Samoa that the Germans built. I wonder what Kolonia would look like if the people who named it had lasted.

The missionary's eyes light up, his face flushes with laughter as he recalls a night in Yap when he and his wife were awakened by noises on their front porch. They found a half-dozen old Yapese men waiting for them there, loincloths, beer bellies, betelnut mouths, lined up as if on a parade ground. *"Achtung!"* shouted one of them, taking the part of some long-gone drill sergeant. *"Brust raus, Bauch rein"*—chest out, belly in. And then, turning to the Kalaus, *"Jetzt, ein Lied."* They sang the old songs. *"Wer will unter den Soldaten, er muss haben ein Gewehr." "Ach das fällt mir so schwer, auseinander zu gehen." "Ich hatt ein Kameraden."* They ended with an explanation. *"Wir waren Deutsche soldaten."* German soldiers, still.

These days, Germany seems materialistic to the Kalaus. He still feels drawn to Palau, his first post. After all the years he senses there was something different about the Palauans. His wife shakes her head. Maybe Oregon or Northern California will do, when they retire. I wonder about their last day, that last trip to the airport, waiting for the plane that will take them away forever. There are horror stories about long-timers' departures: a heroic schoolmarm in Truk, leaving after decades, going home to die, and just three people at the airport to say goodbye. The islands rarely say thank you.

"I'm realistic," he begins. "We do not expect . . ." He stops and starts over. "We know the nature of humanity. The day will come when I leave. I do not expect crowds at the airport. Knowing human nature . . . I do not want to build an illusionary castle . . . it can be painful to people if they expect it. What is important is that I know between me and my god I have fulfilled my duty."

◄ V ►

It rains almost every night in Ponape, hard sudden showers that roll down from the mountains. Sometimes there are lightning flashes and you wait for thunder that you can never hear, it's raining so hard. I piss more often in this weather. The rain induces it, I think. If the sun comes out in the morning, it's like the first day of creation, and Ponape reminds me of some dark, long-haired woman, surfacing after a dive below a waterfall, bounding into daylight, streaming and new. But other days— today is one—the rain stays: clouds impaled on mountains, caught like ships on reefs. Rather than forage for chat in air-conditioned offices, I stay at the hotel, drinking coffee, and try to sort out my thoughts. I caution myself against hasty judgment. Maybe all the reports of money wasted, half-assed projects, short-sighted politics, maybe it's just grow- ing pains. Maybe. The United States had its early turmoil. And a civil war besides. Who am I to judge? Or to cluck about the environment, when the *Pacific Daily News* is all full of the Exxon *Valdez*? Or about deficits, coming as I do from the world's champ debtor nation? Or—god—to worry about drugs and violence, when the last stop on my airplane ticket is Newark, New Jersey. *Sewark,* the stewardesses call it. And yet, there was always the hope that our mistakes might not be repeated out here, that they wouldn't feel so perversely *entitled* to repeat them, that—and here's the scariest scenario of all—under the cover of a dubious independence, with all the prideful trappings that accompany it, flags, diplomatic recognitions, twenty-one-gun salutes, they won't just raffle their islands off. Shit, I'm sounding like a Peace Corps volunteer again, yet through the Marshalls and here in Ponape a line from *Citizen Kane* keeps coming back to me. I can't shake it. "You can make a lot of money . . . if money's all you want to make." And outside is where the action comes from, the deals and the money. I expected this in the Marshalls, small as they are. But in Ponape I thought it might be different, that the essential passivity of islands might be broken in this green and open place. But island eyes turn outward, scanning the horizon, looking to Washington for programs and budgets, to Japan, where people are hooked on sashimi, golf courses, and warm places in the winter.

The rain looks like sweat when it trickles down off banana leaves. Breadfruit go *thunk* when they hit the ground. I wonder what it takes, getting the breadfruit off the tree and onto a table. I love breadfruit. You can boil or fry it, like a potato. On outer islands, they bury it for months, dig it up and eat it, all funky and fermenting. I'd forgotten how disappointing it can be, traveling through the islands, to be confronted with chopped steak, french fries, white bread, instant coffee. There are exceptions: the Village does a decent job, especially with mangrove crab; some Japanese-run restaurants serve local fish. But there's nothing like that look on a tourist's face, sitting on a tropical island, confronted with some canned pineapple from the Philippines and Thailand. I've seen that look a hundred times, astonishment that contains the beginning of wisdom. You picture beaches, you get mangrove swamps. You imagine native markets teeming with fruits and vegetables, you get rows of dusty canned goods, freezers full of rock-hard mastodon meat that could have been carved out of a glacier. Island fantasies go glimmering. Big ideas too. I've seen investors come in with plantations, mines, hotels, fishing fleets on their minds, only to find that land was parceled and entangled beyond belief, that labor was spoiled and scarce, that politics was rife. Economic development, island style, meant marrying outside money, Japanese or American, with outside labor—Filipino, Korean, or Chinese. The local role in all this was that of agent and landlord, something like the minister, organist, and witness at Las Vegas wedding chapels who'll marry almost anybody, no questions asked, for a fee.

Later, on this wet, do-nothing morning, at just the time when taste for coffee yields to thoughts of beer, a legend enters, Budweiser in hand. Matt Mix arrived in the islands a few months after I did, back in 1967. The moment he stepped off the plane in Guam, wearing a straw boater, carrying a guitar, he was famous. A photographer snapped his picture, the wire services picked it up, and the result—this being Vietnam time—was forty-six U.S. newspaper editorials about draft-dodging Peace Corps volunteers. Mix was unperturbed. His arrival in Truk, for training, was like a homecoming to him.

"I loved it the minute I stepped off the DC-4," he says. "I knew in fifteen minutes I was home. I cut my foot on a broken bottle, stepping onto the dock at Udot, and I still loved it!"

The heat, the islands, learning a new language, brewing up yeast and sugar, in defiance of Peace Corps rules, sneaking across the lagoon to drink beer at the old Truk Trading Company bar in Moen, also in defiance of Peace Corps rules, he loved it all. Assigned to Kusaie, he defied the rules again. Later they made it sound like a whole plantation, he complains, those two marijuana plants he had in back of this house. The coconut telegraph turned him into a pothead's Johnny Appleseed. Only two plants, he stipulates. But when a local kid started talking about Matt's cigarettes that made you drunk, the Peace Corps had enough. They yanked him home.

That wasn't the end of it though. After a short visit to his home in the freeze-ass latitudes of upstate New York, Matt found a job at a florist shop, saved his money, and returned to Ponape with twenty-five dollars in his pocket and half a promise of employment from the Ponape Cooperative Federation. He started as a truck driver, worked his way up. Now he's a lawyer, a belching, potbellied red-nosed character, pungent and happy. This morning he dropped one set of in-laws at a farm, harvesting taro. He left another group at a fishing place. He scrounged around town for a spare part, a cylinder for a 1972 Toyota Landcruiser. He's married to a Ponapean woman, a second marriage, has ten, twelve, fifteen kids around. In 1978, in a bill that moved from the Sokehs Municipal Council to the Ponape District Legislature to the Congress of Micronesia to the high commissioner's desk, he became a citizen of the Federated States of Micronesia. Heading out into the rain, he invites me to his home to drink sakau.

Sakau is an elaborately ceremonial drink. Gene Ashby's guide mentions thirty-one different sakau rites, ranging from birth to marriage to death, celebration to atonement. But this turns out to be an informal, down-home occasion, with a couple of six-packs of Budweiser along for company. We sit in a shed, on wooden benches. Laundry droops down from overhead, laundry that stands about as much chance of freezing as of drying. Rain plunks off a metal roof, dogs scurry around, and a radio is playing someplace. Out here, they turn radios on when they buy them and never turn them off: they're like fishnets, set to catch whatever music is swimming around in the dark. While Matt and I drink beer, some kids are at work over the sakau stone, a slab that sits on top of a tire. They take turns pounding the root of the pepper shrub, a rhythmic, hollow clunking, which reduces the wood to pulp. They add water and keep pounding. Then they wrap the pulp in hibiscus bark, raise the pale, wet, intestinal-looking mass, and wring out the ultimate jungle juice. No plastic umbrella, no pineapple wedges, no rum-spiked coconuts with barber-pole straws. Sakau is the color of mud, the taste of earth, and the consistency of slime, spermy and seminal. The first effect is a numbing of the lips, not unlike dental anesthetic. After that comes a certain benign torpor, a thickening of the tongue, a laziness in the limbs, but the mind remains untouched so that you are a witness to your own oblivion.

Sitting here, I face another version of what life would have been like if I'd stayed. This could be mine, this disorderly household, this gaggle of kids and dogs. How did it ever get started, the idea that going to islands is to lead a life of isolation? *Robinson Crusoe,* I guess. But this is more like *The Beans of Egypt Maine, Tobacco Road, All in the Family.* For Mix, the Peace Corps is ancient history now, like summer camp.

"We were young, we were idealistic, fucked up, and wrong," Matt says, waving off our Peace Corps days. He suspects that when the free association money runs down and out, the place will foresake its quasi-independence and seek to become a U.S. commonwealth, "because there's no goddamned source of funding to run the fucking place. What source of money is going to take the place of the millions they're getting now? They're supposed to lose four or five federal programs next year, and they're talking like it's the end of the world." A pragmatist, Matt figures the islands have little more than their presumed strategic location to offer, and "if Gorbachev winds down the fucking cold war, we're fucked. Anybody who goes to bed here and prays for peace ought to be shot."

Maybe this is beer-and-sakau induced hyperbole. Maybe, though, the brew is working fine. Even as body parts winkle out, as yawns start coming in waves and eyelids grow heavy, you see things more clearly. Near the end, I ask if all the years he has put in, his marriage here, his change of citizenship, mean that he's accepted as "one of them." His answer is right on the money; it implies my question was dumb. A dumb Peace Corps-type question.

"Hey," the blue-eyed Micronesian retorts, "good manners are good manners and bad manners are bad manners all over the fucking world, and just because I was born someplace else doesn't mean I have to take shit."

As Matt Mix walks me to my car, some dogs play around the edge of the yard. They eat dogs in Ponape, baked whole, luau style, so you don't get too attached. "When they're nice, they're pets," the old Peace Corps volunteer says. "When they get to be a pain in the ass, they're food."

V

TRUK STOP

Tosiwo Nakayama was just a boy when World War II swept into his islands and his memories of those days have the vividness and awe of childhood, nearly half a century later. He recalls sailing around the *Yamato* and *Musashi*, high and mighty, the largest battleships ever built, when they anchored at Japan's Pacific Gibraltar, the broad and lethal Truk Lagoon. He can still picture his first American, a captured airman of the island of Tol. Tall, blond, blindfolded, his hands tied behind his back, he stood there while a couple Japanese officers looked at papers they'd found on him. Some Trukese kids, just showing off, threw rocks at the American, till the Japanese officers told them to stop. The captured airman was sent over to Japanese headquarters on the island of Dublon, and chances are he died there. There was a hospital on Dublon, and cruel doctors; talk of surgical experiments without anesthetic; talk later—when the islands were bypassed and left to starve—of cannibalism as well.

Nakayama stood on a hillside, that day in February 1944, when the planes came off Mitscher's carriers. The big game—the warships—had slipped away, but dozens of smaller vessels were sunk. Nakayama remembers watching a bugler on a sinking ship, tooting away as the deck slipped into the lagoon, and he does a funny rendition of what it sounded like, a military *da-da-da* turning into a watery *gurgle-gurgle-glug.*

After the war, the Americans came—for good. But some of the Japanese had been in the islands forever, settlers and pioneers in the South Seas, administrators and merchants. Their postwar repatriation was traumatic: they left their hearts behind. And their children. Tosiwo Nakayama's father was Japanese, a storekeeper for a Japanese trading firm, Nanyo Boeki Kaisha. The Americans shipped him home with the other Japanese. Sick at heart, Nakayama watched him go. Some of the Japanese were closely inspected by MP's, stripped and searched, before being shunted onto an LST. Nakayama's father spoke English and was more cordially treated. He went through his belongings, item by item, explaining each of them. This is this, that's that. A likable, obliging man, but in the end, the outcome was the same. He left with the others.

◄ II ►

Half-Japanese, half-Trukese, first president of the Federated States of Micronesia, Tosiwo Nakayama is the man I hope to see in Truk. If he's not there, I'm shit out of luck. "Stuck in Truk," we used to say. The place has an ominous reputation. Start with the paucity of land, just forty-six square miles in all. Add a burgeoning population, close to fifty thousand. Throw in strains of alcoholism, intramural violence, a teen suicide epidemic, a political life bordering on anarchy. Consider the state government, running up a debt close to $20 million, three or four times all the other FSM states combined. Add to that the fact that Truk's weight of numbers gives it an unpopular veto over national politics. That's Truk, the bad boy of the islands, the problem state, paradise refuted or, at least, mightily complicated. The prospect of union with Truk sent the Marshalls, Marianas, and Palau rushing for separate deals with Washington. Kusaie (now Kosrae), Ponape (now Pohnpei), and Yap, Truk's partners in the Federated States of Micronesia, may yet bolt too. Despairing Micronesians shake their heads about Truk: so many people, so many problems, so little land. Tourists—unless they're wreck divers come to see the sunken fleet—pass the place by.

Ah, Truk! My wife still talks about her first morning there, back in the mid-seventies, wondering what that man was doing, sitting outside her hotel room in the dark, till she learned that the governor had posted him there to keep her from being hassled. She has another memory from slightly later that day, staring out across the road to where a Trukese lad stood in a grove of banana trees smiling cheerfully at her, waving with one hand, masturbating with the other. Ah, Truk. It must be odd, a little insulting too, living in a place whose main attractions are under water. Culture, cuisine, friendship, shopping, night life aren't here, not for these visitors in tanks and goggles, their sojourn built around two half-hour dives a day, a bit of snorkeling in between, and a lot of idle time at the nearly inevitable Truk Continental Hotel, fifteen minutes from the airport.

Built as a first-rate resort, the Truk Continental has slipped into an almost-endearing shabbiness, like a cocky kid who's been taken down a notch or two. Plywood sheets cover typhoon-damaged windows. Carpets that may never dry squish underfoot. The rooms, when you open them, have the musty, sealed-off aura of a just-opened time capsule. The property is fenced, and security guards patrol the perimeters. They've been known to handcuff drunks to coconut trees at night. The drunks go free at dawn, apologetic and chagrined. All in all, the place feels like a besieged fortress, with vacationers inside the fence, the reality of Truk pressing on the outside, especially so at night, when there's not much to do but watch videotapes of Smithsonian-type documentaries on underwater Truk. Strange, isn't it, arriving for a vacation and spending nights watching films of the place you're vacationing in, as though to confirm that you've come to the right place.

There's prohibition in Truk. Sort of. It dates from a few years ago, when drunken brawls erupted with such regularity that the weekend mayhem down on the docks was nicknamed "free movies." Now you can get a beer, if you know where to ask, but Budweiser fluctuates between twenty-two and forty-five dollars per case. There's local stuff too, yeast and sugar laced with coffee or pineapple or whatever's handy. Every now and then some unfussy chaps drink the brew early; "before its time," Orson Welles would say. The fermentation continues *in situ,* their stomachs rupture, sometimes they die. Best to stick with the brewskies.

Truk can sound horrible, and part of me wants to fast-forward this next week of my life. And yet it's nice, being back in the loop, sitting out in back of the hotel, talking with some people who know some people I know, listening to yarns about politics and power outages, typhoon relief, suicides, cholera. And torture on Tol: some youths from one village plucked a plant off a grave in another village. A marijuana plant, it was, so we're not just talking desecration. We're also dealing with the pilferage of a cash crop. The avenging posse caught up with one of the culprits, and their punishment was to put fish hooks through his eyelids. Then they threatened to beat the shit out of him if he went for medical treatment. Other Truk stories come to mind. A friend of mine, a bird-watcher, climbed to the top of the Tol mountain, seeking an endangered bird that lived on that cloudy, rain-forested peak, lived in groves of poison trees, where not just the touch of the bark or the brush of a leaf but the very rain dripping off the leaves can raise fierce blisters: it started raining just when he spotted the bird. Truk. Paradise. In Peace Corps days, Truk was just about impossible for an outsider to get laid in—that's good news and bad news—and we used to sit around our cabins over on Udot, sit around while smoke drifted off mosquito coils that burned like incense all night long and one older volunteer, a grizzled veteran of Sargent Shriver's first wave, told us about Trukese lovemaking, strenuous and sweaty, painful too because the trick was to jam a lit cigarette into your arm at the moment of orgasm. I had no way of knowing whether it was true, but I started checking local forearms out, and sometimes I saw a line of round scars, like Japanese flags slapped on the side of an ace pilot's fighter plane. My arms stayed clean, and if you're one of those people who believe you haven't really lived in a place until you've gotten laid there, I guess I never really lived in

Truk. But I fell in love—would you believe it?—and it comes back to me now, as I glance across the lagoon. It's dusk now and it takes my breath away. This is the first I saw of the islands. This is where I got hooked.

A million years ago Truk was one large island, a mountainous mass rising thousands of feet from the floor of the Pacific. Then the mountains sank; only the highest peaks remained. The result was the Truk Lagoon, forty miles across, with eleven main islands and numerous satellites caught in a vast coral circle. And they are out there tonight—three-peaked Udot at the center of the lagoon, taller Tol hovering behind. To the left, Dublon, with its ruined Japanese hospital, its docks and piers. Tosiwo Nakayama once told me that American bombs landed on a Japanese brothel, blasting locked-together torsos into the mangrove swamp. That was the story, anyway. There's Uman, there's Fefan, named for its resemblance to a woman floating on her back, head and breasts and thighs. It pleases me to stand here, to recognize the islands and to name them, one by one. To remember them, whether or not they remember me. This is a landscape I learned by heart, more than twenty years ago, these islands, this lagoon. I saw it on scalding clear-sky, water-boiling days. I saw it on gray wet days, shivering, amazed how cold you could get in the tropics. I saw it on nights like this, moonlit and fine.

At the back of the hotel, some divers are talking, hush-hush, about a sensitive subject, the pornography of wreck diving: bones. Japanese bones. The Japanese comb through Micronesia all the time, gathering remains of war dead. In Truk, this has engendered debate involving dive shop operators and guides, politicians, and divers themselves. Should the Japanese be left or returned? Photographed or ignored? Tonight's group is high-minded.

"People come for ships and the war and the beautiful coral growths," one diver professes.

"Yeah," says another. "I mean, I wouldn't like it if *they* went diving off the *Arizona* to see American bones."

"I've had more than one Japanese diver refuse to go back to the wreck, once he'd seen bones," a guide offers. "He goes out to one of the islands on the reef. He won't go back to the ship."

I decide that, if there's time, I'll go out with one of the dive groups, to see how things turn out. But now I return to my room, to sit on the porch and drink beer with an official whom I agree to call an American source. His job involves keeping an eye on the islands. Ten years ago, when the islands were filled with whispers about the Pentagon, the CIA, the Mafia, such an encounter would have been highly charged. I was suspect; most Americans were. There had to be someone who'd been planted out here, people reasoned, an agent or an asset who was filing reports to Washington, then going about his business as a bureaucrat, an anthropologist, a missionary. Or—clever move!—a Peace Corps volunteer. And if there weren't such a spook, by god there ought to be! These islands were important, damn it, they rated surveillance, they deserved attention! Sometimes the islanders reminded me of that pathetically minor poet in a poem by Brecht, so trivial, so unimportant, that when the Nazis started throwing books on bonfires he pleaded "burn mine, burn mine!" The days of conspiracy fever are over now, I guess, and the American official and I are relaxed, enjoying the clubby rapport that comes from knowing about small places. I ask him how he rates the Federated States' chances. Though the Compact of Free Association still has a dozen years to run, everyone wonders whether this collection of islands will sink or swim. It's as though the United States had given a gang of youngsters a certain amount of money. Go ahead, save it, spend it, gamble it away. If the experiment succeeds or if it fails, either way, Washington can say: *see, well, now you've learned.*

"I think the compact will hold things together for fifteen years," the American source says. "The funding runs until 2001. As we approach the mid to late nineties, we're supposed to sit down and talk. The trends may become more obvious then. There's some feeling you hear that commonwealth may not be such a bad idea, that the price paid in terms of independence may be worth it, in terms of economic benefits—and that was not the thinking of people like Tosiwo Nakayama. The first generation of Micronesian leaders had to band together to negotiate with the United States. The present group didn't have to do that. They think in terms of state's rights—Ponape and Truk, not Micronesia. They could go for a Saipan-type solution—commonwealth. It's something of a sham if you're independent and 90 percent of the money you get is aid coming in from someplace else. I don't think there's any former colonial area in the world that gets the same aid per capita as this place. That hasn't registered in Washington and those of us who are out here are glad that it hasn't."

Things could still go either way, the American seems to think. Check in later. When trends are clear. A dozen years from now, if the islanders have made some sort of minimal progress, if they've reduced their dependence on U.S. aid from 90 percent of their budget to between 70 and 80 percent say, the compact may be renewed, funding continued. Then again, Washington might signal an end to the game. Or the Micronesians might throw in the towel. *No más!* What's the difference, anyway, between Botswana and Bophuthatswana, between the kind of nominal independence that feeds smorgasbord style, off an international buffet, and the outright dependence that hunkers down to some solid 'merican cookin', hot and heavy?

◄ III ►

As the boat cuts across the lagoon, the island turns green in front of me. I pick out the hummocky hills we climbed to find Japanese guns. I spot houses on the shoreline, the village church. Udot is coming up on me just as it did in 1967. The Udot Invasion, they called it then, 150 Peace Corps trainees piling off an LST and onto a twelve-hundred-acre island, met by 900 amused, skeptical, pragmatic, astonished Trukese. There were lessons for all of us. Peace Corps was pronounced Piss Corpse because if they pronounced it correctly, it was an obscenity in Trukese. Female genitalia, as I recall. Or maybe mother's female genitalia. Trukese was a subtle language, some ways.

The Peace Corps built forty-six houses that were to be passed on to Trukese at the close of training. It hired them by the dozens: cooks, construction workers, boat drivers. We were all quite sure, when we left that the island would never be the same. We were "agents of change," weren't we?

Twenty-two years ago. It's almost as far back now as World War II was then. We landed in a DC-3, stepped onto an old Japanese fighter strip, jumped into trucks. I had Proust in my luggage, and condoms and a Panama hat on my head: none of which I needed. I noticed green hills and dusty roads and tin shacks as we drove through Moen. I'd wondered for months what those dots on the map would look like. Now they came to life, glaringly bright, killingly hot. We rode down to some rusting World War II decks and were shepherded onto an old LST, the whole bunch of us, and the war surplus landing craft set out across the lagoon, the sunken Japanese fleet below us and islands all around.

Now I repeat that trip alone, in a fast boat. I should try to settle my feelings about the Peace Corps, I guess. They keep changing. I haven't kept in touch with more than two or three of the volunteers I met out here. There've been reunions, but I haven't attended. I keep my distance now; I kept it then. Membership in the Peace Corps troubled me. I resented Peace Corps staff especially, the ones with yarns about how they did things, back when *they* were volunteers. That and their know-it-all theories about culture and development, their going on forever about what the role of the Peace Corps should be. Did they really believe that stuff about a "new kind of American"?

The longer I stayed, the greater my distrust. The Peace Corps' model of strenuous virtue didn't go down well, in this island heat. It felt like we were collecting for UNICEF on Halloween. I made as little as possible of the Peace Corps. When I was introduced by one islander to another, nobody mentioned I was a PCV. I took the clue. I stopped identifying myself that way. For years, I rarely mentioned the Peace Corps. You'd have thought I was a German, covering up a shadowy war record.

And yet, with Udot in front of me, I feel a flash of gratitude. The Peace Corps got me here, I'll give them that much. I give them some credit. Back at Kenyon College I'm surprised when students come to me to ask about the Peace Corps. I thought those days were over, that college graduates were making shrewder choices. But there she sits, mulling over Poland or Botswana, one of my best students, lively, funny, smart. I tell her to beware of staff, be suspicious of programs, not to take the Peace Corps too seriously. And then I say: go.

Now the boat comes in to the end of the dock, a crumbling concrete finger poking out into the lagoon. Mangroves press against it, weeds grow out of cracks, chunks of rock have tumbled into the piss-warm water. I jump onto the dock and head in toward the village. First I see the schoolhouses the Trust Territory built back in Kennedy days, concrete rectangles with rusted roofs and battered, slatted windows. The school looks abandoned but, then again, it always did, and, coming closer, I see blackboards and chairs inside. The two schoolhouses and the grassy parade ground between them were the center of the village. On the inland side was an old Japanese building, turned into a municipal office. On the other side, right at the beach, was the house I lived in. We slept on the floor, on mats, lighting mosquito coils to protect us through the night. Daily brushing kept the mold off a bound copy of my University of Chicago Ph.D. thesis. An asshole move, bringing that along! We read *Time* and *Newsweek* cover to cover, even business and medicine. We compared draft boards. We feasted on peanut butter and jelly smeared on rock-hard ship biscuits. We drank powdered Tang stirred into lukewarm water, we bathed in rain that ran off roofs into oil barrel catchments. At night we went to the end of the dock to catch a breeze and play the tapes we'd brought from home. My tape had "Ain't No Mountain High Enough" and "A Natural Woman" and—of course—"Dock of the Bay." Odd, in 1967, where you wound up, running from a war.

Our house is gone, I see. A typhoon got it, someone says, and a concrete slab foundation is all that's left. The house on the right that belonged to what the Peace Corps encouraged us to call "our Trukese family," is now a little grocery store selling warm soda and mosquito coils, potato chips, and canned mackerel. A policeman—a uniformed policeman at that—welcomes me enthusiastically, points me to the municipal building. It's odd. My unannounced return is causing a stir. Why? A Trukese girl giggles and places a flowered maramar on my head. What goes on here? Leaning down to accept this welcome, I spot two young men carrying picket signs, flashing messages at me: FSM MEANS DIRTY POLITICS and CINDY, WE STILL NEED YOUR FEDERAL AIDS. Now I have it. It's not a surprise party in my honor. It's something else altogether.

I'm not Cindy, but the day I've chosen to return to Udot is the same day the place is to be visited by the Arizonan Voluntary Medical Team, a red-shirted crew of doctors and nurses led by Cindy McCain, wife of Arizona Senator John McCain. My maramar was probably meant for Mrs. Senator. Tough, Cindy, I got here first. Twenty-two years ago, and today. "Conrata!" I call toward the porch of the municipal building. She was the Trukese woman who looked after us, a dark, shrewd matriarch who rousted us out every morning. "Conrata."

"Steve!" someone replies, getting out of the chair. It sounds like Stiv.

"No, not Steve," I say. "Steve was my roommate. Fred!"

"Fred," she shouts. Fret.

I'm surrounded by faces from back then, Kintoki Joseph, the chief, Masaichi, the sanitarian, and Conrata, sharp-eyed as ever, the mother of eleven. I hand her a bag of things I bought at the Truk Trading Company, a jar of Folgers Instant, a can of Hormel Spam, a can of Ox and Palm corned beef from Australia, and I sit down beside her. Now I'm not a visitor anymore, I'm part of the reception for the Arizona bunch, and this pleases me. While we wait, Conrata tells me about her children, eight still on the island—where the population has swollen to twenty-five hundred—three moved up to the Marianas. I remember them, bright-eyed kids in ragamuffin dresses, who followed us from language class to area studies, endlessly repeating, "Hello, what's your name?" They leaned against screen windows when we sat inside drinking our warm Tang. When it rained they splashed in schoolyard puddles, slid across slick grass, squealing with delight. She tells me about Honolulu, where she accompanied her husband when he was in Tripler Hospital. She liked the flowers, she says, the coolness, and the wind. She liked Waikiki and the Ala Moana shopping center. Every day she went around on the bus, Conrata from Truk, sharing the Number Eight with packs of tourists buying muu-muu dresses, aloha shirts, monkey-pod plates, Conrata the genuine islander in a place of counterfeits, Conrata dark and strong, heavy-bodied, gold-toothed mother of eleven, like a real plant in a room full of plastic flowers.

The red-shirts from Arizona come walking around the corner of the school. The people of Udot shoo dogs off the grass and arise to form a reception line. Conrata, representing a local version of the Red Cross, joins the line and I remain seated, trading stares with a new crop of island kids. "Piss Corpse," I can hear them whispering. Word is out.

It's murder in the sun now. As soon as the red-shirts are received, everybody squeezes back into the shade, except some dutiful adults and a couple of kids who take folding chairs out onto the lawn and sit there while a Jesuit priest gives a blessing and the magistrate thanks the Arizonans for "an act of love bearing fruit on these small islands of the Pacific." Out in the sun, some of the Trukese hold up umbrellas; odd to see black rain umbrellas sprouting on the sunniest possible day. The kids who were seated are down on the ground now, holding the folding chairs they were sitting on over their heads. Meanwhile, Cindy McCain, speaking through an interpreter, thanks the island for its welcome, promising future visits. After that, the whole village lines up for medicals. Besides the Arizona team, there are white-shirted Mormon missionaries helping out, and some khaki-clad members of a U.S. Air Force Civic Action Team. It's the Peace Corps all over again: people on a mission coming to a place like Udot. The island greets them like it greeted us. Everything is familiar: the speeches, the flowers, the lunch. One of the old-timers I share the shade with tells me that Udot is what is known as a picnic island—a place where the main activity is the acceptance of outside benefactions. From navy, to Peace Corps, to Arizona medical volunteers. Typhoon relief, war claims, school feeding programs, Head Start, aging. Whatever. The porch is crowded as a lifeboat. I jump overboard into the sun and take a walk around the island.

"Piss Corpse!" What a bewildering parade we must be, we outsiders who come ashore. We thought of the Peace Corps in terms of our personal history, a two-year episode, that's all. Or we thought of it as a phase in American history: Kennedy makes a speech, and one of the results is that the mouth of an LST drops open in shock and a couple hundred middle-class kids come wading out. But that's only one side of it. There was history here before we came and history that kept happening after we left, the island's own history, and it cuts us down to size. It swallowed our good deeds, our houses, our language classes and waterseal toilets and handicraft co-ops. We were passing through, that's all, and though we didn't know it, I suspect that the islanders knew it all along, from the minute we stepped off the boat: we would go and they would stay.

A guy I know tried to explain what it felt like to be an islander. He said it was like sitting in school and every day it's a new teacher in a new outfit with a new lesson. "Hi, we're going to make soap out of copra this morning." "Greetings class, today we're going to form a fishing co-op." "Now, students, can anyone tell me what community development is?" Or tourism, tapioca culture, cacao, trochus, *beche de mer?* Is there a future in golf courses? Is there profit in military bases? Are gambling casinos a sure thing? So it goes, the promising projects and high purposes.

"Piss Corpse!" At this time of day, walking is a primal effort. I'm drenched in no time. But it was always this way. These withering lunchtimes offset sparkling dawns and gaudy sunsets and moonlit nights you could read by, nights when the whole island stayed awake, on the prowl. Palm fronds were silver on nights like that, like sharpened knives. Banana leaves were gilded platters and taro plants were rustling thighs. That combination of discomfort and beauty were what I learned on Udot, that linking of paradise and irony. Eden needed snakes and Truk needed *benjos,* overwater toilets. You'd walk across a coconut log into a rusted tin shack that sat on stilts above the beach. Sometimes your excreta hit water, sometimes sand, it depended on the tide, but down it went, followed by a torn-out page of schoolbook, *Our California* or something, and you'd glance over your shoulder at the enormous lagoon, those green hunks of island, and you'd maybe see a fisherman throwing a net twenty yards behind where you were sitting, shitting.

Other memories come to me, discomfiting ones like the discovery that Trukese were . . . different. This wasn't about brown skin or poverty or isolation. We could hack that. That's what we'd signed on for. But casual cruelty to dogs rattled us. And laughter at movies, especially during those scenes of pain and suffering that elicited compassion anywhere else. Hearing our hosts giggle, we sensed that those horrifying newsreels of Buchenwald, corpses stacked like cordwood, would have been riotously funny out here. Maybe it was nervous laughter, uncertainty as to how to respond. Maybe. But I remember a guy who sat outside a neighboring house, sat on a bench every evening, leafing through an old *LIFE* magazine as if it were *Playboy,* staring at a picture of some Chinese landlord, down on his knees, about to be beheaded. Chuckling.

Piss Corpse. There are no roads, no cars on Udot, and the island has a slow and pleasant style, even when heat and humidity leapfrog each other into the nineties. At low tide, the mangroves cook and rot. Crabs scuttle over baking coral. I'm dying for a cold beer. Kids scoot out and follow my walk. "Hello, what is your name?" And, from older people, "piss corpse, piss corpse." The way "white angel" followed Laurence Olivier on Forty-seventh Street in *Marathon Man,* "piss corpse" trails me on Udot. "Piss corpse" returning for a last look at the island we thought our presence had changed forever, tourism and fishing co-ops on the way, tennis and volleyball vacations just around the corner. New houses we built for them! It hasn't changed at all.

▲ ▲ ▲

Back on Moen, waiting for a driver to take me to a promised interview with Truk's current governor, Gideon Doone, the Peace Corps stays in mind. Probably this is because the driver is late. I wait patiently and this annoys me. The Peace Corps taught us to be patient. So I get angry at the Peace Corps. They cast us in such a pliant, mendicant posture vis-à-vis the Micronesians. Understand. Forgive. Endure. Were they late? Silly, that was Micronesian time. Did they evade us? We were being too direct! Did they lie? That was because we'd asked the wrong question. Did they, perhaps, steal? Different sense of property, tradition of borrowing, obligations to the extended clan. Fuck-off on the job? Different work ethic. What about that drunk in the bar at the Truk Trading Company, the one who wants me to fix him up with a Peace Corps girl he can screw? Well, we're wrong again. The fellow was using alcohol to break through all sorts of language barriers and neocolonial inhibitions to meet with us honestly, one to one. This was an intercultural situation.

Still no driver, no sign of one, no way of checking. I pick up, toss aside the Anne Tyler novel I've been trying to read: frails from Baltimore, limping through a Frank Capra universe. I'm tired of waiting politely, standing by. I decide to wait another ten minutes for my interview. Well, half an hour anyway. Old habits die hard. It's an intercultural situation, right?

It doesn't matter how long I wait. Nobody comes. I cruise to the back of the hotel to check the sunset, chat with a couple military guys, divers down from Guam, and I buy a drink for a guy in off one of the lagoon islands for some air-conditioned R and R with his girlfriend. I spot him as a Peace Corps volunteer right off, that knowing, slightly hangdog look. Takes one to know one. He teaches at a school where politically appointed teachers, often with fudged degrees, rack up a 50 percent absenteeism rate. That's teacher absenteeism, not student. He's seen bags of concrete intended for seawalls go into private homes. He tells me about "pitcher-catchers," politicians who appropriate money on the national government level, grab it off locally. "He pitches in Ponape, he catches in Truk." There's another saying in Truk, a saying, maybe an epitaph, you can see on T-shirts. *Ka pach, ka tento:* You stick with me, you've got a tent. It refers to politically influenced distribution of typhoon relief. Sometimes it's *ka pach, ka fiber:* You stick with me, you've got a fiberglass boat. My American source had it right. This is not what Tosiwo Nakayama had in mind.

◄ IV ►

He waves to me across the hotel dining room, rises as I come toward his table. I hug him. We've had our moments of distance, Tosiwo Nakayama and I. He knew I was Salii's man, in the old days, and for years there were big differences between the two. When Salii pressed for free association, Nakayama and a few others held out for independence. In the mid-seventies, when the Trust Territory was splintering, Nakayama campaigned for unity, while Salii acquiesced in separation. I suppose that Tosiwo Nakayama is—or was—as close to a radical as you could find in the American-administered Trust Territory. Oh, there were some other minor claimants, back in the sixties. Another Trukese,

Hans Wiliander, wangled a much-talked about trip to Communist China, before it was fashionable. A guy from Saipan spent a little time at Moscow's Lumumba University. And there were two Palauans, the Ulu-dong brothers, who talked a tough anticolonial game. But Nakayama was different. The others dealt in fashions and gestures. In the Trust Territory scheme of things, there were roles available for radicals. There were trips and symposia, a certain notoriety. Attention would be paid. But Nakayama's radicalism was deeper.

I've never understood where it came from. Was it his wrenching separation from his Japanese father? Was it some insult or slight from an early American administrator? Or was it an islander's visceral suspicion of outsiders, loud-mouthed, all-knowing outsiders? All I could say was that there was a distance in him, a sense of otherness. Warm and confiding as he could sometimes be, you sensed that he'd just as soon be left alone, in his house, on his island, thank you very much.

How different he was from the others! Where Salii rushed to confront, Nakayama demurred. Salii's strength was in improvising, changing. Nakayama stood fast, hung tough. Salii dealt in words, Nakayama in silence. Salii was looking for balance between the islands and the United States, the perfect deal. In the process, he reduced the distance between the two places. He could handle both, a juggler. Not Nakayama. He was Trukese. That was that. He wanted independence. That was that. Combine these two men, I used to think, combine Salii's flair and passion with Nakayama's patience and staying power, and great things could be accomplished. But it wasn't in the cards. Now Salii is dead and it's important for me to find Nakayama, the tall, soft-spoken Trukese with Japanese features. Seeing him now makes me realize how much I like him, his shyness and toughness. I wonder if he trusts me. Does he think I'm with the CIA? Never mind. I ask him if we can talk sometime. "Let's talk now," he says and we step out of the dining room, across the yard and up to my hotel room. It's still early. The air in my room was damp last night; now it's musty. Outside it's heating up, inside the air conditioner is leaking a little cold air into the room, not more than a token showing. Might as well open the window and let the heat roll in. Nakayama sits down, at ease. Nice room, he says.

"What do you know about banking?" I ask, kidding him.

"Nothing!" he answers, laughing. There are no presidential libraries in Micronesia, no university chairs waiting to be filled. Joking that he was down to his last pair of socks when he left office, Nakayama became a vice president of the Bank of Guam. He has some reservations about going from the presidency of a country to the vice presidency of a bank, but he seems relaxed and talkative. We chat about Salii's death. Though he attended the funeral, Tos was reluctant to call at Lazarus's house. He went with some other people, though, and when he stepped inside, the place was full of mourning. "Eta!" Tina Salii called out to her dead husband, "Tos is here!"

Salii is dead, Kabua is sitting pretty, Nakayama works for a bank. In power, out of power, gone forever. Nakayama's position is the most interesting, watching from the sidelines as younger men test—and pro-test—the island independence he campaigned for. He's irritated, Nakayama says, with the young fellows who run Truk these days, the ones who want to ditch free association in favor of commonwealth.

"I get disappointed when I hear people say the solution is to change our status and become a commonwealth," he says. "These islands are god-given. We should protect these islands for new generations of Tru-kese. For those who want commonwealth, Saipan is not far away. For those who like a U.S. territory, there is Guam. And for statehood, Hawaii is open. You've got your choice, I say. But please do not change our status here."

God-given islands? Protection of future generations . . . this at a time when the economy languishes, the government hemorrhages, and hun-dreds of Trukese are voting with their feet, heading for minimum-wage jobs in Guam hotels, Saipan garment factories. A few weeks ago, the acting Guam police chief blamed a crime surge on Micronesians. "Com-pact Micronesians," he called them, and he wasn't talking about down-sized bodies, that's for sure. He meant Micronesians, mostly Trukese, who live under—and run from—the Compact of Free Association Nakayama helped negotiate. He still believes in it, too, that with time, with wise leadership and hard work, these islands could wind up with total independence. Meanwhile, though, his people flee; they are the wetbacks of Guam. Nakayama's words fly in the face of facts, as credos often do. I'm not the first to wonder why Truk, the neediest and most desperate of all the islands, produced someone like him, so committed to independence. Salii wondered too, speculating about Nakayama and his ally, Andon Amaraich. "The stone walls of independence," he called them.

Now I look over at Nakayama, holding doggedly to a position that everything around us contradicts. I've hung out in Moen, a dusty, crowded dead end of a place, all shacks and washlines, plastic buckets, dying dogs, dead cars, idling people, and monotonous Trukese music on the radio; it sounds like they're singing the tide tables. A refugee camp, more than a town. I've browsed in the Truk Trading Company, seen those freezers loaded with an item that captures where the place is at. We're talking turkey tails, that look like they've been frozen since the last ice age, selling for about a buck a pound, the rejects of a thousand mainland Thanksgivings. The Trukese love them. They barbecue turkey tails, they boil them in soup, they cut them up raw and eat them sashimi style.

People take shots at Nakayama, now he's out of office. "He must know in his heart the war's over and he's lost," someone told me. "A new group has taken over. Tos and his generation are regarded as the idealists of a past age and maybe the cripples of a past age also. The crazy uncles. They saw themselves as country-builders. Moses in the promised land—that sort of trip. It was sort of a heady time. Now there's a couple differences. There's a cynicism about money, about Washington, about what the prospects of the future are. No one talks about independence anymore. They talk about getting through the fiscal year and getting a better deal after fifteen years." They say Nakayama's out of touch, his time is past. I hope not. He says that people come up to him, ask him to run for governor and save Truk, run for president and save the FSM. He seems reluctant but I've seen him reluctant before. Meanwhile, almost alone, he holds out for distance from America, widening distance, ultimate independence.Why?

"I think if we'd had good Americans from the beginning, we would be a commonwealth," he reflects. "If they had done—not a better job, but a less bad job. They had government vehicles and school buses. Their own commissary store. Their own school. Their own little community with lights and water and telephone. A few feet away, the situation was different. When I visited the U.S., the situation was different. But here . . ."

He pauses. Memories of TT days still dog him, that trembling liver-spotted ineffectual government that left behind more wounds than it could measure. A no-win operation. When it was poor and low-budgeted it was accused of ignoring the islands, condescendingly protecting them, of wanting to preserve the place, keep it as it was, quaint and primitive. The "zoo theory," they called it. The United States was the villain, the islanders the victims. It had to be a conspiracy. Later, when the United States poured it on, when U.S. budgets went to $16 million in 1962, to $25 million in 1967, to $50 million in 1970, to $100 million ten years later, we were accused of buying Micronesia off, turning it into a welfare state. Didn't we realize what USDA food would do to fishing and agriculture? What aid to the aging would do to Micronesian families? That money was no substitute for pride? Once again, villains and victims. Another conspiracy, of course. You wonder if there's any way a big place can touch a little one without harming it. Cuff it, you kill it, kiss it, you smother it. Keep the place pure, you embalm it. Open it up, you destroy it. Nakayama was a product of the poor times. Having gotten so little from the Americans, he wondered, why have them at all? But the people who followed him have done a little better—just the tail of the turkey—and they want more. This, I suspect, leaves the former president in a lonely eminence.

"There were some good people," Nakayama grants. "But many were people with the wrong attitude. If you ask me what motivated me to stay as far away from the U.S., it was people's attitudes. That and the fear of the loss of land. These islands are god-given. Who are we to give them away?"

◄ V ►

Truk is glorious this morning. There's not a cloud in a thousand miles, not a smokestack either. The islands are technicolor, greens and blues too bright to contemplate. A perfect morning to play tourist. I'm no diver, but I borrow a snorkel and link up with some Guam-based Sea-bees who are diving some of the "ghost fleet" wrecks this morning.

"It's the best wreck diving in the world," a local guide tells me. "You've got a lot of ships, which have not been salvaged, sitting in warm water. It may never happen again like that."

About fifty ships went down in the lagoon. Some haven't been found, others are too deep to dive, but forty or so vessels are in reach. Divers can spend weeks picking over what the war left behind—destroyers, freighters, transports, sub chasers. The only regret is that the great *Yamato* slipped out before the American planes came in.

Our first stop is the *Fujikawa Maru,* an aircraft transport sunk off Uman. Its stern mast sticks out above water—we toss a line around it—and the main deck is sixty feet below. The Seabees are ecstatic. Over they go. I watch their descent from above, a bunch of guys turned into a school of fish, headed down, and into, the drowned ship. I swim over to the stern mast. Above surface it's just a rusted pole, scrap metal, but below water it's covered by coral, the mast and crossbar turned into a coral crucifix, attended by a school of phosphorescent fish.

"Awesome!" one of the Seabees exclaims when he comes up. They jabber about zeros all jumbled together in the hold, bullets and gas masks on deck.

"This is paradise!" another Seabee decides. They want to stay longer, forever, move here and live, get a job, any job, and dive forever, hit the deep ships, find the lost ones. I love their enthusiasm. It makes me smile. Truk is their first taste of the islands and, right now, they are hooked. I see my younger self in them. I remember the days when I looked at the map of the Pacific and plotted voyages, when I collected islands, when it was important for me to see as many as I could. It was like a hobbyist's obsession, or—this embarrasses me now—like having women. Each island was another score, another notch on . . . whatever you notch for islands. Even if they all started to look the same, even if they were only one-night stands, it mattered greatly, getting to them. There were islands almost no one went to, hard catches, places like Pagan and Agrihan, north of Saipan, volcanic cones with black sand beaches. There was uninhabited Helen Island, closer to Indonesia than Palau, where birds sprayed out of branches as you walked along the beach and lumbering turtles came crowding ashore to lay eggs, darkening the beach on moonlit nights. I remember a month-long voyage through the outer islands of the Yap District, how I talked my way onto one of a wretched, rusting fleet of government field trip vessels that got me to Ulithi, where brawny teenagers in bright red loincloths stevedored the boat, then sat next to topless girls at the Outer Island High School. On Ifalik, I admired imposing boathouses, cathedrals of thatch, with fishnets spread on the grass in front of them, giving the whole scene the measured beauty of a formal garden. And on Lamotrek, I found a couple Japanese seaplanes on the beach, just above the tide and, nearby, in a shady grove, the grave of one Paul Glaser, off the German raider *Cormoran,* which had ducked in during World War I. We delivered a coffin to Satawal, a woman who'd died at the hospital in Yap. I watched her last landing, ship to shore, the graveyard procession, the coffin declining into the ground, followed by the dead woman's clothing, blankets, sarongs, turmeric powder, and hibiscus flowers. After the burial, the people of Satawal sat among the graves, leaning against crosses, the whole village acknowledging their own mortality, their death on this island and burial in this graveyard. That night I drank coconut brew and slept in a boathouse, next to a half-finished canoe, and awoke on a carpet of woodshavings, and it was Christmas Eve.

Now, as we move around the lagoon, old emotions repeat themselves. They are having a ball, those divers; it's a long weekend they never want to end. The islands are in them now, an infection that will linger, flaring up when they are far away from here. We snorkel a sub chaser, then go deeper, to a sunken freighter. The ships are eery, not just their size, but their condition. If they'd survived the war, they'd surely be scrapped and gone now. Sinking here, they became immortal. And so, too, their crews.

"Did you see where those bones fit together?" someone asks.

"Fit together? You a doctor now?"

"You never saw a skull before?"

"On *Quincy*. Plastic."

"Some brave lad who went down with his ship."

"Paradise," says one of the Seabees as we skate across to the hotel. That word again—and not a trace of the usual irony. Only wonder. "What's the penalty for desertion?" he muses. "Death?"

◀ VI ▶

I love the language of typhoons. They begin as tropical depressions a nice summary of my state of mind, when I think too much about these islands. These tropical depressions become tropical disturbances. That's what we have this evening. Gray skies, sudden gusts of wind, spattering rain that makes a puddle archipelago on the grass outside my room. The palm branches sway wildly, slapping left and right, tugging at trunks, which have metal rings around them, to keep rats from climbing to the top. The wind must be giving them some ride, any that are up there. Sometimes tropical disturbances grow into typhoons. Little typhoons, mostly, banana typhoons, but now and then, 130-mph-once-in-fifty-years-monsters that peel sheets of roofing off houses and send them flying through the air like razor blades. They can strip every leaf and branch, turn a lush greenhouse island into a weirdly brown autumnal place. On atolls, they can drive the waves over the island, swamping the place. People have been known to climb into trees and tie themselves to trunks, like sailors lashed to the masts of sinking ships.

I do not expect Tosiwo Nakayama to appear in weather like this, though we had talked about going for a ride around the island. It looks like another night with *Celestial Navigation*. Everyone knows there are books you read when you travel, on airplanes, in hotels. What needs looking into is the relationship between *where* you travel and what you read. There are hot weather books and cold. Now I want something that's brisk, urban, wisecracky, Joseph Wambaugh or George Higgins. But then, to my surprise, my old friend drives up and we set off in the rain, slowly, no destination in mind; scenery not the point in this kind of weather. Now I see why Salii was so attached to car rides, for cars are private places, confessionals almost. I just wish Nakayama would turn the air-conditioner down. It's freezing. I hope he doesn't have it on for my sake. I decide not to ask. Intercultural situation. We wander through Moen, drive out as far as St. Cecilia's school, where he remembers delivering a commencement speech I'd helped out on. He lost a page in midspeech and bluffed his way through, and later Salii charged me with having written a subpar speech for Nakayama.

We end up sitting in the airport parking lot, an hour before plane time. Nakayama has a letter he wants someone to hand carry to Guam. I'm relieved to be off the potholed roads, so I can take notes on the story I now ask him to tell me, a story he told me years ago, in bits and pieces, the story of his search for the Japanese father who got shipped out of Truk in 1945.

"It's a story I'll never forget," he begins. "When he left, he promised he'd come back. He left us an address for a family home in Japan. When I decided to go to school, the motivation was to learn enough English so I could get a job on a ship and go to Tokyo and find him."

The first contacts were made by others, by Truk-based Americans who went to Japan in the early fifties and found the old man. They brought home a new address, and Nakayama, feeling he was close, followed up with letters.

"I started writing letters to this address," he says. "In 1955 I went away to school in Hawaii. I kept writing in 1956. No reply. In 1957, I got a letter. He said he didn't have the courage to answer before, he felt he'd deprived us. I said I would see him; I kept writing. But he didn't reply."

In 1961, the high commissioner elected Nakayama to help represent the islands at the annual dog and pony show before the U.N. Trusteeship Council in New York. Someone who knew of Nakayama's quest suggested he return home via Tokyo. It only cost an extra thirty-seven dollars, he remembers.

"So I went alone to Tokyo," he says. "Very few Micronesians traveled on TT passports then, but they cleared me quickly at Haneda airport, I spoke just enough Japanese. I went to a place called the New Japan

Hotel, I think it has been torn down now. The bellboy started speaking broken English. I told him I had come to locate my father, we'd been separated sixteen years ago. He got off work at nine in the morning and he went with me, took me in a cab to a police station. He was feeling sorry for me. I think Japanese are sentimental about these things."

The police didn't recognize the address Nakayama showed them. No such place. They went to a second police station, where his story brought tears to people's eyes. "Where does he come from?" they asked. "From way in the Pacific, poor soul." At a third police station, they got lucky. Cross the bridge, turn right, you can walk there. It ended in an apartment in back of a small store, a woman running up the steps, a man coming downstairs in his underwear.

"So you came," the father said.

"Yes. As I promised."

"Well, come on up. I didn't expect you to come so soon."

Sushi, sake, beer, and relatives crowded the rest of Nakayama's visit, his father presenting him as "one of my sons from the South Seas." The word got out. "One of them is here, one of them is here, one of the kids from the South Seas is here."

Fluent in English, the elder Nakayama had found work with the American occupation, first as an interpreter, later as an accountant at an officers' club. At their reunion, in 1961, he was still tied to Japan. "Right now I have a job," he said. "I'm working. But my burial place is Truk. Truk is home."

In 1972, he was ready to come home. Tosiwo Nakayama set up his father in a tiny store. He spent his days reading, poring over his son's congressional correspondence, reminiscing with a handful of other Japanese old-timers around the lagoon. When one of his friends, old Aizawa, died over on Tol, old Aizawa, whose son pitched baseball in the Japanese leagues, faced Joe DiMaggio in an exhibition game once, glanced at Marilyn Monroe, his reaction was stoic: "He left first." In 1979, the elder Nakayama followed. Truk was his burial place. . . .

The airport parking lot is filling up, mostly with pickup trucks. Finishing his story, Nakayama gets out of the car and, spotting the passenger he's been looking for, hands over the letter that's going to Guam. I don't suppose there's any huge moral in his story. He told it straight and soft; I sensed the underlying emotions but I didn't see them. Nakayama is like that. Still, the story pleases me. These islands are . . . well . . . insular; they are at once forlorn and self-centered. You're here or you're not, you come and you go. They shrug off outsiders. "The same tide that brings them in, carries them out." But Nakayama went against the tide; he searched, he persisted, he waited but he never forgot and, in the end, the poor boy from the South Seas brought his father home. This has nothing to do with political status, with independence or common-wealth, and there's no money in it, but it pleases me anyway, this story, which is about memory and integrity and faith. It pleases me when, on our way back to the hotel, Tosiwo Nakayama takes me into his house and we sit while his wife types letters, and some kids—his and other people's—cook pots of fish and rice while sheltering from the storm. It pleases me now, when I am far away, sitting in an English department office at Kenyon College, delaying grading papers, preparing lecture notes, my revisionist look at *To Kill a Mockingbird.* It pleases me when I reach back to the shelves, thinking of my friend from Truk who sailed around great battleships in a canoe and later became a president, pleases me when I pull out an E. M. Forster novel that I've mostly forgotten, except for its haunting, true epigram and invocation: ONLY CONNECT.

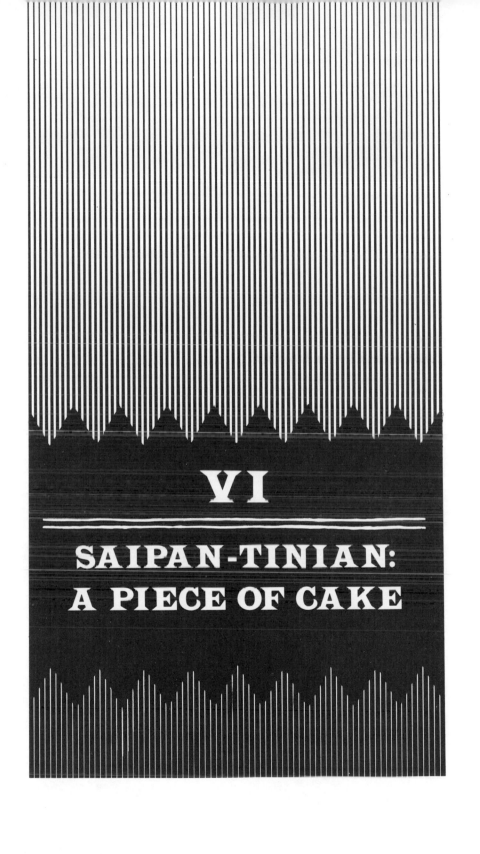

VI

SAIPAN-TINIAN: A PIECE OF CAKE

The Air Micronesia flight from Truk comes into Guam at one in the morning. The plane to Saipan, doesn't leave till dawn. I had hoped for a nap, or some quiet reading, but the transit lounge is packed with Japanese and Korean tourists, hundreds of them, nursing sunburns, snapping photos, pricing duty-free cognac and perfume. They look like they're on a class trip. Why is it that when people go on vacation—people who dress simply and well at home—they all join a worldwide bad-taste fraternity? Why do tourists look the way they do? *I'm a fool and I don't care,* their clothes proclaim, their T-shirts and shorts, their shopping bags and sandals. Anyway, I'm going to be up all night and I'll arrive home—for that is how I think of Saipan—blurry and disoriented.

Majuro, Ponape, and Truk are places I've visited. Saipan is different; Saipan is where I lived, two years in the Peace Corps in the late sixties, a year more in the mid-seventies, weeks on end at other times. I've had a half-dozen homes around the island. I've climbed down to its most isolated beaches, up into its war-littered caves. Driving there at night, cold sober or high, I feel that special, and dangerous, confidence that no harm can come to me. But I know something else, too, which makes me tense about returning. I know Saipan is one of the strangest places on earth, continuously shifting and mutating, so that I think of this island as one of these troublesome relatives who might be showing up in love beads, tie-dyed shirt, denim trousers or, then again, in polyester pants, silk shirt, and gold chains.

Saipan was always different. When I first saw it in 1967, it was already clear that the old battleground island wanted nothing to do with the rest of the Trust Territory. Most Saipanese were Chamorros, as were the people of Guam, largest and southernmost of the Marianas chain. Guam had belonged to the United States since the turn of the century, a prize of the Spanish-American War. We kept it because we needed a Pacific outpost, a coaling station. Guam became an outright U.S. territory, its people U.S. citizens, while the rest of the Marianas chain, all the islands to the north, were run by the Japanese, under League of Nations mandate. After World War II, the division of the Marianas took a new form, with the northern islands thrown into the Trust Territory, tied to places three thousand miles west, a thousand miles south. And all the while, there was Guam, fat and happy, just over the horizon, prospering while the Northern Marianas languished. Guam, "where America's day begins." That was the slogan of the island. Guam had the minimum wage, Guam had military bases, tourist hotels, air-conditioned movies, shopping centers, hamburgers, and pizza. No wonder the people up on Saipan felt shut out, so close to all the good things; it was like watching your neighbors—no, your cousins—throw a wingding party, beer and barbecue, while you were sitting with a gang of rock-chucking wards of the U.N.

Guam appalled me, though for reasons that reflected as much of me as it. I dismissed it as a sleazeball garrison island, a *B*-grade back-door California, the very image of what I hoped the rest of Micronesia would *not* become. That's not to say that I didn't enjoy it—revel in it—from time to time. We can all be had, now and then, by air-conditioning, thick steaks, and smooth roads. Coming in from the districts, I could have fun on Guam. But I hated myself in the morning. There was a lesson for me there, if I'd been wise enough to learn it. If I had fun on Guam, what about those islanders I cared about, marooned in paradise, sans steak and pizza? I should have seen it. Guam was the future, paradise American style, improved, paved, air-conditioned. But I was proprietary about Micronesia. One of the last beautiful places, small, remote, and all that: could we please not fuck it up? Next question, though: what if the people wanted to fuck it up? What if they voted to do so, in one of those democratic elections we were so proud of importing? Guam made me uneasy. It jeopardized my hope that Micronesia would become something other than this road company America.

I wasn't Saipanese, though, and history had dealt Saipan, all of the Marianas, a peculiar hand. Western impact in the rest of Micronesia had been late and glancing, only spasmodically violent. But Magellan had called at the Marianas in 1521, naming them Islas de los Ladrones, islands of thieves. Later, Guam became a way station for Manila galleons. Warfare and disease reduced a precontact population of thirty-five thousand Chamorros to a mixed race of four thousand colonized, Catholicized "neo-Chamorros" with names like Palacios, Cabrera, Sablan.

So the Saipanese were different from other Micronesians, you had to grant them that. Not their fault, anyway. It was when they *boasted* about the difference that things got tricky, when their history of colonization, exploitation, near genocide somehow segued into an air of entitlement, sophistication, privilege. They went out of their way to distance themselves from the other Micronesians, to let us know that their inclusion in the Trust Territory was a historical accident, a case of mistaken identity. Watch out, they warned me, for Trukese men, Palauan women, Yapese magic, and thank god that I'd been assigned to a modern island like Saipan.

Like it or not, there was no holding the Northern Marianas in the Trust Territory. And no keeping them out of a close, permanent relationship with the United States, if that's what we were willing to offer them. And we were. Memories of Tinian and Saipan, "blood on the reef," mingled with worries about bases in the Philippines, Korea, and Japan. When it came to the Marianas we were ready to play, willing to pay. It took a while, though. For a few years, until 1972, the Northern

Marianas remained part of a Micronesian group, headed by Salii, that negotiated future political status with the Americans. Their presence became more strained and artificial each year. The break came at a meeting down in Koror, when Marianas delegates, one of them close to tears, pleaded for the right to begin separate negotiations with the Americans. Our islands are different, they insisted, our culture, our people. Let them go. If it were up to the Trukese, the Northern Marianas would never have gotten out. The Trukese sensed, accurately, that if one district split, others would head for the exit. Still, there was no holding the Marianas in. They *were* different. The other islanders wanted to keep some distance from the United States; they wanted free association that would lead to independence, at least they thought they did. The Northern Marianas wanted to be American. No doubt about it and all aboard.

In 1975, 78.8 percent of voters endorsed a "covenant" that made the Northern Marianas a U.S. commonwealth. The Northern Mariana Islands were going to be as American as Long Beach, California. They were joining us forever. I felt like I was standing at a wedding, toward the back of the church, fighting off the impulse to shout "no . . . wait a minute!" when the minister asked if anyone objected. I'd been on the island when they voted to cast their fate with us and this union made me uncomfortable. The son of immigrants, I sympathized with people who came to America, with the striving that brought them, the work and heart that kept them, whether they were greenhorn Germans coming in through Ellis Island (my father to work as a janitor in Harlem, my mother as a nanny on Riverside Drive), whether they were Koreans who ran vegetable stands or Indians who spent their lives in newspaper kiosks the size of portable toilets. But this felt different. The Saipanese weren't moving toward America—they were bringing it out to their island on terms that lawyers, theirs and ours, negotiated. Their citizenship wasn't earned, it was conferred; it was part of a package. All this was an odd, late, and fairly cynical way of becoming an American, I thought. In the weeks before the plebiscite, I listened to Saipanese discuss their Commonwealth Covenant with the United States. They called it a deal; that's how they thought about it, a bad deal, a good deal, a deal that might be improved or might not ever be offered again. There was no sense that this sort of commitment—a permanent bonding with the United States—ought to involve anything more than a calculation of benefits. Oh sure, there were benefits galore: covenant money, federal programs, 95 percent rebate on federal taxes. They liked the money and who could blame them? But there was more to America than money, some good, some bad, and of this they hadn't a clue.

I got back to Saipan a couple times in the late seventies and early eighties and—though my misgivings lingered—I had to admit the fledgling commonwealth was making out. There was all that money coming in, about $40 million a year in federal programs, aging, nutrition, USDA food, food stamps, Head Start, all in addition to an annual $14 million in direct commonwealth grants. But no one bothered answering—or for that matter, even asking—the questions that seemed important to me, dumb Peace Corps questions, but as long as I kept coming back to the islands I couldn't help wondering: do they like us? really like us? do they want to be part of us? do they belong? or is this another round in the old island game of we-and-them?

The Guam-Saipan flight is finally called. The air is cool, the morning sun, just up, puts Guam in the pink. We lift up, level off, and soon start pointing down. The Mariana Islands are a convoy down below, Guam, a battleship, Rota, a freighter, Tinian—I see the A-bomb strips!—an aircraft carrier. And Saipan, a pleasure boat. Just above the water, we cross the three-mile strait between Tinian and Saipan. The convoy continues north a couple hundred miles toward Japan: Anatahan, Agrigan, Pagan, Maug, Asuncion, and, hindmost, Farallon de Mendinilla, a rocky outcrop the Air Force uses as a bombing target. But now Saipan is right beneath us—the rocky shoreline, tin-roofed farm houses in clearings of tangan-tangan brush. Ahead sits 1,500-foot Mount Tagpochau, meadows of sword grass, patches of forest. It's amazing how each of these islands has its own look. First, you find the atolls of the Marshalls, a cartoon setting, a cartoonish-feeling place. Then, wet, hulking Ponape, ominous and clouded. And Truk, an armada of islands inside a lagoon, aspects and angles changing as you move between them. Now, here's Saipan. More handsome than beautiful, I always thought.

Beautiful is feminine: palm trees, waterfalls, sand. Saipan is masculine: pine trees, flame trees, and the tangan-tangan brush that they seeded after the war, to keep the soil from running off the burned-over island. Saipan is rocky, scarred, fought over and lived in, a bruiser of a place. No pristine illusions here, no easy talk of paradise. Saipan has paid dues.

Bleary and exhilarated, I step out onto the tarmac, toward customs and immigration. Whoosh! The island throws a wrap of hot, heavy air around me. Three shirts a day here, free and constant sweat under a sun that can turn a closed car into a torture chamber, the seat a frying pan, the wheel a branding iron. Glorious, no-nonsense heat, that welcomes me home.

◄ II ►

On my first days back I feel as stunned as a Japanese straggler poking his head out of some hillside hidey-hole, finding the battleground his comrades died on, the place he risked his life, past all hope of victory, now turned into something that no one on either side could have foreseen, a commonwealth of the United States and a playground for ... Japanese. For lemming packs of tourists, more than a quarter million of them a year, funning and sunning along invasion beaches. I am a straggler too. There's no more Japanese army here and no Peace Corps either: both outfits are extinct.

Starting near the airport, I head north along Beach Road, which runs the west side of the island. Once my departure would have been from Kobler Field, a World War II–era strip, but now Kobler Field is Koblerville, a suburban-looking subdivision of concrete houses. It's remarkable how, given half a chance, the Saipanese turn their island into an American suburb. They paint their concrete houses pastel colors, they park washing machines in their carports, cover their sunburned yards with toys. Just beyond Koblerville the scene changes though. I come upon the brand new Coral Point, hotel, restaurant, and golf course, the whole drill, where they joke about vacationing Yakuza gangsters coming in from Japan for sport, a certain floppiness in their golf gloves betraying the trademark absence of a ritually severed digit. Julio Iglesias has called here, taking time out from Far East bookings. Can Willie Nelson be far behind? But Willie was here all along, in spirit at least. Saipan was a country-western island, beery and dusty. The Julio Iglesias element is what's new, glitz triumphant. Down the road, I cruise past what used to be the White Sands Hotel, where we wrote a constitution. Now it's a Miami Beach–scale place called the Pacific Islands Club, a staff of gung-ho "club-mates" helping vacationers enjoy themselves. They've got waterslides and a Disney-esque Spanish galleon picturesquely wrecked on some rocks around the swimming pool. Next I come into the crowded part of the island, San Antonio Village, Chalan Kanoa, and Susupe, a gamut of tourist ships, mini shopping malls, Korean and Chinese restaurants, beauty parlors, discos, gaming rooms, and target-shooting parlors. The road is jammed and there is construction everywhere; not the wishful construction I saw in Truk, where a year-old pile of sand and a few rods of rusted re-bar say maybe we will, maybe we won't, but hectic under-the-gun hard-hatting Koreans and Filipinos working like they work in Saudi Arabia. Then, more hotels, the Saipan Grand, the old Royal Taga, renamed and expanded.

Past Susupe, the road runs close to the beach, too close to permit construction on the ocean side. Here, I find the same placid, grassy shoreline I remember, parked cars and picnic tables under graceful, soft-needled ironwood trees. But right across the road, on the inland side, the hits just keep on coming: car dealerships, Chinese restaurants, hotels and motels, duty-free shops. One continuous blur, all the way to Garapan where there's another cluster of hotels, the ten-story Hafa Adai, the Hyatt, and the Intercontinental, big deals that have spawned a whole zone—the Ginza, it's called—of smaller operations, video rentals, curry houses, soft ice cream, moped rentals, strip joints, you name it: Athlete's Foot, Winchell's Donuts. Flags of all nations fly outside the Duty Free Shopping Center. It looks like an embassy.

I head north, just like the marines headed north, nearly fifty years ago, glancing up a hillside to a house I once lived in. There were avocado trees in back and eggplants on the side fence and dogs sleeping on the porch. At dawn I'd awaken and see if a ship had come in to Charley Dock, maybe a field trip vessel headed for the northern islands. At dusk, cooling down after running, I'd watch the sun crash into the Philippine Sea and realize that it might not be such a bad idea to spend a life in a place like this; maybe work wasn't the most important thing, after all. Maybe living on a hillside over a harbor facing sunsets was something you should build your life around, that or those nights when I'd drink a beer on the porch, under the stars, and feel blessed.

Now I have trouble spotting the place, there are so many other buildings on the hill—homes, office buildings, construction barracks, condominium apartments. I press on past Tanapag village and San Roque, past where workers are finishing off a new hotel called the Aqua Sports Club. Right in front of where the Marpi gate once blocked access to acres of undetonated World War II ammunition scattered all over the northern tip of the island, ammunition that was aimed at Japan, then rendered war-surplus by the A-bomb, stands the Nikko Hotel, three hundred rooms, goldfish ponds, aviary, waterslides, piano bar, shops full of Louis Vuitton and Christian Dior. Japan runs, Japan redux, Japan is rich.

I decide to save Marpi for another day, head back south and turn inland, up toward Capitol Hill, where I used to work. Driving uphill, I suppose this will be my version of that honored literary convention, the-Peace-Corps-volunteer-returns-to-his-village-years-later. Wet-hanky time.

Suddenly the hairpin road winds out of the brushy tangan-tangan and opens up—bingo!—on a San Diego–style suburb, lawns and gardens, smooth streets with concrete curbs, dozens of ranch houses, a community club, a post office. Welcome to my old Peace Corps village. Quaint, no? Lagoon, reef, sea, and in the mornings you can see Anatahan Island, forty miles north.

This unexpected hilltop community has a curious history, part of the underlying weirdness of Saipan. It was built in the early fifties for something called the Naval Technical Training Unit (NTTU), a spooky outfit that restricted access to Saipan and fenced off this whole end of the island. This was where the staff reposed, this is the view they came

home to after a hard day at work, training students in espionage, sabo-
tage, guerrilla warfare; students who flew in without being told where
they were, who were transported around the island in sealed vehicles,
who were tutored in the boondocks of the Marpi District. One old-timer
tells me of watching the Americans build a model home out there, an
American ranch house, furnished down to the last Ozzie-and-Harriet
detail, only to be blown to pieces by an attacking tank. The teachers
were American. The students were Nationalist Chinese, say some Saipanese who glimpsed them. And some darker people too. Indonesians?

When it decamped in the early sixties, the NTTU razed its training
facilities. No records and monuments for this outfit; even the aerial
maps that showed its installations were whited out. No alumni reunions
either. But the housing area, the hilltop mini-America, was turned over
to the Trust Territory government, a Department of the Interior operation, which had been running the islands from offices in Hawaii, later
Guam. Capitol Hill was an American community, a world away from
America, a world away as well from the wood and tin shacks, the
bullet-scarred foundations, potholes, and coral dust in the villages down
below. The place had already run down some, by the time I saw it. Grass
grew on the tennis court, weeds in gardens. The old officers' club was
casualty number one: paint peeling in the ballroom, puddles on the
floor, pieces of its thoroughly vandalized table service showing up at
weddings and baptisms all over the island. Still, it was a piece of America and—America being the uncola of colonial powers—there was
room for Micronesians too, elite Micronesians of the right sort. Why
there were dozens of Micronesian households on Capitol Hill and, as
some American housewives tartly pointed out, dozens of Micronesians
in every household.

I drive around Capitol Hill, along streets that remind me of sleepy
suburbs, past the two-story headquarters building I worked in, the
American flag and the six stars of the Trust Territory of Pacific Islands
flying side by side outside. An odd place to be a Peace Corps Volunteer.
Sometimes Peace Corps staff would come up to the Hill, to parlay
with the high commissioner. They'd drop by my office, notice the air-
conditioning, the secretaries, the coffeepot, and leave troubled. Why

wasn't I living more on the level of the people? Why was I always cruising around in government vehicles? Sure, this was a nice-enough magazine I was putting out, but who was I training? Who were my "host country counterparts"? Now my old office is part of the headquarters of the Commonwealth of the Northern Marianas. A new flag. Across the grass, up a hill, I spot the old high commissioner's residence—highest house on the island—now home to the commonwealth governor. High commissioner: it sounded British. You expected Lord Mountbatten, the Duke of Windsor, or a lesser somebody who'd blotted his copybook back home and gotten shipped into exile. You couldn't picture an American kid dreaming of being high commissioner when he grew up. But that's what Bill Norwood was when I arrived, a Honolulu PR man who was followed a few years later by Ed Johnston, a balding, bespectacled insurance executive who wore fire-red slacks on Saturday nights. I remember the receptions up there, receptions for someone from the U.N., or the U.S. Congress or the U.S. Marines or the South Pacific Commission, a shuttle bus carrying us up the sloping driveway to the high commissioner's home where we ran a gamut, a reception line of aloha-shirted *haoles*—a Hawaiian term for whites—and Micronesians squirming in ties and shirts. The bar was busy, the dining table offered a collection of hors d'oeuvres just large enough to destroy an appetite, never quite enough to make a meal. I behaved myself, at the high com's table. Peace Corps volunteers had a reputation for . . . well . . . loading up on free food, two paper plates in each hand, a doggie bag in their back pockets, right along with the marijuana. The other Americans were always watching, ready to snipe at wet-behind-the-ears college kids who thought they were God's gift. Half the time on Capitol Hill, I felt that the people I needed to win over were the Americans. I didn't mind. The Peace Corps staff had given the Trust Territory regulars a bad rap and the result was intramural squabbling, Americans fussing over turf, each side passing itself off as the real America. They were all screwups, when you got right down to it, but the TT people had been screwing up longer and I kind of respected that. It would take the Peace Corps years of screwing up to catch them, which was more time than they had. The clock was ticking in the islands.

Later, after the party wound down, I'd head to the beach. I lived in the villages, in a series of shacky places, rats in the kitchen and Jesus pictures on the wall. On the way, I'd hit some of the bars down on Beach Road. At Josie's Bar on Beach Road, Kirin sold for a quarter and it was easy to dance and get happy and talk about the real America and, almost as far, out beyond the reef someplace, the real Micronesia. Saipan was neither one. Not then, not now, and at no time in between. The other islands thrashed and writhed as they took the bait that Washington threw them. Free association. But the Northern Marianas leapt right into America's bait box, Charley the Tuna finally conning his way into a Chicken of the Sea can. I remember, when they voted to become American, there was a poster that asked WHO DO YOU WANT TO BE YOUR PRESIDENT? and there was a picture of Gerald Ford and a picture of Tosiwo Nakayama, my friend from Truk.

Past Capitol Hill, the road winds around the back side of the island, a hilly, curving grand prix of a drive, Mount Tagpochau on one side, the Pacific far below, but now there are driveways left and right, mansions, palazzos, San Simeons. All those airy roosts that I thought might someday make a writer's modest bungalow, all my pleasant vacancies have been filled by Japanese wheeler-dealers, American businessmen, nouveau riche locals. I dreamed, they planned. While I was doodling A-frames in New York, they came and bought and built their mansions.

◄ III ►

"Hey, Fred, I'm rich."

I'm sitting at Herman's Bakery, eating fried rice and over-easy eggs, when Manny Muna comes over to talk. In the old days he was a politician, an early member of the Congress of Micronesia. Later he drifted to the edge of local politics, a legislative aide, a jovial wisecracking guy who used to drop by the *Micronesian Reporter* to bullshit. In some ways, he epitomized the Saipan of those days, smoking a cigar and driving one of the surplus jeeps the navy sold to the locals at one dollar per vehicle after the war. Now he sits down for coffee and brings me up to date on himself. He drives an airport taxi, his wife works at Duty-Free, but that's just keeping busy. He has some Filipinos farming down on Kagman Peninsula and—get this—the agricultural extension service is planting some windbreak pine trees down there at no charge.

"If the United States gives money to countries that don't like America, they can give money to Manny Muna," Manny Muna cheerfully reasons. He likes America fine and he's got the papers to prove it, a voter registration card at the address of the house he bought in Seattle. What happened, it seems, is that these Chinese guys came along and wanted to put a garment factory on some land in San Vicente. Muna leased them the land, put five $200,000 deposits in the bank in his children's names and bought some property in that new Saipanese frontier, the Pacific Northwest.

Manny Muna has it right. I keep dropping in on people, liking the surprise my appearance produces. I drive old roads, scowl at new houses, I cruise through government offices, drink coffee, crack old jokes: "CIA here, you're all under arrest." I compose lists of dead bars along Beach Road, Da Place, Saipan Inn, Golden Leaf, Josie's, Saipan, Smiling Bar, Amatugula, Castle Heights, all gone. I prowl new hotels, trail tourist buses, insinuate myself among duty-free shoppers, and Saipan is rich. I'd might as well admit it: all things considered—the way they work, or avoid work, the houses they live in, the Filipina maids they hire at the going rate of $150 per month, the cars they drive, the trips they take—the people of the Northern Marianas are living as good as Americans. How it happened, whether it should have happened at all, whether it will last—I'll get to that. But what I see right now is that coming back to Saipan is going to put me through some interesting hoops. If I were a Peace Corps volunteer returning to say, Turkey, I could measure the place in terms of its own identity. Let Turkey be Turkey. I could nod, smile, and swallow my tongue. But the Northern Marianas joined America—for good. Is this perfect decolonization or the ultimate colonialism?

▲ ▲ ▲

"I'll tell you a story about my island," Escolastica Cabrera says. "The Spanish, the Germans, the Japanese, the Americans . . . why this many nationalities fighting for this mosquito island? On a map, it looks like mosquito manure. But see how the Japanese like it? They're going to buy it back."

I listen carefully. The old people on these islands are more interesting than the young ones. The kids are proto-Americans, wanna be's, outward bound. Some will make it, some won't. But the old people are different. Their English is often shaky, they're not glib, but the way they look at you, that something in their eyes, tells you they have seen it all: wars, foreign powers coming and going, colony, Trust Territory, commonwealth. There's a man I know in the Marshalls who saw his father beheaded by the Japanese. A guy I used to know on Saipan saw Japanese and Koreans and Okinawans, men, women, and children, jump off Suicide Cliff. Every islander past fifty has a story to tell.

Escolastica Cabrera has some of this. I'd never talked with her much, though I saw her almost every day for two years, at the store she ran behind the headquarters building on Capitol Hill. I'd come in at lunch for sandwiches, lumpia, empanada, hard-boiled eggs, cookies, always complaining about the prices: I'm a poor guy, a Peace Corps volunteer, these sandwiches are so small, Escolastica! And she'd give us as good as I got, how times were hard, her years of service unappreciated, she was barely breaking even. Our daily banter. Now, twenty-two years later, I sit with her in the shade and ask her to tell me the story of her life.

She was born in 1930, on a Saipan that was a bustling Japanese colony, covered with sugar cane fields. Narrow-gauge railways trundled cane from field to mill, from mill to wharf. Garapan, the main town, was a pleasant, orderly place, bicycles and cars moving along shop-lined streets, gardens and flowers everywhere. Japanese everywhere as well, Okinawans and Koreans too. They outnumbered the locals, ten to one. "Japanese people treated the Chamorros number three," Escolastica says. "The Japanese were number one, the Okinawans were number two, the Chamorros were number three."

Still, the prewar memories are more good than bad. A cobbler's daughter, Escolastica lived in a tin-roofed concrete house in Garapan, "a beautiful, peaceful town." Though education for island kids was limited, usually stopping at the third grade, Escolastica was bright. "I received a medal from Hirohito, a certificate with red and white stripes." Her family owned a farm on the back side of the island. That is what she remembers best. When I ask her to tell me what grew on the farm the answer comes, not as list or inventory, but as a kind of elegy for a life that used to be. The staples were white and red and brown taro, bananas, yams, corn. Her father grew tobacco, "English cut," which he sent to Yap. Vegetables were eggplant, pumpkin, long beans, string beans, bell peppers, cabbage, tomatoes. "My father was a very hard-working man." They made their own vinegar and soap. "Everything you put in the ground, God gives the spirit to grow." Hot peppers, garlic, onions. Coffee. Betelnut. "I have these things in mind, I'm telling my children, but it's so easy now to go to the store."

The farm is where they went, when the war came. So did many other families, some of whom stayed while others drifted north, keeping ahead of the fighting. At first, when the battle was a distant roar, a matter of ships and planes, they stayed in caves during the day, foraged at night, finding water, cutting and cooking bananas. A Japanese soldier who'd been a sort of boyfriend stopped to say goodbye. "You should hide," he told her. "The Americans will kill the old men and women and take the young girls to the ships for geisha girls."

Toward the end, forty-five people were crammed into a cave, day and night. "You couldn't cook, you couldn't stand up, the cave was small, forty-five people like sardines." They could hear the Americans now, out in the sugar cane, hear them cursing! "Goddamn." "Son of a bitch." Then they saw one of them right outside the cave. "Hey, uncle, there's an American and he's pulling your cow." Everyone was scared. An American stamped his feet outside the cave. "Then my mother put her hands up, saying, "*Paz*, Chamorro. *Paz*, Chamorro." Peace, Chamorro. And a brother who'd spent some time on Guam rescued the situation with broken English. *"Hello, my friend, never mind, I don't know. Hello my friend, never mind, I don't know."*

Smart and resourceful, Escolastica worked as a seamstress and laundress while the Saipanese were still interned in camps. Later, she made handicraft for the Americans, cigarette cases out of pandanus. She worked in officers' homes, opened a series of beauty parlors, dress shops, snack bars. More ambitious schemes to market tangan-tangan charcoal and tapioca starch haven't prospered. But she leased some of her land to a group of Chinese and used the proceeds for a long trip, part vacation, part pilgrimage. She complains about all these aliens leasing land from locals, herself included, all these Japanese, Koreans, Filipinos. "They're buying my island," she laments and brings out the scrapbooks, filled with photos from her travels. Paris, Washington, Kentucky, Oregon. Lourdes and Fatima. There she is, riding a camel at a county fair someplace.

▲ ▲ ▲

Leaving Escolastica's store, I drive out into that special hour, the time of roadside walks and first beers in other districts. Mellow dusk. On Saipan it spells traffic jams along Beach Road, locals in air-conditioned cars, imported workers jammed into the backs of pickup trucks. I join the convoy, remembering when most of the vehicles on the island were Jeeps, when you waved at every passing car, when the whole island listened to the same radio station, the one and only, its staff of disc jockeys working to sound cool: "Okay, chick and doood, it's time now to make track out of here." When all the stores on the island were missing the letter *D*, so that a place was either OPEN for business or CLO3E, which I kind of liked because it hinted a near miss, somebody just around the corner.

I wonder how Salii would react to the way Saipan has turned out. He spent more of his adult life on this island than he did back home in Palau. He lived in a half-dozen houses around the island, all government issue, and he seemed pretty much at home here. Much as I'd like to think otherwise, that he'd be appalled at the pace of development, the gold coast and the ginza, the dust and clutter, I bet he'd like it still, especially the hotels and golf courses. The action. It would have been a tug of war if I'd gone to work for him in Palau, seeing that parade of agents, clients, speculators file in and out of his office.

Who *are* these people? What kind of deal *is* this? I can see myself trailing after him, asking questions, dumb Peace Corps questions. I try to picture his response. Could I have calmed him, slowed him down? Or would he have shrugged me off, avoided me, fired off a few rounds of "you're not a Palauan." It's a moot question now. But I go on hoping he'd have found some balance, if he'd lived, a mix of yes's and no's, a torn man's reconciliations. And now it occurs to me, not for the first time, that I wonder about him too much, for all the good it can do. Let him rest in peace. Trouble is, he didn't live that way and he didn't die that way. Maybe he's at peace now. But I'm not.

Dusk on Saipan. At sea, outside the reef, silhouetted against the sunset, are two mammoth freighters, military charters prepositioned there, ready to take off for the Philippines on a moment's notice. "Cory's tanks," the locals say. I pull out of traffic into a restaurant-disco-massage parlor that serves Cory's food. It's still early and the girls are hanging around in shorts, T-shirts, their hair up in curlers, all Filipinas except a tough-looking blonde with a baby on her lap. Filled up on pork and rice, feeling ornery and down, I head for Hamilton's.

Hamilton's bar is a constant, an eternal, a shrine almost, and I never feel that I'm completely home until I turn off the road near Navy Hill, wind up the driveway into the parklike grounds, step over the sleeping dogs, walk into the bar with the picture of John Wayne on the wall behind the pool table. Everything else on the island is changing but Hamilton is still pouring drinks, drinking some besides, sometimes soaring far above, sometimes just floating along with, now and then—like Nakayama's Japanese bugler—sinking beneath the nightly tide of talk.

I believe—and so does Hamilton—that he was put on earth to run a bar on Saipan, to shrug, shudder, and shout about local goings-on, to regard life with a Tennessee hillbilly's leery, squinting eye, sighting on the bullshit that comes down the pike: U.N. bullshit, Trust Territory bullshit, Peace Corps bullshit, now commonwealth bullshit. He pours drinks, he scowls, he smiles. Some nights he breaks out his harmonica, sings navy ditties, dances Smoky Mountain jigs till Carmen, his Chamorro wife, comes out of the kitchen, intervenes, leads him away.

Twenty-five years ago, he ran the best restaurant on the island—steak, shrimp, chicken—and the place was thronged, especially by Congress of Micronesia members who appreciated Hamilton's fine, blunt disregard. He retired for a while, leased out the restaurant to others who tried and failed. Then he re-created the bar in a different building, out in back, and he was in his glory again.

I arrive and find the pool table busy, the small bar crowded. Hamilton nods, shakes my hand—he's almost forgiven me for being a Peace Corps volunteer—and sells me a Budweiser. The evening chat, briefly disturbed by my entrance, forms up and moves on. An American who brought his girlfriend out to the island tells me he's seeing her off tomorrow. She hates the place, the tits-and-ass bars, the massage parlors and macho attitudes, the leering references to trips to Manila. Though he's staying, he doesn't much like Saipan either. Like many other Americans, he's disturbed by some clauses in the Commonwealth Covenant. While conferring U.S. citizenship on Northern Marianas residents, the covenant stipulated that land ownership was reserved to citizens of Northern Marianas ancestry. Thus, in the Commonwealth of the Northern Marianas, some U.S. citizens—locals—are more equal than others. Outsiders tried circumventing the law by using local agents—buddies, girlfriends, whatever—to buy land, but now the courts are undoing some of those deals, giving these pioneering Americans something else to resent. The locals are walking all over us, they think; they are Americans for some purposes, islanders for others. When it suits them. They want to have their cake and eat it. "Not just their cake," one American says. "Your cake. My cake. Everybody's cake." It's still islanders versus outsiders, us versus them.

"What really gets me," someone volunteers, "is the sense that they are *entitled* to a certain life-style. We're not talking about middle-class America either. This isn't *Leave It to Beaver.* We're talking *Dynasty.* Without doing anything, without producing anything, just by manipulating their relatives and selling their land, they ought to live in a house like *Dynasty.* "

"Fantasyland," a drinker sighs.

"The most corrupt place on earth."

"Everybody should be indicted."

"It's a racially discriminatory fucking law!" a guy cries out. "If they want to be Arabs or Communists or some weird shit, that's something else. But if they want to be Americans . . . what is this shit! I spend fifteen fucking years here and can't buy land and they can go to California and buy what they want?! That's bullshit! And now they go even further . . . they decide I go in with some local, give him the money to buy some land, I work it and develop it and make a profit, that's illegal too. What is this shit?"

"Other places you get U.S. citizenship, you have to study. Night courses. Constitution, history, civics. Here they just . . ."

". . . conferred it on them."

"Fantasyland."

Hamilton listens quietly to the evening noise. It's not his night to dance and roar. Maybe he's heard all this before, this tension between locals and Americans, which has now become a tension between new Americans and old. Maybe he saw it coming. Still, he's here. He stays . . . and worries, and irrigates his worries with Canadian Club. Japanese investors have noticed Hamilton's handsome five-hectare spread. First they offered five million, then eight, and Hamilton fears that his wife and kids may want to deal. "I really don't want to sell this hill to the Japs," he says. He glances out to the kitchen, where his wife sits calmly rolling lumpia. "Maybe I'll wind up in some old sailors' home in Missouri."

◄ IV ►

I remember the look of those first Japanese who dribbled back to Saipan in the sixties. They were shy, polite, a little shell-shocked. They were tentative, always in groups, often in square boxy suits. They appreciated everything, it seemed; they'd photograph a run-over dog in the middle of the road; they'd nod and smile as they piled into tour buses that took them to the invasion beaches, the old Japanese hospital and jail.

Some of them were bone-hunters, sponsored by the Japanese government or veterans associations or religious groups, led around the island by scouts who knew where the bones were buried. It was a bizarre occupation. Japanese died by the thousands on Saipan, thirty thousand in all. They died on the invasion beaches, in trenches and bunkers, they died in the rubble of Garapan and Chalan Kanoa, they died in the ravines and gullies that lead up to Mount Tagpochau. The battle lost, invaders pressing north, they still died. They were incinerated by flame throwers, they were entombed in blasted-shut caves, they committed hara-kiri in bunkers and command posts. Toward the end, they poured down out of the hills, onto the plains of Tanapag and San Roque, armed with guns and clubs, a human-wave banzai charge, right out of the movies. At the last, they died jumping off cliffs, eight hundred feet, the biggest mass suicide till Jim Jones dispensed Kool-Aid in Guyana.

The bone-hunters came to take them home. They were solemn people, off to work at dawn, a convoy of pickups headed into the boondocks, harvesting remains. I had an interview, stiff and awkward, with one group: platitudes about tragic war, hopes for peace, no rest for the living until the dead were home. It sounded morbid at the time, but years afterward when I saw grateful Americans accepting coffins from Vietnam, I understood their passion. At the time, I admired their diligence . . . and the island's charnel house fecundity. What they found!

On a mellow afternoon, early in December 1975, I drove to the north end of the island, parked on an old Japanese fighter strip, and walked in toward a group of bone-hunters. The pyre they'd built was enormous, a dozen feet long, five feet high, all bones. How many cords of bones did that amount to? I was struck by the neatness of it, the way they'd put the heavier bones at the bottom, legs mostly. Lighter bones came next, arms and ribs I guessed, and spinal vertebrae. Then, on top of the pile, an icing of skulls, two or three deep, that looked as though they were peeking over a wall, spying on the living. They were the color of the earth that had kept them, brown and autumnal, save for one that must have been wrested from a souvenir hunter: he was painted pink. The fire started with a sudden whoosh that kicked off clouds of off-white smoke. The skulls turned color, brown to black, a shining ebony; they might have been sweating. At the last, they turned white, ready to be crumbled into boxes and shipped home.

Macabre, I thought. It had nothing to do with me. It was about Saipan, about Japan, about the past, not me. But two days later I got a telegram from Florida, from my brother: POP DIED THIS MORNING. And when I adjusted for datelines and delivery times, I realized that the old man's death and cremation coincided with what I'd stood photographing on the Japanese airstrip. It was his funeral, I realized; what happened to them, happened to him. Could . . . would . . . happen to me. And from then on, I walked around more aware of my own bones, heavy and light, the skull beneath my face, the someday-to-be-burned skeleton in me.

Veterans, mourners, old-timers, the first Japanese were downbeat, melancholy tourists—something like Americans traveling back to Vietnam—and I supposed that, once the bones had been collected, the monuments built, the guilt exorcised or forgotten, once these old-timers were gone, that would be the end of it. I was wrong.

It's hard to acknowledge that where you live, even as—especially as—a Peace Corps volunteer, is someone else's idea of a resort. When we used words like paradise, they were laced with irony. This made it hard to grant that other people could say paradise, straight-faced, and put their money where their mouths were. So when the first real hotel went up, the Royal Taga, old island hands were skeptical, wryly ironic, just like old island hands are supposed to be, watching some outsiders invest their money and get taken for a ride. Chateaubriand for two? Here on Saipan? They've got to be kidding! The prices were too high, the island was a little too hot and a lot too humid, and unless you were interested in, I mean really hung up on World War II, why come here? Which goes to show how little old island hands know. We were living on the Japanese Florida, not knowing it.

Surprise, surprise! And paradox. The Japanese craving for the islands of the south, the warm lost islands of the vanished empire, was born in the years of Japanese control, between World Wars I and II. The trauma of war complicated those feelings, but it enriched and deepened them too: no colony like a lost colony, no love like a lost love. And when the war generation started to fade, Japan sent out new armies of honeymooners, sun worshippers, office workers, golfers. The Kintetsu Buffalo baseball team chose Saipan for spring training, a tattooed Yakuza was found floating off Banzai Cliff, and Colonel Sakae Oba, leader of a band of stragglers who harrassed Americans for a year and a half after the battle ended, returned to visit. Now Beach Road bristles with high-rise hotels and hardly a week passes that doesn't bring the announcement of another big deal development, hotels, condos, marinas, and all. The beaches on the west side are gone and the villages too are being nibbled away at, piece by piece. Now the Japanese are landing on the rough east side of the island, on Lau Lau Beach, and up in Marpi. They're reconnoitering the neighboring islands of Rota and Tinian too. What is happening is eerily like World War II—in reverse. Beaches falling one by one. Locals moving inland. An island-hopping campaign, bypassing some places, slamming into others. A yen for the south brings them, and me, to people like David Igitol.

▲ ▲ ▲

He was my student once. Back in my Peace Corps days, I taught a college extension course for the University of Guam. A handful of short stories: Willa Cather's "A Sculptor's Funeral," John Cheever's "Angel on the Bridge." They didn't travel well, but never mind. Whatever the literary goals, the course became what these courses always become: composition and conversation. Arguments for clean, plain style.

I hear a lot about David Igitol this trip, how he's on the edge of a great fortune, possibly the biggest land deal the island's seen. I find him at work in the commonwealth's finance department, a soft-spoken agreeable guy. He estimates that there are a hundred local millionaires already, a club he may soon join. Igitol's family land, a 4.8-hectare tract just north of Tanapag Village, is the largest beachfront parcel left on the island. It has a white sand beach, a fringe of ironwood trees and, inland, three or four family houses surrounded by scraps of garden, mangos, and banana trees cut into the thickets of tangan-tangan. It was—it still is—a pleasant breezy place, conducive to barefoot walks, beer, and barbecue; a Sunday kind of place that calls for a spread-out blanket or a shady hammock on a lazy afternoon.

The first nibble came from local brokers, middlemen, not surprising on an island where everybody dabbles in real estate. Then the Japanese came along, asking questions. Can we see the land? Can we walk the beach? Hey, nice beach. Do you want to sell it? Lease it? Before long, five companies were bidding. They bought dinner, they offered trips to Japan, volunteered to fly relatives in from the states, offered nine, ten, thirteen million, sixteen, twenty-six, thirty-one million.

"All the beach areas are sold," Igitol told them, hanging tough. "There might be a few 100-by-100 parcels left, but all the rest are sold. If you look left and right, you see hotels and tourists. Tourists in chairs, white legs and white arms. You should be proud to see me between them. I'm the only local on the beach."

It wasn't that simple, though. Igitol was part of an extended family, a family of Saipan Carolinians whose ancestors migrated to Saipan from the far-off islands between Truk and Yap. For years, while Spaniards confined Chamorros to Guam, the Carolinians, relative newcomers, had Saipan to themselves. When the Chamorro diaspora ended, the Carolinians became a minority—darker, bigger, quieter than the His-panicized Chamorros, closer to island customs and traditions, medi-cine, magic. Time has eroded some of these differences, but not all. Carolinians hold land as a family, and the family that claimed this lucrative parcel included fifteen members of Dave Igitol's generation. One cousin wanted to sell a portion of the land as an individual. Family meetings turned tense, lawyers were hired. Meanwhile, Dave Igitol read books on trusts, investments, leases, joint ventures. And he confronted his father, Pablo, who probably didn't want to sell at all.

"Our father was fifty-fifty," he says. "The land is so precious because of its value and because he lived there, we were born there, we worked the land. The Japanese used it for fuel storage, and he fought to get it back when the U.S. conquered the place, because they wanted to con-tinue to use it for storage. He fought in court to get it back. So at first he said he was fifty-fifty about selling. He said he had to follow his father's wish not to sell the land, to leave it for family use, so we can live here and stay together as a family. The family ties are close if you live here. There are not so many Igitols in the world, and once the land is divided and sold that would be the end. The family would start falling apart. . . ."

Igitol pauses. He seems unaffected by the millions that are so close to him. He doesn't even seem surprised. Being rich on Saipan is a matter of accepting the inevitable. Strangers coming to your island, walking the beaches. Sometimes they fight a battle, sometimes they build a hotel. Location, they say in real estate, is everything.

"Deep inside, I don't think he wants to sell," Igitol resumes. "But he said, you're my children, I'm in my seventies. I'll die and you'll be the heirs. Make the best decision you can make. But I still feel he doesn't want to sell the land. As long as he lives, he doesn't want to sell the land."

The Igitols were still in court when I left the island. And the Japanese offer—latest, not last—was up to $40 million.

◄ V ►

The Japanese didn't forget these islands. Neither did the Americans. Sometimes it came in a firm and steely voice: these islands were captured with American lives. Sometimes it was muted, to the point of inaudibility: fall back positions, contingency plans, defensive arcs. But there's never been doubt that if Japanese tourism and investment are what's happening now, American military presence is what might happen again. And that is why no visit to Saipan is complete without a side trip to the neighboring island of Tinian.

People on Saipan shrug when you mention Tinian. Dullsville. It's always been that way. You get nonchalant about history, when history's just three miles across the straits. But I could never look at the place or hear its name without feeling a surge of excitement at the presence, just offshore, of the place from which the *Enola Gay* took off for Hiroshima. No matter that Tinian was sleepy, dusty, dull. If you had a taste for the ebb and flow of empire, you'd go to Tinian, if only for a day or two. And Tinian didn't disappoint. Twenty years ago, you could stay in a ramshackle hotel that had been Curtis Le May's headquarters. You could explore the grid of roads and airstrips the Americans left behind: it was like having the run of an abandoned aircraft carrier. You could sit up nights, talking in German to the aged innkeeper, half-Scottish, half-Marshallese, Henry Fleming, who had seen the Germans and Japanese and Americans all come and go. Or you could visit the Capuchin missionary, Father Marcian, who would point out how part of his church, the clerestory, had been built out of scrap salvaged from the buildings in which the Americans had armed atomic bombs.

Now, I'm determined to go again, and again I'm warned. Tinian hasn't changed much. That's all right with me. Tinian wasn't supposed to change; just be there, heart of America's "defensive arc," a chain of fallback positions we can call home if we lose bases in the Philippines, Japan, and Korea. Tinian is a ghost-ship of an island, a gigantic *Marie Celeste,* ready and waiting for its crew's return.

Oh, they are hustling on Tinian all right, trying to share in Saipan's hothouse bloom. People are applying to build garment factories, just like Saipan, and others are aiming to put in some gambling casinos. A Tinian delegation has just returned from an entrails-reading tour of Vegas, Monte Carlo, and the rest and—surprise, surprise—were mighty pleased with what they saw. They plan to put the issue in front of the voters, soon. Still, most of Tinian's future remains locked up in its past, linked to the magic day the nuclear age began.

The Tinian airport is new, friendly and small. It's refreshing, after Saipan and Guam, to walk through an airport that doesn't have a gift-shop, to rent a car from an agent who leaves right after I do, and to take off down roads that are as empty and exhilarating as I remember.

A word about the roads of Tinian. Back in the forties, the Americans detected a resemblance between Tinian and Manhattan. They gave the roads they laid out Manhattan names, a Wall Street and Chinatown, Park Row, 42nd, 59th, 64th, 69th, 72nd, 86th, 96th, 116th streets, a Saw Mill Parkway, and Boston Post Road. Weeds and tangan-tangan have swallowed much of Gotham since then, but Broadway is still Broadway, a two-lane, island-long thoroughfare through green, rolling country dotted with flame trees and eucalyptus. Cattle graze around old Japanese bunkers, a tori arch stands in a grove of flame trees, and the Japanese Hinode Shrine is in a traffic circle, ringed with cowpies from the local herd. Zooming north on Broadway, not another car on the road, I spot fingers of grass edging out onto the macadam. All of a sudden, one lane is gone, the other threatened. Now the tangan-tangan reaches and meets overhead and I'm driving down a green pipeline, branches slapping against my window, fallen trees menacing my fenders. Sensing I've come far enough, I turn left into a lateral tunnel, which might take me where I want to go or, then again, to someplace I've never been—an antiaircraft gun, a Japanese bunker, a shot-down plane.

Then: daylight, space, eternity. I drive out onto the grid of four eight-thousand-foot runways, laterals, feeders that marked the high-water mark of American power—August 6, 1945. Top of the world, Ma! And I have it all to myself, that's the Walter Mitty glory of it, racing down one strip after another, broad, baking, open runways, with just an occasional island of brush or clump of weeds, the odd fallen ironwood, to make things interesting. I zoom down the runway at one hundred miles per hour. Tinian is the only place I've ever driven this fast, right in the path of the B-29s whose skid marks are still on the runway.

I once interviewed Captain Paul Tibbetts, for a *TV Guide* profile tied to a made-for-TV movie, *Enola Gay*. A courtly executive type, head of a Columbus, Ohio based air charter service, Tibbetts went out of his way to show his life had *not* been ruined, damned, haunted by Hiroshima. I promised to send him slides of Tinian; like most promises reporters make on stories, it was never kept. Now I think of him again, though: a white-haired man of taste and sense, watching Patrick Duffy play his younger self, Billy Crystal impersonate his navigator, Kim Darby enact his long-ago first wife, and Tucson stand in for Tinian. That was the worst performance. All they had in common was the ovenlike air that comes off the shimmering runways.

Sometimes there are arrows painted on the runways, sometimes there's a sign, but mostly I feel my way along the edge of the airstrips, toward the A-bomb loading pits. Twin pits, one for Hiroshima, one for Nagasaki. The holes from which the bombs were hoisted into the B-29s' bellies are filled with dirt, planted with plumeria—a graveyard plant in this part of the world—and coconut palms. Tablets give the date and details of each mission. It's an austere monument, no frills, no whooping it up. You never know when the planes might come flying in again. That prospect bothered me a lot, once. It was too cruel a fate to contemplate, like lightning striking twice. And I assumed that what disturbed me ought to upset my island friends as well, people like Salii. But I may have been wrong. My scruples were luxuries; he had other things in mind.

The last time I saw Salii in Palau, I'd just come from the Philippines, from Olongapo, the jaded, neon town that lives off the huge U.S. naval base at Subic Bay. I'd written a piece for *Playboy,* and I was still all full of the grotesquerie I'd seen. The fleet had been in, thousands of sailors coming through the gate, crossing a river—"Shit's Creek"—and plunging into Olongapo, a horny sailor's paradise: foxy boxing, mud-wrestling, massage, go-go, blow jobs, country-western, hard rock, oldies but goodies, San Miguel beer, satay barbecue. A hive of LBFM-PBRs: little-brown-fucking-machines, powered-by-rice, Olongapo startled me. It also, let's face it, turned me on. Three hundred pesos—fifteen dollars—could buy a nymph in a bikini. In Olongapo, I'd felt a little like I was back hanging off the edge of a cliff in Ponape: fuck it . . . just drop off. Let it be!

Going to Palau from Manila felt like an escape. It was only a two-hour flight, but what a change. From above, the Philippines looked used up, crowded. The mountains had been logged to death, the fields were slashed and eroded, the lagoons turned brown with silt. Then, in Palau, each island was fresh and green, the sea as blue as the sky and then some. I sighed in relief, landed, checked into a hotel and went for a chat with my old friend, President Salii. I started to tell him what I'd seen. "It's a nice place, isn't it," he said. "I wish they'd come here."

Lightning striking twice? There were kites flying all over Micronesia, and hopeful men beneath them. That's the lesson of Tinian, worth relearning: that war brought America to the islands and the prospect of war keeps us in the old neighborhood. A military base isn't the end of the world, not by a long shot. And in between the military interest that was and might yet be, you have this outfit called the Peace Corps, which taught English and fiddled around with small-business advisers, architects, sanitarians. A children's crusade, a one-way citizens' exchange program, a fresh-air fund for liberal arts graduates. A new kind of American, they said, and maybe they were right. "The Coast Guard leaves babies behind," the island saying went, "and the Peace Corps leaves babies behind and worries about it." Now it seems as far away as spelling bees and pajama parties and there's a little embarrassment around, in them and in me, that we were ever once so young. The Peace Corps? We were what came in after the marines. And before the lawyers.

◄ VI ►

I think of these islands as odd places, weird latitudes where irony gets piled upon irony. I ponder thousands of Japanese tourists sunning themselves on invasion beaches. I drive the Tinian landing strips, wondering when the same mighty American tide that swept across the Pacific will come washing back this way. I savor the prospect. Japanese tourism, American military interest: I roll these ironies around in my mouth like wine, I sniff and taste and swallow. In a while, I feel drunk and wise.

Then, though, there are the things that flabbergast me, things like garment factories, the third element in the new commonwealth's prosperity. Who'd have guessed it—dozens of factories, thousands of laborers knitting shirts, suits, sweaters? Fashions of the season from an island without fashions and without seasons.

The credit, or the blame, goes to "headnote 3-A" of the Revised Tariff Schedules of the United States, which permits duty-free import of Northern Marianas products into the States, provided that 70 percent or less of the value of the product—50 percent in the case of textile and wearing apparel—is derived from foreign materials. Headnote 3-A started an industry on Saipan, and an argument. Backers claim that garment factories generate taxes and employment and diversify a tourism-dependent economy. Critics complain about thousands of aliens who come to work in factories, Trukese, Filipinos, Chinese who strain the island's hospitals, its power and water systems. Americans shudder at the very idea of it: Communist Chinese slapping together foreign cloth and Made-in-USA labels. Crafting with pride, you might say.

The garment factories and barracks are all over the island, tucked away off Middle Beach Road, secreted in the hills around San Vicente, but the biggest of all, Willie Tan's operation, sits near Charley Dock in Tanapag. I pull in one afternoon, hoping to talk my way onto the factory floor. Buy a sweater, maybe, and take it from there. I've been warned: you don't breeze into garment factories as though you were going on a winery tour. Owners are a little sensitive about a loophole, offshore, sweatshop reputation. They're nervous, I'm told, and this makes me nervous. For no reason. The good news, the bad news, the island news, is that I have an old friend right in the middle of things.

"P.F.K.!" someone shouts as I enter the factory offices. It turns out that Willie Tan's right-hand man is Ben Fitial. A Saipan Carolinian, dark, round, cheerful, he gave me a mattress to sleep on twenty-two years ago, when I first set up housekeeping on Saipan. A shirt-off-the-back kind of guy, that's how I remember him. Later he had a career in politics, serving as speaker of the local legislature. In his office, I notice a picture of Ben with George Bush, and a framed letter signed by Ronald Reagan, and a photo of my old drinking buddy at a formal banquet in mainland China. Once again, I realize that Saipan has leapfrogged every reasonable expectation.

A tour of the factory? No problem, says Ben. We leave the crisply air-conditioned office and step out into a humid, hangar-size facility where 1,000 mainland Chinese sit at sewing machines, knitting 5,000 dozen sweaters, 20,000 dozen shirts per month. Arrow Shirts, Christian Dior, L.A. Mode, Stanley Blacker: Made in USA. "The made in USA label is important," Ben says, "from a marketing point of view." I look for Ben to give me a wink, a hint that he finds this business as ironic as I do. But he shows me through the plant as cheerful as a Napa Valley grandee giving the winery tour. And, at closing time, he invites me to dinner that evening, at the fussiest place on the island, the tenth-floor restaurant at the Hafa Adai Hotel. I arrive first, around sunset, and the headwaiter frets, scrutinizing his list of reservations, but when Mr. Fitial shows up, provision is made, a corner table with a view of the sea.

Times change, all right. We start with double orders of escargot and smoked salmon. Ben tells me how he stepped out of his post at the legislature and into his job with Willie Tan, an American-educated Chinese with Filipino roots. Now he surely makes more money than I do, shakes important hands, travels widely, and not just to China. Hell, he's been to Norway! Still, there's something of the big-hearted fellow I remember. He calls me "brother" and that touches me. And he proceeds to defend Willie Tan, whom many regard as a sinister carpetbagger. Willie Tan runs a chain of "Fun and Games" round-the-clock poker machine emporia, but Ben says his operations are mostly patronized by outsiders, thus parrying the charge that Tan is sucking the blood out of local families. As for garment industries, they produce taxes, they buy local goods, and, yes, it's true that employees were housed in freight containers for a while, but the containers had been nicely converted, you see, not bad at all. "People who don't like Willie Tan are the ones who don't know him or are jealous of him," Ben insists. "I call him my brother."

Out below the hotel dining room, lights twinkle up and down the gold coast, the Hyatt and the Intercon on one side, the Diamond and Grand farther down the beach. It feels like Waikiki. The only dark patch is a cluster of decrepit government housing that some hotel-building airline is looking to acquire. All-Nippon Airways, I think.

"Do you feel that you're an American?" I ask.

"I was thinking about that the other night, when I flew in here," he says.

"And?"

"Almost."

"Almost?"

"Almost. I like that word."

Dinner over, we walk across the parking lot to Ben's Jeep, modest and scuffed up on the outside, but inside we've got tinted windows, air-conditioning, music cassettes. A symbol of Saipan, maybe, what the frozen turkey tail is to Truk, this air-conditioned Jeep, the high-living offspring of those wooden-sided, lashed-together, one-gear-only war surplus jobs where you could see the road between the floorboards, the road where snails came out at night, popping like kernels of corn as they were crushed beneath the wheels. Now we've got Anne Murray serenading us and we're headed to Coco's, a businessman's club, where the dread Willie Tan is entertaining some associates.

Coco's is easy to miss, unobtrusive, tasteful. Expensive. The Filipino hostesses are svelte, decorous, speak better-than-average English, and drink above-average drinks, six bucks a pop. We find Willie Tan and party in a private side-room. A young man in blue jeans and sport shirt, Tan is flipping through a scrapbook of song lyrics. Coco's is a *karaoke* club: pick a tune, hoist a microphone, sing the words that flash on the video screen. Tan struggles through a Bee Gees tune. I manage "Tom Dooley" in a take-no-chances baritone, flat and safe, and then Ben, the island guy, the entertainer, the garment industry's public relations man, crafts a tune with pride, taking the high and low parts of "That Lovin' Feelin'."

Coco's is a clubhouse for the new, moneyed Saipan, for deal makers and politicians. The bars I knew had country-western jukeboxes, forbidding restrooms with cracked toilets and no paper, sharp-tongued Palauan barmaids. What we have here at Coco's is a bit of Tokyo and a bit more of Manila. Nocturnal predators relax in air-conditioned easy chairs, surround themselves with hostesses, croon ballads as if they were at home singing in a shower. It's a sophisticated place, in its hotshot way, though a hostess assures me—cross her heart and hope to die—that the girls never, never go home with customers. Perish the thought! At closing time, it's straight back to the convent.

The evening's young. We move to the Ginza, to a strip joint called the Starlite, where Ben's Filipina wife joins us, fresh off duty as a cashier at one of Willie's poker places.

If Coco's caters to Saipan's movers and shakers, Starlite is for the guys who work by the hour, imported laborers who sweat it out all day, come to watch imported dancers who sweat it out at night, jiggling tits and spreading legs, their stripteases segueing into fake orgasms, all of it watched with the same hard, experienced eyes you'd see at a bullring or a cockfight. Dark lights and loud music inhibit conversations, but there isn't much to say.

It gets late. My evening on the town with Ben Fitial could have ended a couple times already, after dinner, after Coco's, after this place, but one thing on Saipan that hasn't changed is the custom of closing things out with a valedictory bowl of soup. We head to a Chinese restaurant, where Ben is welcomed heartily and there's no check. No check. The manager is someone else Ben calls "brother." The last I see of Ben, he promises to meet for a Sunday barbecue, which doesn't come off. I show up for a promised chat with Willie Tan. It was important I talk to him, Ben suggested. One brother meeting another brother, I supposed. But Willie Tan is busy. "Where's Ben?" I hear him ask a secretary, and I realize that I am one of the problems Ben is supposed to handle. A second interview fails too, and a third. I'm not surprised. I had gotten closer than I was supposed to get.

◄ VI ►

They are the envy of the Pacific. They are American and they are rich, my old friends, and they did it without moving and without working. Part of me wants to say, fine. Let it be. They are good people, mostly, and the island is good, with much left in it to love. I love the pine-fringed invasion beaches, the battlefield boondocks blazing with poinciana, the shell-scarred solemn cliffs. I love the weddings and baptisms, those long tables of saffron rice and roast pork, breadfruit, taro, chicken with coconut, sashimi with hot peppers and soya, cucumbers with ginger, soup from taro greens. I love the bars and the bullshit. I love the sunsets. Take it from me, the sun that passes over New York and disappears over the Hudson River Palisades, that spins out to sea from Malibu, does not continue around the world from Saipan. It crashes right beyond the reef, about seven miles out, crashes spectacularly, exploding as it falls. It spends its color off of Saipan, all its color; it stops and rests and arises mean and nasty in the morning. It's the surest thing I know.

So I love the place and I say what the hell. It's probably a corrupting, unhealthy relationship, this American enclave half a world offshore. It's a questionable commitment. But we have worse ways of spending money in worse places. If you're going to squander taxes, it's just as well to spend them on islands like these; if you're going to pass out U.S. citizenship for the sake of holding on to some possibly strategic islands, why not pass them out here, to my old friends? This commonwealth isn't something I can defend, but I'm in no rush to attack it either. Not if it makes people happy.

They're not happy though. The island is turning into a resort, land prices are booming, money is rolling in from all directions. Once heavily dependent on Washington, the commonwealth government now generates more than 80 percent of its own revenues. But, there's a surprising undercurrent of complaint: about those alien workers who crowd the garment factories and work in the hotels, two jobs per room; about all those Chinese and Koreans who've set up small businesses on Beach Road, outworking and undercutting local merchants. Ah, that's the rub, that inescapable two-jobs-per-room equation, all those waiters, gardeners, cooks, and hairdressers punching in to Fantasyland. There are as many as twenty thousand of them now—it depends whose figures you believe—and if they don't already outnumber locals they soon will. More coming all the time, coming to stay, going underground when necessary. Too bad you can't just cash in your land, divvy up with your relatives and—well—don't worry, be happy. But word gets around about the Commonwealth of the Northern Marianas. A good place for a Trukese woman to work in a garment factory, a Filipina hairdresser or masseuse, a hustling Korean mechanic, a nervous Hong Kong investor. And that bothers the locals a lot. You can have your cake and eat it. But you've got to bring in bakers who—damn it—draw down power, use up water, crowd into hospitals when they get sick, have babies, conspire to stay. So people on Saipan are edgy, even as they're being enriched. The island is shifting beneath their feet.

I see my share of politicians. It's odd. The other islands chose leaders who were exceptional, one way or another, higher ranking, like Kabua, smarter, like Salii, stronger and more patient, like Nakayama. In the Northern Marianas they elected men who were most like themselves, typical rather than special. Stopping by the high commissioner's old office, I chat with Governor Pedro P. Tenorio, cautious and noncommittal. I drink coffee with his peppery, shoot-from-the-hip Lieutenant Governor, Pedro A. Tenorio. I eat breakfast with Pete Guerrero, speaker of the House of Representatives, who sketches for me the layout of some land he just bought in Tacoma, lakefront property where you can step out back and feed ducks. I lunch with the Senate president, stolid, workaholic Benjamin Manglona, the only politician, he tells me, who has never been on a junket to Manila. And what they say is pretty much of a piece: tension and complaint about Washington. I'd always thought that the Commonwealth Covenant was a cynical deal, bound to bring out the worst in both sides, but I also assumed it would settle things in the Northern Marianas. I was wrong. Nearly fifteen years after voting themselves a commonwealth, the Northern Marianas sends delegates back to the U.N. Trusteeship Council, threatens plebiscites, which would reopen the whole deal, and presents a new view of commonwealth, which revolves around "internal sovereignty."

"It's a tricky question," Governor Pedro P. Tenorio says, laughing, shaking his head. "What is self-government? What is sovereignty? It's confusing." The confusion is about power. Defense and foreign affairs are for Washington, everything else should be under local control, the governor says. But, Lieutenant Governor Pedro A. Tenorio complains, "vested interests" in the Department of the Interior are sniping at the commonwealth, asserting jurisdiction, aggrandizing power, so that "everything goes from Tom in the Department of the Interior to Dick in the Office of Management and Budget, to Harry in the Department of State." Pete Guerrero argues that the trusteeship has not been terminated, that the U.N. still has a role to play out here, that the U.S. has been "chipping away" at the commonwealth's sovereignty. There've been problems with passports, with bond issuance, with turf-protecting bureaucrats, pesky auditors and FBI men who have no business on the island, not unless they've been invited. Don't we realize, asks Guerrero, what these islands are putting themselves through, for the sake of the United States? "You sleep comfortably in New York," he says, "because we are protecting your rights to sleep comfortably." Says Ben Manglona, tersely: "They are like a big elephant and we are like an ant."

So the game goes on. The Trukese, chafing under the Compact of Free Association, whisper dreams of commonwealth. The Commonwealth of the Northern Marianas in turn presses for the advantages of sovereignty. Guam, a territory, forms a status commission to press for commonwealth. Across the world, Puerto Rico plans another vote on commonwealth, or statehood, or independence. The Virgin Islands starts making noises too. Everyone is trying to get the mix down, the timing right. Ants dealing with an elephant, coming to picnic, hoping not to get stepped on.

On Saipan, they wear their status, their citizenship like a new suit, something they are trying on, just checking themselves out in, posing in front of mirrors. Tailor on premises, alterations free. How's it look? Pleats or plain? Cuffs or no? Padded shoulders or natural? And don't forget you promised me two pairs of pants. Far from being settled, their status—their deal—is infinitely subject to refinement and, behind all these specific requests, an inch off here, an inch out there, lurks the bogus assumption that if things don't work out, they can take off their suit, walk out the store, and go someplace down the street, looking for a better deal.

◄ VIII ►

Late afternoons, I drive up to the northern end of the island, up to Marpi, where the WW II battle ended. That's the zone of blown-up caves, flying leaps off cliffs, acres of ammunition, mysterious CIA exercises. A straight old road of the sort the Saipanese now complain about—they used to brag—carries me past the Nikko Hotel, into Marpi. Even here, you can't stop progress. At least you can't stop the people who say you can't stop progress. They are nibbling—no, biting—away at this last green redoubt. There's a golf course, a hotel, a half-finished beachside resort, a dude ranch. Still, the place has an austere beauty: shell-scarred Suicide Cliff, surf-pounded Banzai, your choice whether to die on land or sea. Tourist buses keep humming through during the day, visitors posing at cliff's edge, but by dusk you have the place pretty much to yourself. Most of the live ammunition they used to strip here has been collected; the fruit bats the Saipanese used to shoot out of trees to throw in their soup have become extinct. Where the road runs close to the bottom of Suicide Cliff, there's a row of monuments, Japanese, Okinawan, and, most recently, Korean. Someone on Capitol Hill slipped me a copy of the speech given at the dedication of the Korean monument, a comical sad botch of oratory I've grown fond of: "There was a time of sufferings that a country can't protect the souls from danger at one time. For the souls who by force have been taken off to another's battlefield and have died with bearing the grudge, we come here like this today herewith and with a calmly bow pray for the repose of the departed spirit. . . ."

There are no American monuments in Marpi. America is far away, American visitors are scarce, the Americans who died here have long since been buried someplace else. No monuments. But way above the Japanese memorial, way up above the command post, there's an American flag above the mouth of a cave. How did it get there? The spot looks unreachable: fastened to the limestone cliff face, the flag looks like graffiti some fraternity pledges risked their lives to put in place.

A few days later, Ted Oxborrow fesses up. I should have guessed. No one knows Saipan the way "the Ox" does; no one has crawled, shimmied and, in the case of the cliff, rappeled over it like him. The son of a Trust Territory employee, he came out to the Islands in 1961. Love at first sight. "The air that hit me when I stepped off the plane . . . I could smell plumeria," he recalls. "It knocked me silly. From that day, I began exploring."

He's had a number of jobs in and around the Trust Territory government and, when I first met him, he seemed a likely stayer-on. But something happened. In 1983 a dispute about the management of a local museum turned personal, turned nasty. Threats were made. "Get off the island or else": that sort of thing. Oxborrow packed it in. "We were dedicated," he says. "This was home. This was our island too. There was a time when we said, let's die here, let's invest our lives and kids. We left in two weeks, lock, stock, and barrel."

Ted and Jill Oxborrow moved to Utah, then to California, where he worked for Japanese investors. One day there came a meeting, which his employers apologized for ending abruptly. Sorry, they said, but they had to rush off. Where? To the Pacific? Oh . . . where in the Pacific? Some island you've never heard of. Really? What island is that?

When the Japanese discovered Oxborrow's background on Saipan, they dispatched him to the island he thought he'd left forever. But this time was different. This was business. I find Oxborrow and his wife at the Palms, a golf-course community, a suburban-looking collection of concrete ranch houses selling for $300,000 each, intended as third homes for Japanese businessman-golfers. Oxborrow divides his time between here, Japan, and California.

"There's a cloud of money hanging over the island," he remarks. "The physical island I still love. I treasure it. I suck it up. I inhale it. But the people who've ripped it off, the people are their own worst enemies. They don't know who their best friends were . . . and are."

I like going around with the Ox, not just because he knows the odd corners of the island but also because he flirted with the idea of living here and it didn't work out. He has come back the way I have come back, feeling torn and divided, subdivided; all his secret places are now real estate. One afternoon he takes me up Mount Tagpochau in a Jeep, which he turns in to a field of swordgrass the way a surfer points his board into a wave. He shows me wreckage of a B-29 that came down in bad weather between Tokyo and Guam; he didn't just find the wreckage, he researched the crash. Now, he says, some Japanese are interested in building on the site. Another morning, he rousts me out at dawn so we can visit a special place, Oba's Castle he calls it, hideout of the so-called last samurai, Colonel Sakae Oba. Oba and his band of stragglers harassed the occupying Americans for eighteen months, cutting telephone wires, reversing street signs, stealing food, sneaking in and out of internment camps, and retreating to the secret place where we are headed, halfway up the slopes of Mount Tagpochau.

As soon as we step off the road, I sense that we are on another island, the island that used to be, the plantation island that became a battlefield. We work our way up a dry streambed, stepping over rotting logs, slapping at vines and creepers. Though it is just past dawn, the greenhouse heat closes over us like water over swimmers. Half an hour in the gully brings us to an old Japanese road that once connected Garapan with the summit of Mount Tagpochau. We're soaked with sweat now. It's as though there's a tacit understanding out here that if you sit still and attempt nothing, you'll be comfortable, but the minute you move, the truce is violated and punishment begins. And we are moving, breasting into ranks of trees and vines. Only the coral is solid. Tree trunks crumble at a touch, filaments of vine wrap themselves around you, so that you're untying yourself at every step, like a magician practicing an escape trick. Every now and then, though, you lift your head out of the smothering green surf and see you're in a magnificent place, an upward sloping valley flanked by bluffs with stands of breadfruit, pandanus, banyan, and bamboo.

Now we come across holes burrowed in the side of the hill above the old road, gun emplacements that Oba's sentinels used as lookout points. Clever of him to hide out here at the center of the island, right above the American camp, the stockades, tent cities, ammunition dumps right below. When he finally surrendered, Oba insisted on a proper ceremony. On his return here a few years ago the proud elderly Japanese forced himself up this grueling trail, resting often but never turning back, remembering every detail. He pointed out to Oxborrow where a rice cooker had been left behind. There it was. And there it is, a rusting oversized cauldron.

We cross a meadow, dotted with palms and bananas, then angle up against Oba's mountain, past stone revetments where his machine gunners were positioned. The place is littered with machine gun clips, medical vials, artillery shells. Up here, you can see all the way down the mountain, across the plains of Garapan, out to the Philippine Sea. I wonder what Oba felt when he came back here and saw a line of Japanese hotels, a swarm of sunbathers along the invasion beach. What if he hadn't surrendered? What if he'd stayed, a nocturnal creature, skulking around the island, hiding out while down on the beach a Japanese Miami was a-building? What would it be like, to walk into that? Twilight Zone, I guess.

We rest in front of Oba's cave. Crabs scuttle over rocks, red birds flit through bamboo, and Oxborrow remembers what it was like, falling in love with Saipan, the odd games he played out in the boondocks. What he tried to do, he says, is put himself in the head of the island's Japanese defenders. "I'd be going over the same turf, the same territory they'd been in and I'd say, 'Here they come!' And 'What do I do . . . quickly!'

And 'I've got to get out of here, they're coming!' I'd go to a place . . . and the bones are there. It's almost psychic. As if I were called there. I found eight complete skeletons . . . quiet deaths in little ravines . . . the actual belt still buckled around the torso. . . . Sometimes, of course, where they threw a grenade, there are bones splattered everywhere."

Covering the island, Oxborrow became an expert forager, bringing his finds to the museum that later led to his undoing. He brought in buttons, scraps of cloth, leather cases, eyeglasses clear and dark, a toothbrush—"always a toothbrush"—medicine bottles blue and amber, rubber shoes with the rising sun on the sole, five different types of canteens, some dating back to World War I, mess kits with names scratched on them, turtle shell buttons, helmets. Soon his name got around. When American veterans came back, they sought him out, as did bone-hunting parties organized by the Japanese Ministry of Health. He spent four days with one old marine, retracing his battle step by step. Seabees and bomber pilots looked him up. Colonel Oba. A Japanese kid whose father had died on Saipan came with a picture of himself in his father's arms.

Japanese bone-hunting has subsided now. Support waned when some bone-hunters were found smuggling guns back into Japan, guns stashed underneath plastic bags of cremated bones. Then, too, time passes, generations roll and, anyway, the easy pickings are gone. To get to what remains remain, you'd need . . . well, you'd need the Ox.

"It's amazing how many are left," he muses. "There's plenty rough areas on this island. If someone said they'd give me a million dollars if I'd find five of them, I'm sure I could."

▲ ▲ ▲

My morning with Oxborrow makes me thoughtful. Add all my stays on Saipan, it comes to three years, which is probably about the same time that Oba spent here. And what I wonder about, getting ready to leave again, is who owns the island. Maybe it's all the buying and selling that's going on, the rub of old-timers and newcomers, locals and outsiders, that and all the nattering about "internal sovereignty." Start with the

locals—the Chamorros—who got moved off this island by the Span-
iards, moved off and nearly exterminated. Then the Carolinians, sailing
in while the Chamorros were away. They have their claim on the island.
But so do the Japanese, the claims of blood and money and so, too, the
Koreans and the Chinese, cobbling together small businesses, and the
Filipinos, the sweat equity of maids, construction workers, and bar girls.
And the Americans have their claim too, because what I am starting to
believe is that an island doesn't belong only to the people who are born
on it or who claim the right to own—and sell—it. An island belongs to
the people who think and care about it, though they cast no votes and
own no land. That is the sovereignty of the heart. Everything else is
money and noise.

◄ IX ►

The local crooked politicians with the help of the Yakusa are pillaging and
raping their own people. The only thing that matters to these slimy scum-
bags is to stay in office, milk Uncle Sam, and get fat. Once these islands
are completely sold out to the Yakusa, these political abortions will hightail
it to their newly acquired properties in the States. They keep cussing out
the United States, but that is where they want to wind up. . . .

Bare-chested, a can of light beer at his side, Guy Gabaldon sits at a word
processor in the front room of one of the old typhoon houses in San
Antonio village. A lively guy, short, agile, military-retired, Gabaldon
chats with Oxborrow while I glance around the office, which is a sort
of trophy room. There's a picture of Gabaldon on movie location with
Jeffrey Hunter . . . who portrayed him . . . on one side, David Janssen
on the other. Funny—both actors dead and Gabaldon still alive, back
on Saipan. *From Hell to Eternity.* There's a poster on the wall, bearing
the endorsement of Audie Murphy. Elsewhere, I see letters, medals,
trophies, and clippings.

Gabaldon is a soldier returned to Saipan to write his memoirs and
press his claims, which are substantial. Growing up in East Los Angeles,

Gabaldon learned Japanese from boyhood chums, vernacular street-smart Japanese, which came in handy on Saipan where, according to the manuscript he gives me, he killed thirty-five Japanese and induced hundreds, thousands more to surrender. A lone wolf, a pied piper, Gabaldon brought in many more prisoners than World War I's more celebrated—and more decorated—Sergeant Alvin York, yet he was denied the recognition, the promotion, the Medal of Honor he feels he earned, probably, he suspects, because of his Hispanic background. In his manuscript, sometimes vivid, sometimes argumentative, he presents his case against the Marine Corps. But that is nothing, compared to his case against Saipan.

"I came back here like a kid, really," he says. That was in 1980. Before then, he'd done a variety of things. He operated a motel, hauled seafood in planes from La Paz to Ensenada. He dabbled in politics, running for sheriff, running for Congress. "I came back smiling. I'm back where it really happened to me. Wow, these are the best friends we have in the world, I bet. They must love Americans. When I came here in the war, they were truly grateful. They were on their knees."

No kneeling, not much gratitude, this time around. A job at Saipan's Department of Public Safety, their police force, turned sour. As chief of intelligence there, Gabaldon says, he found "that everyone on the island is corrupt, especially the politicians." He also learned that everyone was connected. "You hit one guy, you hit a hundred, and pretty soon you've got the whole island on your back."

Now he's once more soldiering on Saipan, outnumbered, beleaguered, wandering between the lines. He snipes at local popinjay politicians: "The Commonwealth of the Northern Marianas is run by semi-illiterates, whoremongers, gangsters, and anti-Americans." He excoriates the "wimps in Washington" who let this uppity commonwealth get away with murder. He threatens to bring out some old buddies of his and set up a breakaway enclave on the northern island of Pagan. He plans to erect a war memorial over on Tinian, an A-bomb shrine, with lifelike figures dripping blood. "My wife says that'll scare the hell out of visitors. That's what I want."

One afternoon, we stroll down to the beach behind his house, the same beach he remembers landing on. There are still some landing craft out on the reef, a tank or two in the lagoon behind the new hotels. Gabaldon is not at peace, not reconciled.

"Four thousand of my fellow marines were killed taking this island away from you," he writes the Japanese. "I will make sure that they did not die in vain. I demand . . . that you build a four-lane highway completely around this island, repair our harbors, furnish scholarships to the best universities for our youth and THAT YOU BUILD A MONUMENT PARK TO HONOR THE FOUR THOUSAND MARINES WHO DIED KICKING YOUR ASSES HERE ON SAIPAN. . . ."

◄ X ►

Three weeks gone, three days to go. I plan to leave quietly, like someone slipping away from a loud, crowded party. I know that I cannot live here. No, check that. I can live here, like I could live in Guam or in Florida or lots of other places. What I mean is that living here would not be magical or resonant in the way I wanted it to be. Saipan had that feeling once, when it was part of the Trust Territory, when the Congress of Micronesia was in session, big dreams and proud talk. The time when I met Lazarus Salii. Now Saipan is an American place, fat and shrunken, querulous, and crowded with new players. So I will close my notebook and leave.

But then word comes on my next-to-last morning. *The canoes came in. They landed this morning.* I jump in my car and head down to Beach Road. Garment factories. Internal sovereignty. Japanese honeymooners. A-bomb shrines. Tax rebates, land booms. And three sailing canoes pulling up on the sand, a stone's throw from the traffic-clogged road, outrigger canoes that crossed the hundreds of miles between this El Dorado and the tiny island of Satawal, where men build canoes of breadfruit wood and steer by the stars, retracing the route that brought their Carolinian ancestors to Saipan hundreds of years ago. Now, they arrive again. A message, a connection, a reproach, all the way from there to here, from then to now.

I glimpse the three boats on the sand. I can't miss the crew—brawny, dark-skinned men in red *thus,* some sprawled asleep in a shaded portico, others chatting with relatives who've driven up to welcome them. I have a friend among them. "Freddy!" He calls my name and walks toward me grinning. "Freddy!" It was worth it now, all the Peace Corps time that could have been spent in real countries, all the magazine articles I pitched to editors who didn't care, all the time I've spent returning here rather than moving on. Lino Olopai was a Carolinian language instructor back on Udot. In later incarnations, he was a school-teacher, an airport security guard. Fifteen years ago, not liking the way Saipan was turning out, he escaped with his wife to Satawal, where they spent three years. Then he came back to Saipan and he still didn't like it. He fled to Hawaii this time; his Saipan marriage ended, and he worked in the Marianas Liaison Office in Honolulu. A tangled man, one of the torn ones. He walks toward me, a red loincloth, his skin brown, his body gaunt, one of his ears pierced. He wears a good luck amulet around his neck and on his legs I see the dolphin-fin tattoos that are the mark of the outer islands. Small world, his smile implies. He'd been back on Satawal several months before making this voyage, he tells me as we sit down. Nearby I spot the legendary Pius Mau Pialug, the navigator who guided the *Hokulea* from Hawaii to Tahiti a few years ago. Though he's been at sea for days and probably been drinking since he came on land, Pialug never seems to lose his poise, his sense of control. Father Costigan, the Ponape Jesuit had the same aura. And so—I think—did Lazarus Salii.

Lino's ex-wife Vicky and his son Typhoon are waiting to take him home for a shower, his first chance to wash properly in a week, but Lino Olopai has island courtesy. He sits and talks to me about the voyage. Suddenly, there's no rush. His time is mine.

They left Satawal five days ago, he says, three ships, the longest twenty-nine feet, thirteen men in all. After the first day they stopped at West Fayu, an uninhabited island where they caught four turtles. After that they were in Mau Pialug's hands, which he can dip into the sea the way a farmer runs his hand through soil, making judgments about temperature and texture, current and direction, past and future. By day, the shape and direction of the waves were their marks and signposts; seaweed, driftwood, fish, birds, butterflies. At night they corrected for any mistakes made by day; at night they steered by the stars.

Once they were nearly swamped, another time the little fleet got separated in the dark, signaling to each other by blowing conch shells and flashing lights, in vain, only to be reunited at dawn. The voyage felt long: sweltering days and unexpectedly cold nights, long periods of silence without rest or sleep. "I don't think I ever slept an hour," he says. "You close your eyes, but you always have that feeling, when the outrigger comes up higher than usual." From the *aimwim*—a perch opposite the outrigger—Pialug directed the voyage. "He never leaves the *aimwim*. Not to help the crew, not to prepare food, not to bail water. He doesn't do these things. He sits there in his place." Pialug tells the others where to stand, where to sit, where to curl up and sleep, or try to sleep. Sometimes, when the weather was good, boats moving in a rippling wind, they'd get in what Olopai calls "a singing mood." Someone would start a song and other people might join in or, listening, they'd ask the singer to repeat a verse, or they'd come up with a verse the singer had forgotten. I ask Olopai the names of the songs. Imagine, Don Ho's "Beyond the Reef" sounding out from small boats in a dark sea.

▲ ▲ ▲

Respect and a tinge of guilt mingle in the way the duty-free Commonwealth of Saipan receives these thirteen men who come sailing out of the past. It's the way New Yorkers feel about the Amish, I suppose, suspecting they've got things right and surely knowing that we're too far gone to do much more than visit, nod, and leave.

On my last day, I drop by the beach to say goodbye. A handful of people visit, but nothing to compare to the busloads that get herded in out of Hakubotan or Duty Free. Still, they keep the Satawalese in chicken and fish, rice and breadfruit, beer and whiskey. Tributes. I sit down with Olopai and ask him what it means, his going to Satawal or Satawalese coming here. He's not sure he can put it in words. I ask him to try.

"It's the traditions," he begins, tentatively. "The sharing. Even of the smallest thing you have. The knowledge and the . . . what do you call it . . . knowing that people will help you one way or another? Especially the old people. The whole system includes them. Knowing that even if you don't go fishing with the men, there'll be something for you when they come back. There's respect for elders, respect for nature, respect for the ocean. The prayers and ceremonies before you go on an ocean voyage. Respect for a breadfruit tree, before you cut it down to use it for a canoe. They set food at the base of the tree before they cut it, speak to its spirit: 'I'm going to take you to be part of a canoe I'm building.' The same with taking a plant for medicine. 'I'm taking your roots and vines to make medicine for my daughter, who's having a stomachache. . . .' "

Satawal isn't idyllic. There are political tensions. Some people don't get along with the chief. There are disputes about outboard motors and federal programs, both of which Olopai has argued against, with only partial success. I know better than to kid myself about small islands, especially with Budweiser and Cutty Sark on the table. Earlier, I sat through a meeting in which Olopai and Mau Pialug dickered with government officials about how much money they'd get for restoring a canoe; later they will bargain with education officials about how much for teaching a course at the community college. There's gamesmanship they bring up from Satawal, grantsmanship, a certain playing upon guilt. Lino Olopai smiles and winks when I ask him how the meeting went. "A piece of cake," he says.

Our paths have crossed so often, I know that we'll meet again, Olopai and I. Anywhere. Clear-cut people are predictable; as to torn people . . . you never can tell. A whiff of coconut oil on the subway? The sight of tattooed legs off Malibu? I will not be surprised. And no matter what, my first question will be when he left Satawal. And my second, when he's going back. Now I shake hands and give him a hug and turn into the traffic leading toward the airport and the plane to Guam and Yap. And Palau. Lazarus, I am coming.

VII

YAP, AND THE END
OF THE WORLD

I'll tell you a story," says Petrus Tun. The betelnut he chews gives his teeth a red, bloodstained look, turns his smile carnivorous. "It's a true story. It's no joke."

We've been drinking beer for a couple hours, sitting in a place on the water in Colonia, Yap's sleepy, almost sullen, district center. There's Tun, Yap's governor, and Hilary Tacheliol, an aide in charge of outer-island affairs. Bill Acker's been by too. A Texas-born businessman with a betelnut mouth, he first came out as a Peace Corps "business adviser" on Ulithi Atoll. "There was no business," he says, "so I read paperbacks, chased girls, and went fishing." And there's Jonas Olkeriil, a Palauan lawyer, nicknamed "Never Die." In younger days, it seems, Olkeriil was smitten by a girl who was unacceptable to his family. Forbidden from marrying her, he tried suicide. Twice. He jumped out of a tree with a rope around his neck, but the branch broke. Later, he swallowed battery acid. In vain. Thus, "Never Die." It's been a good evening, moving from subject to subject in a way that seems logical at the time, baffling in retrospect. Example: Hilary Tacheliol is talking about phallic symbols on outer islands, carved, painted shafts pointing out across the water at rival islands. Then we're talking about hermaphrodites—why is it I have to travel to Yap to talk about *important* stuff?—and someone wonders whether a hermaphrodite could impregnate him/herself. "Maybe so," Tun allows. "But it's still masturbation." And somehow that gets us to Tun's story, which is about the end of the world.

A Yapese stationed in Hawaii, a medical referrals officer, sits watching television. He sees a newscast that reports that the Russians have kidnapped the president of the United States. War is imminent, World War III, the end of the world. He snaps off the TV before he can find out that the newscast was make-believe, a movie scene. Thoughts turn homeward, toward tiny Yap, midway between Guam and Palau. He reaches for the phone, places a long-distance call to his father to say goodbye. The father calls an assistant attorney general, who calls Governor Tun. The local operator, monitoring the overseas call, gets busy and spreads the word. Before long, Yap braces for Armageddon.

Now Petrus Tun is a shrewd, practical-minded man, a graduate—in biology, not political science—of the University of Hawaii, a longtime member of the Congress of Micronesia, a key player at the Constitutional Convention, which led to the Federated States of Micronesia of which Yap is now a part. As Yap's governor, he deals with local politics, with elected leaders, with still-powerful traditional chiefs. But he isn't prepared to confront the end of the world. Leery from the start, Tun nonetheless calls Yap's Washington representative. The man in Washington thinks that President Reagan is in New York, campaigning for George Bush; this contradicts the kidnapping report. Still, he agrees to call the Department of State. You never know. "They don't share everything with us," he admits.

Meanwhile, panic spreads in Yap, and Tun's wife Carmen urges him to do . . . well . . . do something. Tun balks.

"It's either all-out war or it's selective," he reasons. "If it's number one, we're finished. If it's number two, why would the Russians waste a missile on Yap?"

Tun wants to go back to sleep, but his wife suggests they ought to store water, put it away before nuclear fallout contaminates it.

"But if the air goes bad, the water will go bad too," protests Tun. His wife keeps at him.

"If there's a war, they'll blame you," she warns.

"If there's a war, everybody will be dead and no one will be left to blame me."

"You could go on the radio. You could alert people so that families could come together and prepare for the end. They could pray."

That's ridiculous, Tun thinks. "Some guy is sleeping with his girlfriend and I should wake him up so he can go home and sit with his family and wait to die?"

Thus Yap's governor faces the question we've all asked ourselves: what would we do if the end of the world were a few hours away? Make love? Pray? Get drunk?

The governor goes back to bed. He sleeps while Yapese all over the island call relatives in the western United States to bid adieu, relatives who wonder why, if the third world war is coming, people in Yap should find out about it before people in California. And next morning when Tun goes to his office and people ask him if he's heard about the war, he nods his head. Yes, he says. He's heard plenty. And he goes about his business. That's Tun and that's Yap.

▲ ▲ ▲

Yap has always been "good copy," a place where travel writers could knock out three features and a sidebar between planes. Start with that betelnut Tun was chewing. He's in thrall to the stuff; so's everyone here. Throw Tun a curveball of a question on economic development, say, or the future of the Federated States of Micronesia. See him stare a moment, as though he's wondering why he's bothering with you. Watch him reach into a pouch for that green, acorn-sized nut, which he splits and places on a peppervine leaf. "We say, in Yap, when you don't have an answer chew betelnut," he says. "There's wisdom in betelnut." I don't know if it's true, I don't even know if it's a saying, but it buys time. Now he finds a jar of powdered limestone—it looks like talcum—and he sprinkles the stuff on his leaf and nut. He then wraps the thing up—leaf, nut, and powder—pops it into his mouth, bites down. The result? Wisdom? Maybe. For sure: a reddening of the mouth, a mild, lifting buzz, a certain serenity, somewhere between chewing tobacco and marijuana. Other results: the need to spit. Around public buildings, walls, sidewalks, lawns are stained red. And the used-up chews, red-rusty and fibrous, litter the place like used Kotex. You can keep your smile white if you brush regularly with the industrial strength tooth-paste smokers use. Or you can say, what the hell, and see your teeth go brown, go black, go period. The oldsters carry little hammers and cups that they beat the betelnut up with, before slipping it between their aging gums. Sometimes at night, walking past the men's meeting houses in the villages, you can hear the elders tapping out a signal that seems to say it's all right, living on an island where good moods grow on trees.

Another feature story from Yap: stone money. Donut-shaped slabs of rock, taller than a man. Quarried in Palau, brought here on rafts, they line the village roads. All the money has customary value, and though it's almost never moved from place to place it still figures in transactions and has been pledged as collateral in bank loans. Some pieces even have names, and, though it sounds corny, some roadside collections are captioned stone-money "banks."

Third feature story: toplessness. Yap is a conservative society, nearly feudal, but its concepts of modesty run south, not north. A bikini is scandalous, bare breasts are not. So there are topless women shopping in stores, riding motorbikes, playing volleyball, and lots of wry anec-dotes about bras that got turned into slingshots and betelnut holders. That's Yap, at a glance. Good copy.

There's more.

◄ II ►

It is morning in Yap and a German tourist sits in the second-floor lobby of a hotel, watching rats scurry across the first-floor roof. "I stopped counting at fourteen," he says. "It's like a union meeting."

The German's not happy here, I know. Yesterday, coming in from a tour of Yap's limited tourist attractions—a stone-money bank, a coco-nut plantation, a men's meeting house, a couple Japanese zero fight-ers—he complained about the guide. "A *sehr unfreundlich Führer.*"

Whenever the German wanted to take a photo, the guide shook his head, shouted "private land, private land," and kept driving.

I wish the German luck and take off for a dawn jog around Chamorro Bay, the ocean inlet around which Colonia is built. Nothing stirs except dogs picking at the squashed remains of mangrove crabs that got run over during the night. Too bad about the German, I think, but then Yap has never gone out of its way to accommodate outsiders. Old-fashioned—traditional, conservative, primitive, whatever—is one thing. Stupid, they are not. You want betelnut, you buy it at the airport. You want to take pictures of the stone-money bank, it costs you. You want to swim, forget it. The beaches are all private, for one thing, and many villages are closed, and photography is by permission, sometimes at a charge, often outrightly denied. And there are no more hotels now than there were twenty years ago. There's the E.S.A., which has half-decent food and no bar. There's the Rai View, which has thin walls, mediocre food . . . and a bar. That's the Hobson's choice of Yap. If you have a choice at all. When I arrived, both hotels—about forty rooms in all—were full and it took a personal plea to the owner of the E.S.A., a Palauan related to Lazarus Salii, to get me in.

I jog past the road that leads up to the Rai View Hotel. Some of the partitions are flimsy and incomplete, more like the panels that separate men's room toilets than proper walls. Years ago, one of the guests got lucky and brought a woman, an ardent lover, back to his room. "Hurt me!" she implored her mate. "Hurt me!" Again and again, her plea sounded up and down the hall. Then, a response. "Go ahead," someone shouted from another room, "give her a good poke or none of us will sleep tonight!"

I don't know if this stop in Yap makes sense. Yap hasn't changed much, everybody told me, the old culture of stone money, betelnut, toplessness mottled by jukeboxes and beer cans and motorbikes. But after a month on Saipan and a week in Guam, it appeals to me, coming to a place that hasn't changed. Sprinting just ahead of rising waters, a tsunami of garment factories and tourist hotels, I decide to hop onto a scrap of land that hasn't been inundated . . . yet. That, and get ready for Palau.

I'm reading the perfect book, at last, rereading *All the King's Men.*

Another meditation on politics and ruin. The closer I come to Palau, the more I feel like Robert Penn Warren's narrator, Jack Burden, trying to make sense of grand and awful things. More and more I feel the power of the place. I have a strong sense of Salii. I carry it around with me, can't shake it, a stronger sense, by far, than if he were still alive down there, one flight away. Again and again, I try to picture his last minute. Raising that .357 magnum. Slowly or quickly, I wonder? Did he feel the point of the barrel against his head? Have time to hear the shot that killed him?

Salii stories find their way to me as I travel the islands. It's one of the reasons I came in this way, a little at a time, closing in on Palau, knowing these stories, stares, accusations, conspiracies, and silences would come homing in on me. Not all of them bad. On Truk, a priest who taught at Xavier High School—Salii was in the first graduating class—remembered a cocky, sharp youth. Pitching in a softball game one day, Salii faced a priest who was instructing players in the endangered art of bunting. Salii insisted that a pitcher who knew of a batter's intention to bunt could make things hard, real hard. Go on, just throw it in here, the priest insisted, and Salii winged a fastball that caught the Jesuit in the nuts, end of sermon. Some other memories. One Saipanese politician recalled Salii urging him never to forget where he came from, never to forget he was an islander. Another Saipanese pictured Salii chewing up Americans who claimed to be experts on the islands, reaming them out: do your homework if you want to talk to me. People remember Salii when he was sharp, eloquent, pressing the attack; others when he was relaxed, congenial, reminiscing about trying to learn Russian at the University of Hawaii, about working odd jobs in the kitchen of an old folks home. I remember Salii telling me about taking around some Americans who showed up in Palau hoping to find traces of their son, a flier who'd gone down over the islands, chasing rumors, going home empty-handed and in mourning. There was another mission years later, Salii told me about. Three Elvis Presley impersonators were booked into a costly gig at the Palau Pacific Resort. Palauans shunned the show. They weren't stupid, they knew Presley was dead, so who did they think they were, these people putting on what was billed as "The Elvis Presley Show"? The trio was stranded, broke, till Salii bailed them out, swapping a free concert at Palau High School for tickets out. It intrigued me that there were three impersonators traveling together. The first was the young Elvis, lean and mean, the second the movie star Presley, the third the bloated and about-to-die Presley. Three different Saliis face me now: the young idealist, the battling politician, the beleaguered president. And not all the stories that come to me are tributes. There are hints of deals and payoffs. Speculation that Lazarus had dubious investments in the Philippines, gambling debts in Las Vegas, secret bank accounts in Hong Kong. Scuttlebutt, all of it, hearsay and rumor. But it gets worse; that he was a drug trader, a drug user, out of control, sullen to the point of paranoia, moody to the edge of schizophrenia.

In Guam last week I found Lazarus's widow staying with one of her daughters, an Air Micronesia stewardess, in a tract house in a subdivision out beyond the brand new Micronesia Mall. Tina was taking real estate courses, she told me, something to do while she planned the rest of her life. She poured me coffee as I explained my purpose. I'd have understood if she wished me luck and left it at that, but she gamely went through the events of August 20, 1988, the morning coffee, the cigarettes smoked outside the house, the grilling of a fish, the noise that sounded like a rock slamming against the roof. She didn't commit herself exactly, but I think she believes that Lazarus killed himself.

"It's what he wanted to do, that's what I think," she said. "He never did anything he didn't want to do. It's a decision he made, based on so many things . . . that's the way I feel about it. Lazarus did many things I wouldn't do, but he made the decision, good or bad. Lazarus did his own thing. Everything he did was his own. He kept the problems to himself. 'As long as my politics don't get into the house, I'm okay.' "

She paused and reached for a Kleenex. We got through the last day of his life okay, but the memory of his last few weeks brings her down: the solitude, the sense of being under siege and—what still hurt, I guessed—her husband's refusal to talk to her about what he was going through.

"It bothers me a whole lot," she said. "For the last few months, it started to bother me. I felt sorry for him, but I was afraid to tell him. On the job . . . in the courts . . . nothing goes right. But he says as long as I don't have a problem, it's fine. But I have a problem . . . seeing him not sleeping . . . staying up all night to make a call. He's so smart . . . but if he's so smart . . . how come so many people were against him?"

What I remember most is her picture of Salii, sitting in front of a TV in the wee hours of the morning, watching Muhammad Ali tapes. "When nothing amused him," she said, "he watched those tapes." The loneliness makes me shudder. Island loneliness. Loneliness *in extremis.*

On my second lap around Yap's lagoon, I chat with another runner, a Peace Corps volunteer assigned to one of the outlying villages. Yap's villages make visitors feel impertinent. The German who visited a newly built cultural center—a meeting house with some museum artifacts on display—tried to amble through the neighboring village. Kids were called in off the path as he approached, reappeared behind him after he'd passed. When he turned onto a lesser path, someone waved him away. Yap accommodates visitors in Colonia, but the villages are still off-limits. That doesn't mean they're immune. "Things are changing," the Peace Corps volunteer says. "They're fighting it. They're losing. But maybe that's because they have more to lose."

I pull into the hotel. In a place like Yap, there's no point in showering right away. It takes half an hour for the sweating to stop. I kill time in the lounge, watching the Germans depart for the airport, muttering about having to pay for breakfasts that were supposed to be included in their tour price. *"Schweinerei!"* The van rumbles off, and at breakfast I have the place pretty much to myself. The *Pacific Daily News* carries an account of a Palauan delegation kicking up its heels at the United Nations. Vice President Kuniwo Nakamura charges the United States with failing as a trustee, with unkept promises, with shoddy infrastructure. *Infrastructure* is a magic word out here now. In the old days, the magic word was *per diem.* Per diem meant freedom, travel, adventure for blithe spirits with white shoes and belts—"tap dancers"—who wandered the world, conferring and fact-finding. The U.S. was their sugar daddy and their whipping boy. Those were the red-eyed, white-shoed, globe-trotting days. And now: *infrastructure.* Narrowly construed, it means water and power systems, roads and docks and airports. But in it's broadest sense it's a catch-all for the United States' failure to replicate San Diego out here, to give the islanders everything they wanted. Infrastructure. Big word on Saipan. I got tired of it after a while, the chorus of petition and complaint. The navy-era roads are falling apart, they say, the utilities falter under the strain of hotels and garment factories, there are blackouts and brownouts and the water doesn't come out of the shower like it should. And part of me flares up and invites commonwealth citizens to Manhattan for a tour of Civil War–era waterworks, a stroll across the collapsing Williamsburg Bridge, a call on the emergency room at a Harlem hospital, a courtesy chat with our charming mayor who would say aloud what I keep thinking: *Give me a break.*

Speaking of infrastructure, the power in the E.S.A. hotel just went out. I drink coffee with a couple Americans who are trying to get a gold mining operation going. There's gold on Saipan, Palau, and Yap, where they are looking at the village of Gagil. They propose to put up the money, pay expenses, and split the profits with the locals. While we talk, I spot the bartender for the Marina, the best restaurant in Yap, who tells me the crew of a New Zealand naval ship bought $2,000 worth of beer last night, three times the previous record held by the U.S. Navy. They didn't care whether the beer was warm. But I do. And the power is still out; the hotel's turning into a sauna. These concrete block buildings depend on air-conditioning; it's not a luxury, it's a life-support system. There's an air conditioner in every room and a pail outside, underneath the air conditioner, catching the water that drips out. Every morning, the first thing that Silbester Alfonso's maids do is walk from room to room, hefting the buckets and heaving the water out into the lagoon. It's a pastoral ceremony, like country girls gathering buckets of fresh milk at a dairy farm.

The van returns from the airport with another load of tourists, bubblingly enthusiastic: some contract teachers from Guam, in search of quaint, and an engineer who's supposed to check leaks in the local water system, and a pair from San Francisco who "collect countries." There are 308 possible countries, they say, although country is loosely defined, Hawaii and Guam each counting as one. The game is to rack up as many countries as you can, and some fanatics have been known to dash around the conference table at Panmunjon, just to add North Korea to the list. Others—this is hard to picture but I believe it anyway—run around the North or South Pole, garnering all the nations that claim the place. Vacuuming their way through America's Pacific mutant states, this couple are marching through their second hundred countries.

The day rolls on. Petrus Tun said he'd be by sometime today but he didn't say when and so I am caught in another of those island situations, waiting for someone who may not come; not knowing whether I should have just appreciated the expression of an intention to come and gone about my business. But I have no other business. Colonia is poaching and I don't feel like crashing around the villages. So I'm back in the Peace Corps again, reading a paperback book and waiting for a Micronesian who may or may not show. I don't want to sit in the sweltering dining room, though, where sweat pastes my forearm to oilcloth tablecloths. And upstairs the Guam teachers, loud and hearty, have staked a claim to the lounge. I don't want to hear them talking about how Yap is like the Hawaii of fifty years ago, or the Guam of twenty. It's lunchtime in Yap. I walk out to a grocery store where the light bulbs are dark and the fans are motionless. The woman who owns the place is dark and motionless as well. Whoops, watch it, there! I can feel it coming on, though, a spell of the island meanies, one of those moods in which I plot revenge on places like this. I devise jukeboxes with nothing but chamber music. I visualize blizzards blowing in across the reef. I plan menus that the locals would hate: espresso coffee, boiled tongue, pickled beets, chopped liver, steak tartare. . . . The storekeeper nods toward the freezer. I open and close it quickly: the cold is more valuable than the beer. I grab some ship biscuits and a can of corned beef and retreat to my room in a foul mood.

GREAT WALL CORNED BEEF. I used to love this stuff. Back in New York, missing the islands, I'd go digging into this amalgam of flesh and fat, skin and bone, plus the odd unidentifiable something that might have been a volleyball. But that was nostalgia in New York and this is an airless, unconditioned room in Yap, and the Great Wall people make a hard-to-open can. I tear the key off the top, pass the key around the end of a metal strip that runs around the edge, right over a picture of a cow cheerfully grazing on the fabled prairies of the People's Republic. With the second turn of the key, a cloudy fluid squirts out onto the floor, where it will certainly draw ants. I am forced to sacrifice my one and only E.S.A. hotel towel to mop up the spermy, fatty goo. Hey, wasn't there a scene like this in *Moby-Dick,* Ishmael up to his elbows in whale gism? Now I use the towel to secure a grip on the can, slippery and treacherous. I manage to open the can about halfway before the key breaks off in my hand. There's just enough of an opening for a couple fingers to reach inside without getting sliced on the severed edge. But wait a minute! What about the ship biscuits? The cellophane wrapper defies me. I jab my ballpoint pen into the package, breaking the first two biscuits. I reach further in, pull out some survivors. All now is in readiness. I'll just wash up a little, the grease and sweat. Only there's no towel left. And no soap, at least none that I can see, because the lights are out.

Calm down, I tell myself. I pull a chair out onto the balcony that runs around the front of the hotel. It's raining now, which means that my legs, propped up against the railing are in for a soaking, but the rest of me stays . . . well, not dry exactly, but not rained on. Across the street, a single Yapese kid is out on the Protestant Mission basketball court, dribbling through puddles, shooting hoops in the rain, missing again and again. Maybe one shot in ten goes through the hoop. Moments like this, I find myself thinking about Salii. Little things. The books I sent him. Joe McGinnis's *The Making of a President.* Chinua Achebe's *Things Fall Apart.* Going to the Oakland Coliseum in 1970 to see Vida Blue pitch in his one great season. A time I cooked a pot roast for him in Truk. How he always wanted to visit Omaha, because it was the most landlocked place he could think of. All that land. Could it be this simple: that people in big places long for small ones and people in small places long for big ones? Is it that mundane? If that's the lesson of this journey, I've come a long way for a short slide.

Yap was a mistake, I guess. I grant that now. Yap's fine for a travel hack between planes. It's okay, too, for an anthropologist to hunker down in a village for a couple years, getting down the intricacies of land tenure and kinship patterns, before they disappear, holding a tape recorder up to catch a culture's death rattle. But I'm in the middle range, a writer, ex-Peace Corps, sitting here in a puddle of sweat, right in the middle of nothing at all. But anyway the power comes back on and I can stretch out on my bed, watching a Mets-Cubs game that's six weeks old. The long day wanes. Yap was a mistake. But then Silbester Alfonso is knocking on my door. Amazingly, the governor is waiting for me downstairs. I can't believe it.

Tun apologizes. He was up in a village and he's headed back there now and maybe on his return trip we can . . . I'll go with you now, I say, hopping into Tun's Mitsubishi, with the license plate reading GOVERNOR, and we head north, out past the end of the paved road, past Yap's new hospital, past some mangrove swamps, through the outskirts of Fanif and then up into the red-clay and pandanus terrain that is Yap's high country. Our plans are vague, but they involve beer and fish and talk, which are the three main reasons I come to Micronesia these days.

Traveling through Truk and Ponape convinced me that the Federated States of Micronesia are troubled places, floundering some days, floating and drifting the rest; less like islands than like lifeboats, left behind by a large ship's sinking, paddling in circles, waiting for something to show up on the horizon, a continent they can land on or a rescue vessel that will toss them a line. To this Yap is an exception. A modest and partial exception. Part of this is because they are small; they lack the clamorous pressures of Truk; also, they are well-led—or at least smoothly led—by a collaboration of traditional chiefs and high-ranking elected leaders. Because they are conservative, they are prudent; because they are small, they are careful. While Ponape and Truk go head to head, fighting for money and power, Yap mediates and pleads for unity. When that doesn't work, or even if it does, they return to an island of almost deceptive tranquillity.

"What we do here," Tun says, "is we all come together and discuss things, and if we agree we do it. Other people do their part, I do my part. We do it together or we don't do it at all. And we don't spend eight dollars when we only have five."

What Tun describes is sometimes called the Pacific way, decision by consensus, island style. If it works anywhere, it works in Yap. Maybe too well. Some people speculate that there's "too tight a fit" between Yap's elected and traditional leaders. They sense pressure building down below, in Yap's younger generation: a violence, alcoholism, resentment, and anger that the tight little island can't discharge. So, though there are some who say Yap is doing well, there are others who say it's changing too fast and still others who say it hasn't changed fast enough. You hear people argue that change is inevitable, desirable, fatal. All of them persuasive.

Now Tun drives past the old Coast Guard Loran station, abandoned and boarded up. He's turning the facility over to Reverend Kalau, who plans to develop a Micronesian Maritime Academy. "Kalau will be successful where other people will fail," Tun says, "because he will stick to it and stick to it and stick to it."

The road dips down toward Gagil. We leave the cowboy country behind and come into a different place, Gagil at dusk, the ancient village sitting in darkening shade while the sea, glimpsed through ranks of palms, is a sheet of splashing light. Gagil is a cool, secluded place, the road ending in narrow lanes bordered by croton, hibiscus, and bananas, slabs of donut-shaped stone money leaning against the curb like discarded tires. These Yap villages are special. Other island towns feel like camps, Hoovervilles at worst, Levittowns at best. But you feel that Gagil has been here a long time. You sense it in the stands of palm, the stone paths, the gardens. This is somebody's home. Has been. Is. Will be.

Still, even here, you sense change. Gagil now is plugged into something larger, connected. Roads lead in and out. The same road that brings us in carries Yapese out, to Colonia, so this ancient village, stone paths, meeting houses, stone money, and all is a commuter suburb, a bedroom community, tied to the Yap state government in Colonia, just as Yap is tied to the Federated States of Micronesia, which is tied to the United States. Gagil is caught in a net that leads all the way to Washington. That changes things. It's not just beer and cars and T-shirts. It's attitudes. When a place like Gagil becomes part of something larger, it feels its own smallness more acutely.

"It's changing in the villages," Tun acknowledges. "People with jobs don't spend time in the villages. People are somewhere else. Young people leave, there's not much going on. What used to be normal life and traditional activities, you rarely see anymore. People working on each other's houses, or community houses, or dancing in the evenings. People don't have the time. They've switched from thatch to concrete, wood and tin; easier to work with. There aren't many canoes anymore, they've switched to fiberglass boats with outboard motors. We use taxis and buses all over Yap. People are moving around, which is why you don't see them in the villages anymore."

We step into a small store for beer. The owner attended school in the United States, Denver or Seattle, I forget. Then we go down the road and pull into Tun's place, a weekend shelter that he plans to replace with something better one of these days. We nod to relatives, say hello to Tun's wife, then carry our Budweisers out to the beach. The sunset is happening on the other side of the island, spectacularly I guess. We walk to a shoreline covered with beer cans and coconut shells. A pig is tethered to a tree, and some of Tun's kids are eating Cheez Doodles, chasing each other up and down the beach, digging a hole in the sand, covering the hole with a palm frond, covering the palm with a thin layer of sand. Then, when no one comes along to step in it, they take turns trying to push each other into the trap they made. I ask Tun about other traps, the fish traps I always used to see when I flew into Yap, underwater stone walls that sat out in the lagoon, arrow-shaped, as though pointing out directions for incoming planes. Tun takes a stick and starts sketching in the sand. He enjoys discussing practical things. In the States, I bet, he'd be one of those people who enjoys giving road directions, complicated lefts and rights. Some of the traps pointed in to land, others out to sea, still others up and down the beach, always depending on the movements of the fish, which swim into the trap at high tide and never find their way back out, forcing themselves into smaller and smaller places toward the point of the arrow, where they can be caught in bamboo cages, or netted, or gathered by hand.

The traps aren't what they used to be, Tun says. People don't maintain them, for the same reasons they don't build village meeting houses or dance old dances. These are commuter villages linked to paid jobs.

The fishing isn't what it used to be and neither are the fishermen. Tun is talking to me about a world that's slipping away.

"Our conservation measures were stronger than yours," Tun reflects. "Of course they were based on superstition. If you were going fishing, you weren't supposed to get taro or breadfruit the same day—if you did, you'd be unlucky. Something bad would happen to you. If you were drinking or you were with a woman the night before, you weren't supposed to go fishing. Your mind had to be clear. You weren't supposed to be thinking about anything but fishing. But today, if you were screwing around and drinking and you woke up in time to catch the tide, you'd go fishing."

"Anything goes?"

"Anything goes."

"What about the turtles?" I ask. I'm uneasy about turtles, I admit. In New York, I'm at a distance from the death of animals, but here in the islands I've heard the outraged bleating of pigs being slaughtered, I've seen a just-bludgeoned tuna turned into sashimi, slivers of flesh dipped into soya-lime sauce while the fish was still heaving its last breath. But what bothers me most is the death of turtles, the epic, ocean-crossing swims they take, only to be caught on land, flipped over, their shells cut open like the tops of soup cans, meat, blood, viscera, still-beating heart drawing flies while flippers weakly gesture protest.

"With the turtles," Tun says, "there are certain people who are supposed to get the turtles. You bring the turtle to them and they'll divide it. You might get nothing, or just a little piece, even though you caught the turtle."

"Is it still that way?" I ask, wondering why so much of our conversation is about how things used to be. An inventory of loss.

"It's still that way in the outer islands," Tun answers. He tells me what happened out on Ulithi when some people from one island, Falalop, caught and ate a turtle without bringing it to the island of Mogmog, to whom the turtle "belonged." Mogmog imposed a dire punishment. Falalop people were denied access to the sea. They couldn't sail, swim, or fish in it. They lived on canned mackerel until the ban was lifted.

Our backup beers have turned warm, so Tun and I leave the beach, hop into his Mitsubishi, and head back to town. Gagil is beautiful at day's end, tradewinds blowing in from the east, people walking ancient stone paths, and I suppose I must reconcile myself to tin roofs and piles of beer cans, to cars parked in front of houses where VCRs flicker, firelike, in the Yapese night. On the way back to town I talk to Tun and Carmen about Salii's death. Like others I've spoken to, Kabua in the Marshalls, Falcam in Ponape, Nakayama in Truk, Tenorio on Saipan, Tun has a hard time accepting the death as a suicide.

"He looked like a normal person and one who wouldn't for a minute think of committing suicide," Tun reflects. "But something went wrong. I can't imagine what. When he was elected, I said Palau is really going to move ahead now. But politics there is something else. Who knows?" I leave it at that, for now, but I'm struck at people's reactions to Salii's death. It's as if a plane had crashed. Was it mechanical failure? Was it pilot error? There's lots of wondering.

Tun and I drop Carmen and the kids at home. We plan dinner out. But the Marina restaurant is closed and the Rai View is closing and the E.S.A. is dark and dry. We set out on a search for fish to prepare at home. We want fresh—"iced"—fish, not frozen. You can pop a frozen fish in a microwave, Tun says, and even though it cooks okay it somehow doesn't *look* cooked. One store has nothing. We go to a second store, which is also a laundromat. No fresh fish here either, but the owner makes some phone calls on our behalf, while the governor shoots the breeze with some Yapese who are hanging around the store. I hear him telling the others who I am, a courtesy of explanation in which I hear *New York Times* bobbing around in a flow of Yapese.

Now we get word of fish. We drive home to pick up his wife and the family checkbook. When the American district administrator lived here, it was an orderly outpost of *Good Housekeeping.* Carmen was a maid. Now it's an island house, amiably cluttered, an army of shoes on the front step, the second Spinks-Ali fight on TV. I spot piles of yams and taro, portions of cooked fish and pork wrapped up in banana-leaf pouches, enough food for a medium-sized wedding reception. We could stop and eat right now, but I know islanders well enough to accept that the rumor of fresh fish is irresistible. Out here, the love of fish combines appetite and lust. A fish uncaught, a caught fish unbought: there's no denying. So we head to a tiny store above the E.S.A. hotel and Tun quickly buys twenty-four pounds of reef fish. "Tun gets nervous about having enough fish in the house," Carmen says.

Back home, Tun goes to work on a parrot fish, tearing scales off with his hands, yanking out the spine, plucking out the liver—a choice morsel—and chopping the white-fleshed fish into chunks of sashimi. Then we sit at the table, washing down fish and rice and purple yams with beer, while Tun talks about Yap. Despite Yap's reputation as the darling of the Federated States, Tun goes out of his way to stress how mixed the record is.

"Almost everything the government has touched so far has been a failure," he begins. "Years and years ago, we tried ceramics. We have people with skills here. It can be done, but it can't be done profitably. We started a soap project making three kinds of soap, two bath soaps and one laundry soap, from coconut oil. We privatized it. The new owners dismantled it and it hasn't been reassembled, so it doesn't look like a success. There was a coconut fiber project, producing ropes, brushes, door mats to start with, but the rope was too big for local people. You pull it and it doesn't stretch. Yapese people didn't like the rope and the brush market was insignificant and we couldn't meet the outside demands for quantity. In other words, somebody made a boo-boo somewhere. . . ."

Boo-boos! A funny word coming from the governor of Yap, whom you'd expect to be going into an "infrastructure" rap. But boo-boos nicely covers all the botched enterprises that come and go here, outsiders' efforts to invest, locals scrambling like bad magicians to pull scrawny rabbits out of small hats. Actually, there have been some winning gambits. Tun mentions a government-backed slaughterhouse that might yet work out, a print shop that's running successfully, a fiberglass operation that makes outrigger canoes from molds.

"People say we're traditional and conservative and all that," he says. "But when we want something and see it's good we're the first to go for it."

What they are going for now is bigger deals: Okinawans running a fishing operation, Malaysians building a hotel, a U.S.-Chinese-Yapese-Thai cannery, a Sri Lankan garment factory. The same wave of outside investment and alien labor that washed over Saipan is rolling toward Yap, and there are some people who think that what is happening is an outrage. Still, I believe—I want to believe—that there's something in Yap that might spurn, shrug off, if necessary throw rocks at what challenges its sense of self. Something that will keep beaches closed, cameras shuttered, and tourists off all but the most beaten paths. There's a chance, just a chance, that Yap may hold its own. And survive the end of the world.

◄ III ►

Now, Luke.

Along with Lazarus Salii and Tosiwo Nakayama, Luke Tman was one of the islanders who most impressed me, back when I thought greater things than garment factories and hotels would be accomplished out here. Also, he was my friend. While I sat on Capitol Hill, editing my magazine, Luke was a few desks away. What did they call him, anyway? Special assistant to the deputy high commissioner for public affairs? Something like that, I think. Anyway, he was an elite Micronesian, promotable and presentable. God, was he presentable! Killer good looks, sharp dresser, a golden boy with a handsome wife and a nice house on Capitol Hill. If America made any sense in Micronesia, if Micronesia itself made any sense, Luke Tman would be Exhibit A. The others, all the others, were only provisionally Micronesians. Micronesia was an abstraction: like South America. When the chips were down, they reverted to being what they were born, Palauans, Trukese, and the rest. After that, the identity dwindled further, from district, to island, to village, to family, to self, implosion after implosion. But Luke was Micronesian. Born in Palau, half-Japanese, half-Palauan, he'd been adopted and raised in Yap; educated in Hawaii; groomed on Saipan. He included and transcended those categories that contained so many others. He embodied the promise of Micronesia. And, for a little while, the promise was substantial. I saw him deal shrewdly with Trust Territory bureaucrats, traditional chiefs, with drunks and barmaids. Nothing he couldn't handle. Nothing, for that matter, he couldn't do. He wrote elegant memos, talked smart politics, played a devastating game of chess, danced the meanest cha-cha on the island. And—what I liked most—he seemed to be able to stay in touch with the place he came from. In Yap, one time, he didn't show up for a meeting. Well, what the hell, Micronesians were always blowing things off. The next day, though, he told me his father had summoned his son—Luke's son, that is—to go fishing for the first time, and this, Luke said, was a ceremony of some importance, a seven-year-old boy's introduction to the sea, and the gods of the sea. And when the young fisherman comes home for the first time, much is made of his catch. That first fish, however small and ordinary, is presented to the oldest women. "This is what Matthew caught," they say.

When I returned in the mid-seventies, we crossed paths again. That was at the Micronesian Constitutional Convention, where Luke was an effective, though controversial, figure. An ace parliamentarian, unmatched in knowledge of legislative feints and shifts, Luke was appointed floor leader of a meeting that was separatist and fractious. With some districts already heading for the exits, Luke labored on behalf of unity. He pushed or slid things through, first reading, second reading, committee of the whole, move to adopt. Some people thought that Luke's role had gone to his head, turning him curt and arrogant, although it was hard to avoid some sympathy with his irritation at the tangles that less polished delegates got themselves into. Still, there was something prickly about him, arriving at the convention with a wrinkled brow, eyes covered with sunglasses, and a general aura of touch-me-not, don't mess with me. He was drinking then, scotch not beer, and the word was that when you sat down with Luke Tman you weren't just lifting a glass. You were exercising a death wish.

A wish come true, almost. Word about Luke isn't good. The drinking continued, his marriage failed, and—most surprisingly—he managed somehow to accomplish the unthinkable: he lost an election in Yap, which is like Jesse Jackson failing to carry Chicago. I hear that the powers-that-be put out the word it was time for Luke to come home. For his own good. "If you care about Luke, you'll vote against him." Now, I'm warned, he's in bad shape. "You look at him," says one Yapese, "and you say . . . any time now . . . any time."

I want to see Luke, though, because I want to pay my respects and let him know I remember him, because I waited too long to see Salii, and because—any one of these reasons would suffice—I'm hoping he can give me some idea of what happened to Lazarus. I want him to reach back, if it's only for one word, an explanation I can carry with me to Palau where there will be many words and many explanations. What happened to him, Luke? Is it the same thing that happened to you? Or the opposite? What? Just tell me and I'll go. Or I'll stay. Whatever.

Luke is a clerk of courts these days. His job has to do with deciding which disputes should go through a Western-style court system, which should be kept in the villages for traditional settlements. The first time I go looking for him his desk is empty. I'm not surprised. There's such an air of irrelevance in government offices out here, of Gilbert and Sullivan, it's easy to see how a smart man, or a tired one, might shrug off the daily charade. The second morning, though, I get lucky. I see him standing outside the courthouse, talking to a Yapese elder dressed in loincloth, carrying a bag of betelnut the way a Wall Streeter carries an attaché case. I get out of my car and walk toward him, see that he is surprised and touched and maybe dismayed. We weren't supposed to meet again.

"I'm fading away," he tells me first thing, and though I laugh it off there's no denying it. My old friend has lost most of his teeth. There are sores on his arms, infected-looking swellings on his face. Once I thought of him as a brother. I envied him all his choices. Could he have chosen this?

We decide to go around together, one of those island drives I'm getting used to, as if to test the dimensions of the place, maybe make sure it hasn't grown any overnight. He asks me to stop so he can buy some cigarettes. I wait outside, wait too long, see him knocking back a breakfast beer at the cash register. Carrying a six-pack, we resume our drive. Where do I want to go, he asks. It hurts me to be cast in a tourist role, as though stone money were my object, or a sandy beach, or a topless Yapese woman to stand next to in a snapshot. It's Luke I've come to see. I wish he'd understand that. Maybe he does. No place special I need to go, I tell him. He decides we should drop in on a Palauan cousin of his who runs the local Mobil Oil operation. After visiting there, we visit another relative—an uncle, I think—who runs a grocery store in one of the villages. While we sit in front, watching a Yapese motorcyclist tool up and down in front of us, the uncle tells me about plans to bring in some Filipinos to grow tomatoes, beans, and eggplants. Why is it, I wonder, that all these island projects involve outside money or outside labor or both? Ultimate passivity? Utmost calculation?

I get the feeling that Luke is looking for help in dealing with me, a help that people who still care for him gamely render, so we are dealing with two or three kinds of solicitude this morning, his to me, theirs to him, theirs to me. We talk about old days on Capitol Hill. Who was the biggest playboy? You were? No . . . No . . . it was you. We remember barmaids who are matrons now, Trust Territory bureaucrats who have disappeared into retirement. And, at the end of it all, I drive him home, not to the security of a village but out across the old airport—weeds and potholes in the runway, skeletal Japanese fighters bleaching in the grass—and past the slaughterhouse Tun told me about, no killers and victims in sight today, and we stop in front of a dreary metal-roofed shack. We sit out back at a table and, Christ, it's red clay, washtubs, hanging laundry, chicken pecking at red clay, hot winds coming off the pandanus, like the exhaust from another island's air conditioner. Luke Tman looks at me as I'm about to go. Our promise to meet again, though it won't happen, relieves us of the obligation to say goodbye.

"What are you going to say about Eta?" he asks. Eta, Salii's nickname, jars me. I get tense.

"I don't know," I tell him. "I was hoping you could tell me. Because I know you knew him. And I know you're a thoughtful man. It's why I stopped in Yap." I wait, wondering if this is my chance to ask and to learn. Whose fault is it, what happened out here, Luke? I come from a time when hopes were high. Remember me? When it seemed that

America would leave a clean smell behind, that the islands would develop sensibly, that good people would take command and look after
a place that, war notwithstanding, was a clean, unwritten page. One last,
small chance not to fuck things up. And you were part of that time, that
teeny Camelot, you and Lazarus. What happened?

"Palau is a mystery wrapped in intrigue," he says, reaching way back.
"Churchill."

". . . wrapped in an enigma, I think," I say, hating myself for making
a correction I'm not even sure about.

"Well, close enough," he says politely. He has told me all he can I
guess. I'd wanted him to produce a secret, to pull some illuminating
disclosure out of the depths of island life, those depths that swallowed
Lazarus. But he is sinking now himself, and a quote from Churchill is
what comes floating to the surface.

So I leave him, sitting in back of his house, sipping on a Budweiser.
He sits motionless at a table, staring out into the heat as I drive away.
I have no idea how he'll get through the rest of the day.

VIII

HOME AND AWAY: PALAU

◄ I ►

Now only Palau is left in this trail of islands. I sit in the Yap terminal, waiting for the southbound flight from Guam, watching rain lash the runway, ready to enter my realm of dreams. Palau has haunted me for years, tempted and reproached me. Whenever I've been unhappy someplace else, I wondered if I wouldn't be happy in Palau. Whenever I was happy, or thought I was, happily married, books getting published, movies in the works, I wondered if some greater happiness didn't await me in Palau. The place could reach me, wherever I was, forcing me to question my life's direction. Even in New York. Especially in New York.

It isn't the beauty of Palau. There are lots of beautiful places, postcard pretty. It's not the friendliness of the people, that's for sure, because there are many people more hospitable than Palauans. Not the climate, hot and funky, not the food, not the culture. It's Palau's sense of itself, its pride, malice, opportunism, mystery. "Those satanic Palauans," a friend calls them. Travelers expect to be judges. Traveling is a series of verdicts, one place compared to another, all of them eventually measured against (no place like) home. Not in Palau, where something says: *I didn't come to you. You came to me. I'm from here. You're not. My island, not yours. My court, my game, my rules. Now, let's play.*

I'm anxious to reach Palau, but in Yap, the plane lands and sits. No one goes out to it, no one comes off, not through these sheets of rain. Yap. The pilots used to buzz the field before landing, to make sure the pigs were off the runway. Now, they're finishing a new terminal right next door, dedicating it next month. Yap joins the world. Traditional dancing and dedicatory speeches. It should be some party but I'll be in Palau then. An airline employee walks out, carrying umbrellas, and now the plane slowly empties, passengers carrying the umbrellas to the terminal, handing them to boarding passengers. No rush. I purchase two packages of Yapese betelnut, highly prized in Palau. And I think of two other men I've talked with about the next stop south.

▲ ▲ ▲

"I was a hot-shit Peace Corps director," Dirk Ballendorf recalled. This was last week, in his office at the University of Guam's Micronesia Area Research Center. A round, silver-haired live-wire guy, full of ideas and projects, a master at getting grants, Ballendorf qualifies as another in my gallery of stayers-on, though he was Peace Corps staff when I met him here in 1967. Before then, he'd done a volunteer hitch in the Philippines. He's stuck around the islands, first in Ponape, at the Community College of Micronesia, now here in Guam. In the world of scholarship, Micronesia is a mighty small patch, but Ballendorf cultivates it vigorously. He's about to leave for Russia, to chat with some Pacific experts, then on to Germany for a guest spot teaching Pacific history. There's a trove of papers and handicraft the Germans have stashed in Leipzig; he wants to look at that. And then, down the road, there's that business in Japan, a panel of experts convening to decide, once and for all, if the Japanese know more than they've ever said about Amelia Earhart's death back in 1937. Ballendorf keeps busy and with Palau's search for a future political status running more years than a hit TV sitcom, he figures to stay busy for a while yet. We'd spent an hour schmoozing about Palau. Much of what he said was critical. Like me, Ballendorf goes out of his way to be tough on the islands of his affection. "They're just as fouled up as the other Micronesians are," he said. "They don't do their home-work. Their politics are opportunistic. And the high-clan people think that they're above the law." But then I asked about his first perception of the place, and he told me about the time some auditors came out from Washington.

"I'd just had a volunteers' conference up on Kayangel, and I'd ar-ranged for the local people to feed the volunteers for three days. I paid them the way they wanted to be paid—a generator, some baseball equipment, stuff like that. I didn't do it by the book, cost per meal, cost per day. So there were discrepancies. And these auditors, they made me empty my pockets and count out the cash. 'Where'd you get your accounting system?' " one of them asks me. 'The Phoenicians,' I say. Well, he was a diligent man and I was a wiseass Peace Corps punk. I got my ass chewed out.

"At the same time, they were auditing the Palauans' books. Three auditors who sit all day in front of adding machines. They were met at the plane. I saw it. These three guys stepping off the DC-3. An honor guard of policemen with chipped, dirty M1 rifles. And beautiful Palauan women with leis. These wilted, white-shirted guys step off the plane and they're welcomed by these . . . graceful little birds! And they're saying, 'Wow, look at that!' " We went to the Royal Palauan Hotel that night. We ate turtle, drank vodka and gin. Everybody got snockered and we had a blast.

"Then, the next day, it's 'OH, MY GOD!' and 'LOOK AT THESE BOOKS!' and 'THAT'S AGAINST THE LAW!' and 'WHERE ARE YOUR ACCOUNTS RECEIVABLE!' And the Palauans are perfect. 'We don't know your culture, but we're trying.' And that evening, there's another party, after a trip to the Rock Islands. Maybe the auditors got laid, I don't know. And they say, 'Okay, we'll let you go this time, but never again. If you fail to account for money, you go to jail.' And when the auditors leave, we all go to the district administrator's house and have another party. The auditors go back to Washington and report that the books cannot be audited. They say they don't know where the money's gone. And, at a higher level, somebody decides, oh, screw it, write it off.

Anyway we're keeping the Chinks and Ruskies out. What the hell. And that happened over and over."

▲ ▲ ▲

Palau story number two. Now a lawyer on Saipan, Kim Batcheller was the last American to run Palau. He was district administrator for a couple of years in the late seventies. He dealt with the arson at the courthouse and radio station, with a long, bitter strike against the local hotel, which involved attempts to burn the building's generator, short out its powerlines, and blow the hotel itself to kingdom come. (The bomb, a contraption involving a mosquito coil and a stick of dynamite, failed to go off.) Batcheller dismissed seven department heads. He fielded death threats. And—now we're getting unforgivable—he balanced the government books, even showed a small profit. But this story is about his first day at work in Palau.

"I was there on time, seven-thirty, sharp," he recalls. "And I waited around till eight-thirty, when people started showing up. I thought, well, I'm the first guy here, I'll make coffee. The secretary is sitting there, watching me, and I decide I'll show her I'm the kind of guy who chips in, doesn't expect everything to be done for him. Where's the pot? I ask. She gestures. The sink? The cord? The outlet? I do all this and she's watching me and I think I'll make a good impression on the staff. So finally, it's all set up and I ask her where's the coffee. 'We don't have any.' That's how I found out that Palau was quite a different place."

▲ ▲ ▲

The rain slackens and we board the Palau flight, which is almost empty. A veteran of many Air Micronesia island hops, I rush up and down the aisle, ferreting under seats for a left-behind copy of that day's Guam newspaper, the *Pacific Daily News*. Oh, joy: I find one. And it's got a page of baseball boxscores. I take my time, like a chocolate lover working through a box of bonbons. I put my finger over the line that shows runs scored, inning by inning, and study the lineups, checking who got hits, how long the pitchers lasted, trying to figure the outcome, enjoying the beautiful symmetry of the game's accounting system, a symmetry that Washington's auditors couldn't find in Palau's bookkeeping.

We pass over an atoll—Ngulu, I guess—wriggling like an amoeba in a laboratory slide, a filament of sand and green in an amniotic sac of light blue lagoon. Such tenuous places. Now the ocean is empty and dark again, with banks of clouds lowering in the south. In America, when I see clouds on the horizon, I picture imaginary mountain ranges, a high country, rolling up to heaven. Here, flying over the deepest part of the Pacific—Mount Everest could drown below our wings—the clouds cast shadows on the water, imaginary islands and ships at sea. In a while the clouds will thicken and the real Palau will emerge from out of them.

◄ II ►

I don't go in for graves. In 1967 my father scattered my mother's ashes around a spruce tree in Berkeley Heights, New Jersey. He did it on the sly, so as not to spook his grandchildren. Eight years later, his own ashes were cast to sea, somewhere off Fort Pierce, Florida, by someone he didn't know, who didn't know him. I was in the islands at the time. I don't know about graves. But I mean to visit Salii. The last leg of my trip.

From Koror, Palau's capital, I hop a small plane that carries me south, over the Rock Islands. I am recently enough arrived to find them stunning, lagoons and coves and inlets, bright green hillsides. Paradise, again. Looking down from above, I try finding marine lakes. There are more than a dozen of them, I know, hidden pools screened by limestone cliffs, connected by subterranean passages to the lagoon outside. Eerie, mutant places. Ahead lies the battlefield island of Peleliu, like an egg frying in a skillet of hot sea, its blistering ridges popping against the sky and its punctured yolk of sand running off to the south. The plane starts descending, passing right over the limestone hills whose honeycombed caves and tunnels the Japanese turned into a perfect fortress. No wonder a three-day battle took three months. There's the monument that the marines perched on top of Bloody Nose Ridge, a stone pillar with some letters missing. LEST WE FORGET THOSE WHO DIED. Minoru Ueki didn't. He's a physician in Koror, a sharp, lively gent who told me that whenever he needed a skeleton for teaching purposes after the war, he went into the caves. A medical supply house, the caves of Peleliu, well-stocked with skeletons. I've crawled around in those caves. They scared me, the dripping rocks, the slippery footing, the puddles and crags and chunks of metal, the sandals, belts, bottles, and unidentifiable stuff you stepped past rather than probed. The bats, the rats. But what I remember most is the feeling of being trapped, two or three times over. Trapped on an island, trapped in a cave on an island, enclosed in the guts of a living thing, dark and earthen, wet and warm, that would pull you out of the daylight, swallow you whole, and shit you into the lagoon, out into the mangroves, where fiddler crabs could pick at you before the tide rolled in. More Peleliu: a glint of metal roofs, roads running down to the old invasion beach, Orange Beach, pronounced *oh-ran-gee* by Palauans. Peleliu looks green and sleepy. It's not pretty, though. The battlefield islands out here—Tinian, Saipan, Peleliu—have a scuffed-up, second-growth look that never leaves them. Even the colors of the island seem tentative, as though something knows that these are islands of newsreel footage, black and white, right out of *Victory At Sea.* Somewhere down there, they buried Haruo Remeliik, Palau's first president. And somewhere ahead, across the channel, Lazarus Salii is buried on Angaur. Island by island, dead president by president, the place claims its own.

Pancake-flat, outside the main lagoon, Angaur sits across a deep blue channel, with an opening in the treeline along the beach. That's the airstrip, World War II vintage, grass growing in the military's aging footprint. We land and park at the end of the strip. There's no terminal, just a guy with a University of Oklahoma T-shirt dozing on a bench beneath a banyan tree. "Maybe the agent is sleeping," he speculates. "Maybe he went fishing last night." He resumes his nap. The pilot opens the cockpit doors, leans back, snoozes. My kind of place. A rusted truck pulls in and a schoolteacher gets out, carrying papers with names and grades. Finally the agent arrives; the plane departs. I rent the agent's pickup truck and set off on a maze of dirt roads that would be bewildering anyplace else. But Angaur is small—that's for sure—and I will find my way to Lazarus, find him without looking. That's for sure too. Though I have reduced the distance between us to a mile or so, every day that passes widens the other gap between us, that which separates the living and the dead, and it's as if the brief silence we had in our long-distance phone calls, those annoying, echoing intervals when our voices bounced off orbiting satellites has now stretched into something that will last, and widen, forever. "Fred." I can still hear it, hoarse and low. No small talk. The minute I heard it, it made its claim. "This is Lazarus."

There's the grave and no avoiding it. That's where he wound up, at the intersection of two dirt roads, in a kind of corral, surrounded by three dozen wooden stakes, each with its wreath of plastic flowers. I walk into the enclosure, toward where a mound of fresh cement is piled high with flowers and some sunbleached ribbons upon which I can barely make out his name. Three electric light bulbs dangle over the grave—proxy, maybe, for an eternal flame. I trace the electric wire back away from the grave, toward a basketball court. Farther back, there's a school, beat-up looking, like all the standard-issue government buildings out there.

With faded, purple and white bunting around the outside, plastic flowers bleaching in the heat, the grave looks like a booth left over from a carnival that passed through town. Or maybe the dais of a high school graduation. His widow is planning a mausoleum monument. I've seen the plans, drawn up in Manila, for a skyward pointing spire that would sit over Lazarus's grave. I hope at least they plant some trees. Right now it feels awkward being here. Awkward for him too, if he could feel, the man who believed in change and motion coming back to square one: Angaur. Standing here, my thoughts seem forced. The sun's damn hot. And some women are watching me from a nickel-and-dime store across the road. Enough. I kneel, touch the concrete, walk back to the truck. Corny moment. I drive down to the dock, a couple hundred feet beyond the grave, and walk along a stone breakwater, which faces out to the south. They loaded phosphate here. I see rusted tracks and tumblers that poured the wealth of the island into offshore ships and created a trust fund that sent bright kids like Salii off to school.

"Anguar in the years before the war was a very prosperous island," he once recalled. "There was a large community of Okinawans, Koreans, people from other districts, especially Truk, who lived in a separate area from the native people. My memories of that period are very good memories. We had a very good life there. . . . and it was just fun from morning to evening as a boy of seven and eight years old. I still have desires from time to time of going back to those days."

Salii saw the war coming, saw the omens. He looked forward to it, confident the Japanese would win. He respected them. "You bowed your head, not grudgingly but because this was a superior person you were talking to." He admired what the Japanese had made of Koror, the uniforms, the bustle, the buildings. Years later Salii would have reservations about the Japanese, who were well on their way to assimilating the islands. "In five years," he said, "Palauans would have been in the same situation as Hawaiians." But that came later. Now he was all eyes, waiting for the Japanese to show their stuff.

"We had to practice air raid warnings and we were told to dig air raid shelters. There were more troops coming and we would see fortifications coming up, and it was just a question of time. Everybody was ready for it, waiting for it to happen, and nobody was scared. The Japanese couldn't be beaten. And I think a lot of people were looking forward to seeing some action. It was that kind of atmosphere, thinking it was going to be exciting, not really dangerous, thinking that the Americans would be beaten badly."

In March 1944, air raids began. "The American planes started coming, coming at dawn." Salii learned the air raid system: one blast at first report, a second when the planes came closer, a third when it was time to head for shelters. He saw dogfights overhead, Japanese planes rising up—though in dwindling numbers—to protect nearby Peleliu from the incoming swarms. You could tell the Japanese planes by the sound of their engine, "a machine gun sound." One of them, a zero, came crashing into a breadfruit tree on Angaur.

Most of the Anguar people, Salii included, were evacuated from the island before the fighting. On his way north, to a village on Babelthuap, Salii passed through Koror, or what was left of it. "We had just stopped at the dock to fuel or to pick up some people, but we didn't go into town. Koror had very few trees then and from the ocean you could see the whole town. It was a real mess. That part of Koror was still smoking. It looked like a dump that had been burned. . . ."

Up on Babelthuap, Salii climbed a hill at night and stared south, where a glow of fires and searchlights lit up the battlefield islands of Peleliu and Angaur. He wondered what was happening down there. Ten days of bombing, three days of naval bombardment had given Peleliu such a pasting that reconnaissance pilots wondered whether anyone was left alive. "An immense broken graveyard," one pilot said. Then: coconut log cradles, concrete pillboxes, tank traps, barbed wire, mines, and aerial bombs. Tanks and mortar. After the capture of the beaches and the airfield came the nightmare of Bloody Nose Ridge, a limestone ridge honeycombed with caves—five hundred of them, some nine stories high, barred by iron doors, lit and ventilated. That was Peleliu. Angaur was more lightly defended. But I wonder if it didn't get to Salii, though he was just a kid; if he didn't resent being shunted to the sidelines while the issue was decided.

Koror and Babelthuap were bypassed, though planes dropped leaflets that claimed American victory down on Peleliu and Angaur. Finally, word came that the war was over. On foot and by boat, 360 Angaur people made their way south, Ngraard to Airai, where they waited for an LCU to take them home. Captured Japanese officials counted heads, the vanquished consigning Palauans to the victors. Then came the boat and a scene Salii never forgot. His first American.

"The front of the LCU opened up and it was the first time I saw a blond human being, a tall shirtless young sailor with yellow hair and blue eyes, his hands on his hips, a big smile on his face. An order was shouted by one of the Japanese officers in charge of the evacuation onshore, and the line of people began to move toward the boat. Leading the procession was Dirbelau, wife of the chief of Anguar, somewhere around ninety years of age, half-blind and bent, taking slow painful steps down the ramp with the help of a stick. 'Welcome aboard, ma'am,' grinned the handsome sailor as he moved to assist the old woman. She dropped the crutch, extended her right hand toward the sailor and in a strong, loud voice responded 'Thank you.' "

The LCU headed south, past Koror—"in ashes and heaps of collapsed concrete and tangled steel, with smoke still billowing from various parts of the island." They passed the Rock Islands, then Peleliu, which Salii remembered as "just a white mass of rocks." Then, the one-ship convoy crossed over to Angaur and home, which had been utterly—and delightfully—transformed.

"To our surprise, when we got there, there were two villages, trees had grown, Quonset huts were lined up." The Americans had restored much of the island, built a little America to replace the ruined Palauan and Japanese villages. "We had our house assigned and we moved right into the house with everything there—beds and mattresses. No kitchen utensils, but we were told there was a galley at the center of the village."

Those early, postwar years, those first impressions of the Americans—the military—were indelible. "Free food, free movies, free transportation around the island. We began to go out into the jungle to play and hunt for wild chickens. Almost everywhere we went, we ran into warehouses full of food—it was just like having picnics every day in the boonies."

No wonder, Salii recalled, that the Angaur kids tried to imitate this race of generous winners. "They let their hair grow long. The popular haircut under the Japanese had been the 'bozu,' where the hair was clipped to its roots, nearly shaven, and a boy walked around with a shiny head. Now every kid grew his hair, and bleached it blond, or as nearly blond as possible. With the aid of lemon juice, chlorine in the water system, and almost daily swimming on the beach, this part was easy. Almost overnight, nearly every boy turned blond."

Like the others, Salii struggled to learn English. Later, he succeeded utterly. He was as close to bilingual as any Palauan I met. But he started out, like the kids who followed me around Truk, shouting, "Hello, what's your name?" again and again.

"When one of the Americans passed by in a Jeep, you stopped him and asked, 'Show tonight?' He'd invariably respond, 'Yes, sir.' Everyone knew that movies were shown every night, without miss, but if you had nothing else to say, or could not say it, asking a sure thing never failed to establish rapport and reaffirm friendship."

For several years, the picnic-honeymoon continued, and it's hard not to believe that this early demonstration of what America could do, at the height of its power, stayed with the later political status negotiator.

No wonder he got testy, with those other Americans, "Micronesia experts," people with lots of cultural concern and very little funding, the advocates of go slow, save the islands, protect the culture. Salii had seen Angaur transformed—presto—while the locals were away, hiding out on Babelthuap. And he mostly liked what they'd done.

"War surplus had left Angaur rich, much more so than before the war. There were two camps, now turned into villages, with lighted and paved walks, and rows upon rows of housing, some made of boards and plywood, the rest consisting of the well-known Quonset hut. The houses were equipped with indoor plumbing, flush toilets, and running water. There were warehouses all over the island filled with canned and cardboarded foods: corned beef, chocolate bars, milk and candies, and cigarettes. And clothing: Army fatigues, T-shirts and shorts, helmets, socks, shoes, belts. Other warehouses brimmed with carbines and M1's, .45 caliber handguns, ammunition, and hand grenades. There were open dumps jammed with troop transports, half-ton trucks, bulldozers, Jeeps, tires and inner tubes for all of these, fuel containers, canisters. Never before had the people seen or enjoyed such abundance. For the next three years, living on Angaur was like living on paradise on earth. For the kids, especially. . . ."

▲ ▲ ▲

I head out on one—any one—of the dirt roads that crisscross the island, about all that's left of the wartime settlement Salii described. There's nothing like a village on Angaur, only scattered houses that could be from Georgia or south Jersey. At midday, the sun is brutal and the silence is deafening. I understand my old friend's restlessness. After a few weeks here—I don't care how many books he brought along to read or boxing tapes to watch—he'd be stalking the island as if he were in a cage.

Odd that he came back here at all. An office on Saipan, a hotel room in Hawaii, a golf course anywhere might as well have been his resting place. But now, remembering his account of what happened here when the Americans came, what happened to him, I see the logic of it. This place formed him.

It always bothered me, that Salii didn't share my suspicion of the U.S. military, that he could negotiate with them so cheerfully, put up on Guam and golf with the admiral, mingle easily with men in uniform. The Pentagon's interest in returning to Palau worried me more than it worried him. Sure, he could hold forth about these poor, scuffed-up islands that had suffered from wars not of their own making . . . but that was stuff I wrote. For him, Palau's military importance was a bargaining chip. There was something in Salii that loved action, loved anything that would break the torpid stasis of island life. He never got over that sense of anticipation, down on Angaur, war rumbling in his direction, or his surprise at how the American forces transformed his island after they captured it.

Military historians contend that Peleliu was a battle that should not have been fought. MacArthur was anxious about his return to the Philippines, felt threatened by the Japanese on Peleliu, who were no threat at all. They could dig in and defend tenaciously, but their offensive abilities were nil. So Peleliu was an unnecessary battle, Angaur was a sideshow to Peleliu, and postwar Angaur was the aftermath of a sideshow. Accident on accident. But that was the paradise that Lazarus remembered. It wasn't thatch roofs and outrigger canoes, copra making and celestial navigation. It was rows of Quonsets, Americans in Jeeps, food in the galley, and movies every night.

Meandering around in my pickup truck, I come upon a last vestige of American military power, so gone to seed I don't even recognize it until I get out and walk the overgrown grounds, the puddled driveway, and see that these one-story official-looking buildings have numbers stencilled on their walls. God, it's the old Coast Guard Loran station. I peek inside. Linoleum floors, torn screens, peeling institutional paint. Someone wants to turn the place into a resort hotel, I hear. Other schemes for Angaur: casino gambling, renewed phosphate mining. I get worn out by this kind of talk. Right now, the Coast Guard station is home for wasps. Their mud nests spatter the walls and ceilings like bullet holes.

It takes about half an hour to drive around Angaur. The houses aren't much: cars parked on grass, washlines flopping, dogs running out in the road. Yet, outside the inhabited areas, the place startles me. On the south side, the dirt road runs along a splendid shoreline, sandy beach, green fringe of grass and trees. On the north the coast is rocky, all blowholes and tidal pools. What's most surprising, though, is the area where phosphate was mined. Time has taken a landscape of pits and pillars that reminds me of what my teeth would look like if they lost all their caps and fillings in one day, and covered this jagged, broken zone with vines and brush and ferns, a garden in the wounded earth. Trees arch over the road, monkeys hopping from branch to branch. The wild chickens Salii hunted dart in front of my truck. It's like a children's storybook version of a haunted forest.

I drive to the airport in midafternoon, an hour before the plane back to Koror. My business here is over. I have driven around the island— twice—and paused at Lazarus's grave—twice. He would understand that it was time to go. I can almost hear him saying, "See, I told you, that place is small." He used to treat airplane tickets like supermarket coupons, peeling off whatever he needed to use. He boasted he'd flown more miles than the average stewardess. What defines islanders is not the way they live on islands but the way they move between them.

I have the airstrip to myself. On Angaur, when they hear the plane land they think about driving to the airport. I like it: it feels as though I've come as far as possible from Newark Airport. I hop into the truck and drive down the runway—try that at Newark!—right to where it ends at a rocky cliff. I find a grassy spot above the water, sit in the shade of an ironwood tree and watch the waves come pounding in, the sun gleaming on wet rocks, every wave like a new coat of gold this time of day. Across the channel I can see Peleliu and the beginnings of the Rock Islands and I know that Angaur is too small a place for Salii not to have stood here too, sighting across the water, realizing that his future lay in that direction.

The plane comes in low over Peleliu and slides into the old runway. Sounds more like a flying lawn mower than a plane. In a minute, we lift off and head back. I'm the only passenger, so the pilot agrees to fly right over the Rock Islands. Angaur falls off to the south and I fill up with a sense of friendships gone awry, chances missed. Leaving him down

there, back there, I feel sadder than at his graveside. I believed in him.
We were linked. A low-caste guy in Palau, an immigrant's son in America: he must have rankled at high-caste Koror when he got to it, the way
I bridled at Kenyon, the fraternity boys walking the planet with their
gentlemen's sense of entitlement. A scholarship guy too. He took off
from Angaur, cocky and confident. He racked up victory after victory,
at high school in Truk, college in Hawaii, politics and government on
Saipan. What happened to us anyway, what broke that string of wins?
He came back to Palau and, like a rocket failing orbit—some burn-out,
some loss of equilibrium, some five-cent part missing—he fell back to
earth. And now I'll try to find out what happened to him in Koror. I could
learn a thing or two there.

◄ III ►

At dawn, I'm out on the road, running through Koror, over the causeway
to Malakal Harbor. You get high tide early in the morning, and the place
is bright with promise, green islands spread out south, ships in port,
small boats bobbing at their moorings, all things seem possible. I need
this morning hour, short as it is, to remind myself of how handsome this
place can be, bright green and true blue, that I wasn't just kidding myself
when I remembered Palau.

By the time I get back, around seven o'clock, though, Palau's brief
dispensation from heat is over. The sun is blasting and we are entering
that time that seems to stretch out endlessly, ten hours wide, ten hours
before quitting time and dusk, before happy hour and the amnesty of
darkness.

Don't tell me that the locals don't feel the heat, that it's only outsiders
who find paradise about a dozen degrees too hot, too humid, not when
I can see the heat smothering their economy and work ethic, irradiating
their political life, warping their architecture and confronting them with
the same question every morning: how the hell do I get through the
day? They retreat into air-conditioned bubbles, cars with tinted windows, government offices, homes, and restaurants. They don baseball

hats and sunglasses, heft umbrellas—hell, grow mustaches, *anything* to keep the sun off the skin and the sweat inside their bodies. If you see someone working in the heat around Koror, chances are he's Filipino. For Palauans, cars are ambulances, offices are forts, homes are pillboxes in the daily battle against the heat.

Government is the first refuge, employing more than half the Palauans who work for money. Government is what happens to Palau during the day, the religion *and* opiate of the people. There's the national government's executive branch, now run—rather quietly—by Salii's successor, an older businessman, Ngiratkel Etpison. Etpison barely nudged out Salii's old rival, Roman Tmetuchl, for the presidency. Across Koror, there's the legislature, the Olbiil era Kelulau—"meeting place of whispers," in Palauan. The O.E.K. is often at odds with the executive branch. In between is the judiciary, tucked in an old betelnut-bespattered Japanese courthouse, a busy, chatty place. Palauans sue a lot. There's more government: departments of education, public works, and so forth. The Commission on Future U.S.-Palau Relations. The U.S. State Department Liaison office, the Department of Interior outpost, the Capital Relocation Commission. Then there are the Koror offices of Palau's sixteen state governments. Politicians' offices. Law offices.

I tell people I'm looking into what happened to an old friend. And before they can challenge me, I grant I'm not an expert on Palau, that anyone who says he is is looking for trouble. I'm not a lawyer and I'm not a detective. I don't plan to crawl around Salii's house looking for fingerprints and second bullets, forced entry or signs of struggle. What's more, I tell them, I assume everyone who lives in Palau knows more about it than I do, more than I'm likely to find out. Oh sure, I say, they've got me beat in all ways but one, just one, my narrow expertise, the one thing I know more about than they do: how they look to me.

It mostly works. Some people talk to me because I'm a writer, some people talk to me in spite of it. History is a matter of opinion here. The newspaper is what comes off the plane from Guam, something you read to compare what it got with what it missed. I think my project amuses people. It's flattering to be asked to sit for a portrait that you're under no obligation to buy. I press on. I sit and drink coffee, start talking and—at that certain point, the writer's equivalent of reaching behind a girl's back to unsnap her bra—I pull out my notebook and start scribbling. Sometimes the conversation dies but more often the girl is willing. What were you waiting for? she seems to ask.

Most mornings I start out at the Arirang Restaurant. "We served lobster and crab" a note on the menu advises, one of those endearing misprints that kicks off huge conjectures. I settle for coffee and French toast and, across the room, spot a familiar figure. Though he's sitting with his back to me, busy talking to a tableful of old men, I recognize the lean, fit body—no beer tumor for him—and the close-cropped curlier-than-normal hair, which might be traceable to a Papua New Guinea grandfather five generations back. Roman Tmetuchl's back in Palau, back from vacation in Bali. The governor of Airai, the sometime status negotiator, three-time presidential candidate, shrewd, high-born businessman politician who was Joe Frazier to Salii's Muhammad Ali, he recognizes me, leaves the table, and pops onto a neighboring stool.

"Palau could be Bali!" he declares when I ask him how he liked his trip. "Better than Bali. I used to think God was unfair to me, because I was born in Palau, because of the treatment we received. I don't think so anymore. Palau could be better than Bali."

Planning, work, discipline, that's what it would take. Roman Tmetuchl is a driven, work-ethic kind of man, with no patience for his fellow Palauans' dithering. "Palauans are worse than monkeys in a cage in the zoo," he complains. Tact was never his long suit, or small talk, which might be why the presidency eluded him. "Monkeys fight sometimes, but they live together, eat together. Not like Palauans."

An older Palauan man, a *rubak,* comes over and Tmetuchl addresses him in the barking vehement style which is his asset . . . and his problem. He's 78 rpm in a 33-rpm world. When the first Japanese came tiptoeing back to Palau in the fifties, Tmetuchl was ready for them, fluent in Japanese. He gave them what was called his "samurai speech": *You taught us, you ruled us, we learned your language and your culture and then you abandoned us. . . .* A masterpiece. But his deals made other Palauans wary of him. He built businesses in sand, gravel, concrete, branched out, prospered, profited. He had a power base in Airai, chiefly status and electoral clout, but Palau has a way of tripping up a man who moves too fast. Now his secretary comes to tell him he's got a call from Yokohama. Before he leaves—we are to meet again later—he mentions prospects in real estate, hotels, airlines. He claims to be resigned to his thirty-eight-vote loss in the last election. "I stated my case," he says. "What's that song? . . . Frank Sinatra? . . . I stated my case . . . of which I'm certain. . . ."

Salii and Tmetuchl. Angaur versus Airai, ordinary versus high caste, scholarly whiz kid versus clever island capitalist. A classic duel. Both smart, both driven: no wonder the island wasn't big enough for both of them. Salii was a product of the American period, though, and Tmetuchl was formed by the Japanese. Salii liked Americans; I'm not sure Tmetuchl feels that way about the Japanese.

"I was born in a Palau where the Japanese outnumbered the Palauans," he says, a little later in his office. "The place was filled with Japanese. We were pushed down to the mangroves. We were called natives, just like savages. Maybe we were. School stopped for us at the fifth grade. I wasn't happy, knowing that was the end of my education. I was willing to study. I wasn't stupid. I was willing to challenge the Japanese. I'd played with them. They weren't that smart."

Tmetuchl was smart, a quick study, who learned Japanese by the age of four. Everything they threw at him, he learned. Abacus and semaphore. He worked as an office boy at the Japanese newspaper in Koror. Later he ran errands for the Japanese police. He interpreted, sometimes he deliberately misinterpreted, if it served a purpose. He learned things, saw things. He washed dishes, swept floors, cleaned bicycles, and sometimes he operated the fastest boat around Koror, racing around mangroves, flags flying, taking salutes from "stupid" Japanese who never knew who they were saluting.

Forty years later, he's still working with the Japanese. He reaches for two rolled-up sets of blueprints and sketches, two Japanese-backed resort hotels on opposite sides of the channel between Babelthuap and Koror. Sumitomo on one side, Taisei on the other, a half-dozen hotels, more than two thousand rooms, a convalescent home, a marina, a golf course. And a theme park. "They made a mistake putting Disneyland in Tokyo," Tmetuchl explains. "No one goes there in the winter."

Something must show on my face. Talk about life imitating art. Bad art. A Disneyland in Palau! Maybe it'll be something like the Polynesian Cultural Center the Mormons run in Hawaii, native huts, tapa-cloth demonstrations, dance shows, poi-and-coconut luaus. Or perhaps they'll go for something more distinctively Palauan: they'll stage plebiscites on the Compact of Free Association, throw in power outages, lawsuits, strikes, and demonstrations. Guest appearances by U.S. congressmen, auditors, U.N. visiting missions, everybody taking turns caring about Palau, searching for—or imposing—their version of the final solution for the last Trust Territory. A tropical Oberammergau, enacting its peculiar passion play, year after year.

I know there are a half-dozen hotel projects floating around town, three golf courses too. Most will fail, investors scared off by political instability or land tenure problems. Land disputes are to Palauan development what the tsetse fly was to parts of Africa. It can take a dozen lawsuits to obtain clear title. But what if Tmetuchl pulls this off? Is this the way he wants things to be?

I look over at him. He's a man of discipline and taste. He lives in a handsome airy house in Airai, dark wood, big windows, view of the sea. Every morning first thing, he walks up and down his driveway through groves of mahogany he planted, a pedometer at his waist: his goal, ten thousand steps a day. At night, he plays a lean, mean game of tennis on the court next to the Arirang Restaurant. He's fit. And smart. This is the man who brought in John Kenneth Galbraith as an unpaid consultant on political status. Now bring a Disneyland to Palau? Is this his joke on the Palauans, who failed to make him president? "I wish I didn't have to do this," he says, poring over the blueprints. "But my people are spoiled . . . the cash economy." Or is it his revenge on the Japanese? That would not surprise me: Tmetuchl the savvy islander conning and manipulating the heavy-hitters down from Nippon. Toward the end of our talk, his Disneyland blueprints rolled back up into diplomas, he says something that strikes me. "I haven't forgotten what happened when I was a small boy," he says. And we leave it at that.

▲ ▲ ▲

By far the most popular place for lunch—thank god it's neutral ground—is the Nikko Hotel. Built in the late sixties on a gorgeous bluff it shares with the ruins of an old Japanese temple, the Nikko—originally the Continental TraveLodge, later just the Continental—was Palau's first luxury hotel. The years have not been kind. Outflanked by cheaper motel-type operations on one side, by the lavish Palau Pacific Resort on the other, the Nikko is a place of musty corridors, sealed rooms, empty swimming pool; a Miss Havisham of a hotel, great expectations on hold. But, funny thing, in its decrepitude, the Palauans claim it as their own. Maybe it's outside ownership that makes them comfortable, or the overall aura of unprofitability that relaxes them, but at lunch the place is jammed with people of all parties, government ministers, business-men, legislators, bankers, secretaries, state governors, lawyers, eyeball-ing each other, tablehopping, checking to see who's got hooks into some Japanese or Chinese investors just off the plane.

So the Nikko is where I talk to people about Salii and, no matter what else they tell me, one statement always comes up, one constant refrain: *Salii was smart, but. . . .* Salii was smart but he didn't do this, he did that, he listened to him, he didn't listen to me, he forgot something, he remembered something. *Smart, but.* They speak of him like a fallen tightrope walker. *Smart, but.* And the but's are all over the place. I carry them with me back to my hotel room after lunch. I know better than to be out in the afternoon. I close my door, strip down to my underwear, work through this amazing pile of papers that I'll have to find some way to ship home. Letters, memos, budgets, court cases, contracts, cables, newspaper clippings. Souvenirs of Palau. Come late afternoon, the hotel fills up with returning divers, bubbling with talk of sharks and coral, places like the Blue Corner, the Tunnel, Emily's Wall, Jellyfish Lake. Lightweights, I used to think. But now, sifting all this political confetti, I wonder if they haven't got it right after all.

I could say that what I'm doing is like putting together the pieces of the puzzle, but that doesn't get it, because the picture on the outside of the box, the picture that shows what the completed puzzle should look like, that picture got lost somewhere, so some people say that what I'm putting together should look like a windmill. But others cry no, no, it's a sailing ship for sure.

Evenings in Koror. At the Arirang, I hear raucous consultations from the youngbloods who are in Palau's latest status commission, long arguments, half in English, half in Palauan, about the next move to put on the Americans. I spot Moses Uludong, glaring, gesturing. "Let's cut out the bullshit," he pleads again and again. Once an advocate of Palauan independence, he now favors a commonwealth deal like Saipan's. Across from him sits Ignacio Anastasio, an anti-Salii legislator who spurns America's latest offer. "Cosmetic changes" are all the Americans have made so far, he says. "They didn't even change the bra and panties. They just put on lipstick."

The talk goes on from bar to bar, Arirang to Cave Inn, Pirate's Cove to Kosiil Landing to Olbukl, the essence of Palau, beer, conspiracy, and cha-cha music: the Palauan cha-cha, a home-grown artform that goes on forever on crowded dance floors, amid dull, deafening music. It takes years to master. It takes more. To be truly authoritative, you need a beer tumor, you need that stomach in front of you, something you can steer, maneuver, make your statement with, combining substance and importance with a cheerful, hippity-hopping grace.

You can't help feeling you've come close to the heart of the place, watching the cha-cha that goes on forever, politics and business and sex all tangled together, people changing positions on issues the way they shift partners on a dance floor, enough of an alteration to generate gossip but never surprise. And, after a few weeks, I've learned, or relearned, a few island lessons, which I suspect apply elsewhere, as true of the nation I live in as the places I visit. But I think of them as island lessons.

I've learned that everything is connected, that everybody is related, that no change is permanent. I've confirmed that means matters more than ends, and are more fun too, that rumor beats truth, any damn day. I've learned that people matter more than principles, which isn't as bad as it sounds, it all depends on who the people are, which leads to another lesson: some people matter more than others. Palauans matter more than foreigners. That's easy. Some Palauans matter more than other Palauans. That's where things get tricky.

Koror bars shut down at midnight, with whoops of laughter, whispered dealings, pairings off. Cars empty out of the potholed parking lot, radios blaring, some peeling off to an after-hours place across the bridge in Airai, the Crocodile Lounge, others heading to the old Japanese seaplane ramps to sit out and drink, others to boats and beaches and motel rooms. There are taxi drivers who carry obscene snaps of Filipina hookers; you like what you see, they can deliver the woman in half an hour.

Now, in the half-cool hours of the night, sitting outside a closing-down barroom, my old loves come to me. Island girls. All the nights I waited outside other places, just like this, to see if she would or wouldn't come, seeking a yes and more than half willing to accept a no, where maybe was the name of the game. On Saipan, a few weeks ago, I talked to a suntanned regular who takes Japanese out sportfishing. "Going fishing," he ventured, "is like chasing pussy: they're out there, but it's all a question of being in the right place at the right time." I wasn't that smart when I came out in the Peace Corps. I didn't hustle well, didn't press things. Still, the islands were generous then and I got lucky often enough: a giggling sprint across a parking lot and she'd be next to me in the car and then a drive, then some wooden shack, tin roofed—her place or mine—and the sacrament of the mosquito coil and a night of sex that started late and ended while it was still dark, with a furtive drive home before islands eyes were open. And I remember the way old people who were sitting around when we came in—it didn't matter how late, they never slept—the way they looked at me, or through me, nodding and not seeing, as if they knew that this would pass, this season of life, this visiting American.

IT WAS. A Palauan expression for old flames. IT WAS, used as a noun. IT WAS. More casual relationships, one-nighters, generated lighter usages: WANTEDS, U-DRIVES, SPARE PARTS. But there was something fine and solemn in IT WAS. I found my IT WAS on Guam last week. We've kept in touch. It's important to me. This time it's a bar near Agana, a place with free popcorn, Pac-Man, pool table, dartboard, and Al Jolson singing "April Showers" on the jukebox. I loved the look of astonishment when I came through the door, the unabashed staring, the outright inventory old lovers go through. I see the same wide, pleading eyes, upturned button nose, moody off-and-on face, emotions close to the surface, like Salii. A tall, high-caste Palauan—unlike Salii—she carried some of the island's haughtiness with her. "Palauan people respect Peace Corps volunteers," she told me once, "but not very much."

I first saw her in a bar, a long time ago, a Koror bar called the Evergreen, down on the old Japanese road nicknamed Geisha Lane. I'd been stood up by someone else and fell in with a bunch who were drinking there. Palauans were optimists, come Saturday night. Small as the island was, they were always moving along to the next bar, and when the bars closed, it was off to where Japanese seaplane ramps slipped into the sea, where breezes were lively and mosquitoes stayed away. I remember beer and whispers and bits of song. I had to pinch myself, I was there. Overeducated, inexperienced, bad haircut, short-sleeved shirt, white baggy slacks, rubber-soled zoris. And her: tall, thin, high cheekbones, long fingered. She had one American in her past, gone now, and a daughter at home and now she was with me, another American, making the same mistake again, maybe.

I have pictures of us I've never thrown out, others have memories also. Coming through Hawaii, I met a Palau volunteer who remembered us driving around town, my girl and me, in some rented Japanese car with a tin can body and a sewing machine engine. He was hitchhiking, it was raining, we picked him up. Years later, he recalled how happy we were, driving around in the rain. Palauans had a name for *everything,* my girl insisted. Oh yeah, I said, steering into one pothole after another. Koror roads were awful then: when old tires wanted to scare young tires, they threatened to send them to Palau. What's the name of this pothole? I pressed. And this one? Laughing together and riding around town, that's how he remembered us, naming potholes.

So we met again in a bar last week. We talked about my woman, her man, we talked about weight, her Jane Fonda workouts, my jogging. And Palau. Why is it that the handsomest and smartest of the islands was the least able to contain the people who were born there? Why does it bring them down, like Salii, or chase them off, turn them into refugees? That is how I think of my old friend, though she might dispute me. She keeps her distance from the place but she keeps in touch as well. Every now and then she returns to visit her grandmother, chew betelnut, talk, eat fish, tapioca, and taro, and then it's back to Guam. It bothers me that this is where she landed, though I understand the reasons. I pictured her traveling farther. Or staying home. Guam feels like a half measure, a broken journey, a light bulb blown out in a projector halfway through a movie.

▲ ▲ ▲

I pull out of the parking lot and head home. These are the small hours of the night, Salii's favorite time, the air still heavy and moist, but cooler now, the place quieting down, cars mostly off the road, not much stirring but stars and breeze and tide, which comes in glorious, high and blue, washing in through the reefs and which, pulling back, leaves flats of mud and stranded puddles, rusted cars and dirt-crusted tires and all the drowned, heavy things that couldn't float back to sea.

Okay. I'm ready now.

◄ IV ►

In bad weather, sometime on the night of August 9, 1783, the *Antelope,* a packet-ship of the British East India Company ran onto a reef at Ulong, an uninhabited island southwest of Koror. Under the command of Captain James Wilson, the crew moved into small boats. At dawn, they went ashore. During the next two days, the crew salvaged what they could from the disintegrating *Antelope.* On August 12, 1783, the Palauans found them.

Chinese traders and Spanish explorers had probably brushed the islands before, but the wreck of the *Antelope* was Palau's first substantial contact with the world beyond. It went well. It went famously. In a century of casually genocidal exploration, the trading and parlaying between the British and Palauans, between captain and chief, was a model of courtesy and reciprocal benefit. It went so well that when the strangers left Palau, five months later, sailing off in a smaller, new-built vessel, a chief's son, Lee Boo, went with them. He carried a rope along. Whenever he saw something remarkable, he would tie a knot in the rope which would then become a memory aid, a kind of rosary, when he told his story back in Palau.

There was plenty to remember. "The Black Prince" was a celebrity in London. He lived in Captain Wilson's house on the Thames, attended school. He saw St. James Palace, he watched an Italian soar over London in a balloon. Lee Boo impressed everyone he met with his warmth and charm. Then he ran out of rope. Less than half a year after arriving in London, smallpox killed Lee Boo. Still, he merited a tomb, and a street named in his honor, and an epitaph written by a future lord mayor of London:

> Stop, Reader, stop!—Let Nature claim a Tear—
> A prince of Mine, Lee Boo lies buried here . . .

There were books about Lee Boo and plays. Samuel Taylor Coleridge was said to have wept at his grave:

> My soul amid the pensive twilight gloom
> Mourn'd with the breeze, O LEE BOO! o'er
> thy tomb . . .

That was Lee Boo. But my thoughts go to Palau and to the fate of another man, the other half of the transaction that brought Lee Boo to London. Madan Blanchard, a seaman of the *Antelope,* asked to stay behind in Palau. Captain Wilson was reluctant. Inoffensive, illiterate, good tempered, Madan Blanchard was no one special. But with Lee Boo going to England, Blanchard's stay in Palau was readily arranged. The chief of Koror promised a house and two wives. On leaving, Wilson exhorted Blanchard to be Christian, to be English, to maintain his skills, his dress.

What then? While Lee Boo had his short season in London, what became of Blanchard? Some say Blanchard sickened and died, others that he was murdered. Lee Boo's death was noted, his grave was marked, his story written. Blanchard's fate remained obscure. No poems or plays for him, though a century and a half later E. M. Forster mused about him: "The depths of the sea, the darkness of time, the ends of the earth, you have chosen all three."

Forster's melancholy reflection on civilization and escape, light and darkness, isn't the last word on Madan Blanchard, though I wish it were. A few years ago, I found the American captain Amasa Delano's account of a series of voyages to Palau from 1790 to 1793. And his journal carries an account of Blanchard's fate in Palau, which is every bit as ill-starred as Captain Wilson had feared.

"This man was much caressed by the king," Delano says, "and every body was compelled to pay him great respect by the royal order. He became arrogant and licentious, as persons are apt to do, when suddenly raised to unusual power and consequence. The natives told me, that he would take their tarra root, yams, cocoa nuts, canoes, wives, and every thing that he chose; and if they made any complaint, would contrive to have them beaten and disgraced. What little address he had for the purpose of justifying himself with the king was greatly assisted by the fear, which the king entertained, that Blanchard might be able to make the English believe on their return to the islands, if he were offended, that the nation had been insulted through him, and that vengeance ought to be taken. He continued this course of abuse for nearly three years, when he went over with a rupack, who was his favorite, and with six or eight men to a small island, where the people had been injured by him. They intended to spend the night there, as was supposed, in some pursuit of selfishness and vice. In the evening a quarrel arose, and Blanchard and his party were put to death, except two who escaped in their canoe."

That was the fate of Madan Blanchard, the first stayer-on, the first outsider to test his fate in Palau. I wonder how much he learned, before he died. For outsiders, the history of the islands begins with our arrival in them; we call it discovery. But there were forty thousand Palauans living in the islands then. There were two warring capitals, Koror and Melekeok, two rival chiefs, the Ibedul and the Reklai. Three times, while the English stayed, they accompanied the Ibedul on northward raids. They were modest conflicts, battles announced in advance and usually ended after one or two deaths, though the execution of prisoners was grisly, one man beaten to death with his severed arm. I wonder how many battles Blanchard fought after he was left alone. Did his power last—his house, his two wives—only until his guns rusted?

Blanchard was the start of a long line. He set the pattern. Palauans dealt adroitly with what came over the horizon, the whole parade of shipwrecks, traders, missionaries, colonial administrators, tourists. Cheerful and resourceful, confident and predatory, they took what they could use. Delano describes his first reception in Palau. "Our vessel was crowded with natives of both sexes, and the water was covered for forty of fifty yards round with canoes, which they perfectly filled. They came on board with great eagerness, and with as little fear or suspicion as a child would enter a parent's house."

Before long, though, Palau changed, or perhaps its true nature asserted itself. On a later voyage in 1793, Delano found Palau declining. The islanders dealt more cleverly with outsiders than with each other. "They were divided into parties and were frequently at war with each other. They were still friendly to the white people, but had lost the spirit of confidence among themselves, and were the victims of alternate stupidity and the violence of contest."

In a century, Palau's population declined drastically, to as low as four thousand by one estimate. There were limits to cleverness, alas. Still, Palauans adapted to their foreign occupiers, prayed to the Spanish god, planted coconuts for the Germans, moved aside for the Japanese. Under the Americans they attended schools, formed parties, held elections, took government jobs. But there was always another life under the colonial surface, native conflicts that Joseph Conrad called "a play of shadows," which outsiders ignored at their risk. What I suspect happened to Blanchard happened to others, to lawyers, businessmen, volunteers who were car-bombed, burned out of their houses, threatened, and run out of town.

The old Trust Territory of Pacific Islands was a perfect arena for Palauans. They didn't know it at the time. They thought they wanted to be on their own. Do their thing. Palau for the Palauans. A separate Palau, separate Compact of Free Association. Independence, maybe. Independence of all the other districts, that's for sure, especially those belligerent, numerous Trukese. But when that happened in 1980, their world shrank. They lost all the other islands where they could start businesses, take jobs, pour drinks. They lost that porous, comfy headquarters on Saipan, that safety net of a Trust Territory government that offered a home—and a job—away from home.

Palau for the Palauans led to the sort of implosion that might occur if all Jews came to Israel, came and stayed, end of Diaspora. Suddenly, old rivalries took on a new intensity. No Palauan would ever blame another Palauan for ripping off a foreigner. But now they were contending with each other, and Koror sometimes seemed like one of those Western movie towns where enemies faced off on the street. "This town ain't big enough for both of us." In Palau, they were right. It wasn't.

Four foreign occupations had muted Palau's intramural tension, but as the end of the American period neared, you could feel things heating up. This time it wasn't canoes and muskets, it was election campaigns, tests of strengths in which T-shirts, plane tickets, barbecues, beer and rice, and tuition payments were weapons. Elections were grotesque, venal combinations of TV game shows—*Family Feud* say and pot latch ceremonies. Last week, a Palau senator told me it had cost him sixty thousand dollars to capture his seat. Politics was war by other means. But it could still turn bloody. Consider this account of a 1970 election violence, in a Christmas letter to me from Salii.

"Homesteading of land in Koror emerged as one of the hottest issues in Palau," he wrote, "along with war claims and personalities. The first has continued to have repercussions, the most interesting of which so far, being an attempt on Senator Roman Tmetuchl's life. Foxy as he is, he managed to escape unharmed, but two innocent and unintended victims were wounded by gunshot. One of the two was a girl who worked at the former Kirin Bar, now Max's Cafe. I believe you know her. She's half-American, slim . . ."

Koror seemed to fill up with politicians jockeying to get an edge, scowling, self-important whisperers. There were famous shouting matches, fistfights. Palau for the Palauans wasn't a winning goal: it was kickoff time. Which Palauans? Which island, clan, family, individual? The place started going a little crazy. You weren't sure you knew Palau anymore and you began to question whether you ever had.

"The Palauans fooled us," reflects an American who's watched the place awhile. "For years we said they were the Jews of Micronesia. The Chinese. They were dynamic, they were aggressive, they occupied positions of responsibility in the Trust Territory government. We always pointed to them as the model. They were in the forefront of change in political status. We thought they had it together. But they don't."

As self-government neared, Palau's ties to the Trust Territory loosened. Washington and Saipan gave the islanders more and more rope, playing it out by the yard. The Palauans quickly tied it, tangled it, yanked and raveled; one man's lasso was another man's noose. By now the basics of Palau's political future were set: a deal with the United States, money for military rights, all of it under the vague cohabitative rubric of free association. It was pretty much the concept that Salii had announced in 1969, the same concept that the Marshall Islands and Federated States had already adopted.

Cutting a deal with the Americans was just the beginning, though. There's never been a bargain that can't be bettered, if you're willing to wait and love to bargain. And, even if you accept that there's no point in further haggling, there's always the question of personalities: who gets the final cut, the featured billing, the name over the title in the movie poster. Early on it looked like Salii who started it all. Then Roman Tmetuchl captured control of political status negotiations. A free spirit, Tmetuchl had earlier espoused independence and commonwealth, though not at the same time. Now he pressed for free association.

It didn't matter though: merits, timing, outside counsel. Palau resisted closure. A love of extra innings kept the game alive. Then, when it came time to write the Republic's constitution, a love of doubleheaders. Balking at instructions that the constitution mesh with Tmetuchl's Compact of Free Association, Palauans at the Constitutional Convention came up with a document that banned nuclear materials from the island. Now, Washington had a problem. They passed the word along: constitution or compact.

To this day, you get arguments about what that nuclear-free clause meant. Some say it reflected tiny Palau's gallant commitment to a nuclear-free Pacific and a peaceful world. Others say it was a bargaining chip, that's all, something they could use on the Americans. A third explanation is that Salii, or his allies, inserted the nuclear-free clause to thwart Roman Tmetuchl's rush to wrap up status negotiations. Whatever the explanation, the antinuclear constitution fomented a couple years of court cases and bitter elections. First it was adopted, then set aside in favor of a second constitution, sans antinuclear clause, which was then rejected and replaced by the antinuclear original.

In January 1981, Palau became a republic. Granted, it was still also a Trust Territory. The Compact of Free Association hadn't been passed; Congress and the U.N. hadn't signed off on the place. Still, down came the stars and stripes, down came the six-star Trust Territory flag, and up went the flag of Palau, a yellow sun against a field of blue. Up, too, the banners of some sixteen Palauan states, each entitled to its own governor, flag, and automobile license plates. The mouse that roared was also breeding, despite the smallness of the nest. By some measures Palau was the most overgoverned place on earth: gold chains and Gucci loafers the national dress.

When they selected their first president, the Palauans bypassed the mercurial, high-flying Salii, the fast-talking mover shaker Roman Tmetuchl and settled instead on a man of the people, a gentler sort, one of their own. A dark, steady, competent man, Haruo Remeliik had been an assistant district administrator in the old Trust Territory days. Unlike Salii, who'd lived on Saipan for years—frankly, he seemed more comfortable away from Palau—and unlike Tmetuchl, who aimed to turn Palau upside down, Remeliik was a product of things as they were. Tmetuchl spoke like a machine gun; he was quick to fire on dissenters. Salii was an awkward campaigner, too conscious he was an upstart from low-caste Angaur to feel comfortable soliciting votes on Babelthuap. Excellent men in their ways. To deal with Japanese businessmen, you'd want Tmetuchl; to dazzle and impress Americans, there was no one like Salii. But to run Palau's government, it seemed, people wanted someone who could sit in villages for hours, chew betelnut, talk story, not be in such a damned rush, someone who scrupulously observed customary obligations, small gifts and courtesies, a five-dollar bill in the pocket of a departing student, wish him luck, urge him to work hard so he could come home and work for the good of Palau. A fishing man, a sociable chap, whose strengths and faults they were comfortable with. There'd been too many leaders lately, too many battles revolving around the constitution and the compact. Now they wanted someone calm and

you the right to screw up. The Palauans hadn't listened to warnings—
"warnings without solutions," one calls them. They didn't want to hear
what sounded like improvised, stopgap alternatives to IPSECO's
scheme. "Yes, they warned us a little bit," Alfonso Oiterong admits. "But
they didn't give us alternatives. Some secondhand equipment in Arizona. . . . We were really tired of hearing about this secondhand stuff.
I was really mad. Just because we were Trust Territory people we
weren't important."

There was more. There were reports of payoffs, contracts, high times
in London and Paris, all connected to the power plant deal. Palau, it now
appeared, had bought a larger plant than it needed for more money
than it was worth and Haruo Remeliik's vision of power in Koror, lights
up and down the coast of Babelthuap was turning into a nightmare.

Now, though, another ship loomed on the horizon, another source of
rescue, from America, a well-armed, nuclear-powered vessel that had
sought landing in Palau three times before: the Compact of Free Association. The compact provided enough money to pay for all or most of
the power plant. Pass the compact and the power plant problem goes
away.

Now they were linked, IPSECO and compact. The compact was the
solution, advocates claimed. And compact opponents—the ones who
wanted a better deal from the Americans, or no deal at all, or the same
deal under other auspices—cried foul, cried conspiracy, cried trap. It
was all too neat, wasn't it? It smacked of conspiracy. Seduce the young
republic into buying a high-priced power plant and then . . . when the
bill comes due . . . shove the thrice-rejected Compact of Free Association at them. Now, in islands where politics were couched in whispers,
voices were raised in anger, Palauans and Americans, partisans on all
sides, journalists, activists, lawyers lining up to fight. Before long, someone was going to die.

▲ ▲ ▲

Palau is an island of omens, warnings, which may not be heeded but
are remarked upon and remembered later. That time, for instance,
when a group of status negotiators were trapped in a stalled elevator

at Honolulu's Ilikai Hotel. There was a message in that. The time some of those same negotiators were on a plane that crashed at Yap. Another message. That rainstorm that came out of nowhere, just as Secretary of State George Shultz, stepped off the plane in Palau, to be greeted by Salii.

In late June 1985, old women looked up, looked south, and shuddered at what they called a matted sky, full of closely woven clouds, like the funeral mats placed around a fresh grave. Someone high, someone from the south, someone was doomed to die. Late on the night of June 20, Peleliu-born Haruo Remeliik was met outside his home on Koror's topside ridge. Shot four times, the dead president rolled down a slope at the side of his driveway.

No unequivocal acts in a place like Palau. Three men, one of them Roman Tmetuchl's son, were later arrested, convicted, then released on appeal.

The courts solved nothing, just added another level of argument, one painful stratum on top of another. A troubled presidency led to a shady murder, which led to a series of unsatisfying trials. Old issues remained unsettled, new developments only compounded old divisions. Palau bristled with intricate, elegant theories involving drugs, power plant, bribes, spies, hit men. But the murder of Palau's first elected president was unsolved.

I wonder what it feels like, being a Palauan and knowing that the island's first president was murdered, that his killers went free. Does Remeliik's memory trouble people?

In February 1986 I stopped in Palau. My arrival coincided with a ceremony. I drove up to a knoll that overlooks Koror, parked at the side of the road, joined a crowd of pedestrians walking up to the grounds of the Palau Museum, a tiny, gallant operation that preserves the souvenirs of another time, its adzes, grass skirts, tortoise shells, and beads. (A major showpiece, a traditional Palauan *abai,* or meeting house, had been burned to the ground a few years before, at a time of political tension . . . another unsolved crime.) On the lawn, they were unveiling a statue of the murdered Remeliik. His genial, stoic face sat atop a pedestal, which carried a line from one of his speeches, something about unity and pride. The statue gave him a more Japanese face than I remembered: the sculpture came from Japan, though. There were speeches that sweltering morning, and prayers, and at the end of the ceremony a black sedan pulled out onto the driveway and stopped as it came to where I stood. The tinted window rolled down and there behind it sat Palau's second elected president, my old friend Lazarus Salii.

◄ V ►

"Salii was very smart. . . ."

I'm having another one of those conversations, this one over breakfast at the Palau Pacific Resort, at a table well away from a swarm of Japanese tourists. The speaker is John Ngiraked. He was a sometimes ally, sometimes enemy of Salii. High caste, Babelthuap based, Ngiraked served as Salii's foreign affairs minister. Just before Salii died, Ngiraked was reported to be planning his own bid for the presidency, though he denies it. That's not to say he didn't declare after the death, placing somewhere in the middle of the pack, with seven hundred votes or so. There are hundreds of people in Palau who will vote for John Ngiraked as long as he can open his mouth. Ngiraked is an orator, almost legendary for his adroitness in Palauan. I think of him as the Hubert Humphrey of Palau. Or William Jennings Bryan. I, too, like to hear him talk, though it's in English. This morning, he describes Palau's status negotiations as "loitering at a dead end." I like that. He calls the effort to sweeten the compact "tedious and controversial." The whole business, he says, has become an "endless picnic." He should have been a preacher. I ask him to tell me about Salii. His response is dutiful, no particular feeling behind it. Whatever he felt about Salii is over now.

"Very few people in Palau equaled his intelligence," Ngiraked declares. Brown skinned, bearded, turning portly, he might be a Ghanaian reminiscing about Nkrumah. "But every failure of Salii comes from one thing. Salii is very emotional. You rub him on the wrong side, you forget the day. You go home and approach him tomorrow. He's very moody, very emotional, ever since I met him as a young man. You take that away and he's a number one politician."

Salii's presidency started well. He was experienced, shrewd, decisive. He wasn't the kind to dawdle and placate, waiting for a consensus. He didn't cater to his constituents. "If they found a guy sleeping at work three times," one official recalls, "Remeliik would say, 'Can't you transfer him, he's got nine kids, please don't release him.' Salii, he'd say 'Get him out of there.' "

Put aside that Salii was from Angaur. You don't forget it, but you put it aside, for later use if necessary. Forgive, at least for the time being, all those years that he'd been away from Palau, on Saipan. Forgive that, even now, the president seemed more at ease with people he'd known outside of Palau, that he surrounded himself with Palauans who once worked with him on Saipan, the so-called Saipan Mafia. Forgive his impatience with Palau, his itchiness on the campaign trail, his admitted mediocrity as a public speaker, the sense that he always seemed to want to get someplace else, that—as John Ngiraked puts it—"Salii has a very high taste in life, he likes the sound of the jets, he likes the hotels, he never appreciated the home setting. Time spent at home was time lost." Put it all aside and grant that a dose of Salii is what the stagnant, stillborn republic needs. In 1985 Salii seemed like just the man to arrange Palau's two main problems—IPSECO and its unresolved political status. Even Ngiraked felt that way.

"In Palau, we don't settle things with talk, with arguments and counterarguments," he told me. "It's not who has the last word. It's the feelings *after* the last word. In Palau we've had bombings and burnings, the presidential office turned into a pile of charred rubble. We've had police firing into crowds of strikers. We've had radical and outrageous things. We've had our first president assassinated. Now people are exhausted. It's over."

In office, Salii made a likable, confident president. "I just want to say that I intend to get Palau moving forward, to progress, to make it a paradise on earth," he told a reporter. His highest priority was to press for compact approval. His first attempt to break out of the nuclear-free clause was a legal ploy. The compact, it was now agreed, would permit

U.S. nuclear vessels only to "transit" Palau. And, though transit was a vague concept—intentionally so—the implication was that, by forbidding long-term storage, Palau would be nuclear-free, more or less, sort of. The conflict between compact and constitution would be evaded, and the compact wouldn't require a 75 percent passage; a majority would suffice. In February 1986, 72 percent of Palauan voters endorsed the compact. Salii celebrated victory, urged the United States to terminate the trusteeship, came to New York and had me write a United Nations speech, which was basically thanks and so long. But anticompact Palauans took him to court and won: the transit clause didn't work.

Salii now sensed that 75 percent of Palau's voters would never vote for the compact. A majority would, three quarters would not. Thus, a basically popular agreement with the United States was at the mercy of a minority. Salii's solution was to have the island legislature, the O.E.K., reduce to 50 percent the margin required. For once, the legislature obliged. In two votes, the people followed, endorsing the change in procedure, then endorsing the compact itself. Once again, Salii claimed victory. Once again, it started to slip away, compact opponents challenging that the legislature had acted improperly. Now, things got bad fast.

What Salii confronted must have been something like what Woodrow Wilson went through after he came to America from the Paris Peace Conference in 1919. They both had succeeded abroad, been heeded and hailed. They returned with documents that expressed that victory. And then they were ambushed by their own people. Some people didn't like the compact, some didn't like Salii. He could handle Americans all right. The Americans weren't the problem in the end. It was his own people, all the usual suspects, all the usual suspicions, another round of island warfare, but now the level of the game had gone up a notch. The closer Salii came to clinching his deal with the Americans, the more his Palauan enemies resisted him.

I can guess what it felt like, I can feel it in my bones. I can picture him—the hand over his heart, massaging nervously, the furrowed brow, glaring eyes. He'd been dealing with lawyers, congressmen, and diplomats, and now he confronted the same small place, the same scowling faces he'd known since childhood, and the same arguments he'd been hearing forever. I can feel it growing as I trace those last three years, Salii's irritation mounting into anger and finally despair. If he'd had Amata Kabua's rank or Tosiwo Nakayama's stoic calm, he might have endured. If he'd had patience. But patience was exactly what he lacked. It was one of the things I'd liked about him, that restless drive, but now it brought him down.

"He was impatient," says Kuniwo Nakamura, a Salii foe who's now Palau's vice president. "In politics the head and the tongue are important. But you need patience, especially in Palau. Especially if you're from Angaur. He was impressive outside. But when he came back, he was just a guy from Angaur."

A pissed-off guy from Angaur, I guess, a thinker thwarted by what he saw as nonsense, an intellectual brought face to face with intractable opposition. To hell with them! Salii started playing hardball. He hired an adviser, a lawyer whose goal seemed to be turning Palau into Hawaii as promptly and profitably as possible. He went ahead—this the ultimate sign of contempt for those who opposed him—as if the compact had already been approved. Forgot those snipers in the O.E.K.; put aside competitive bidding practices, budgetary procedures, normal schedules. There were telephone contracts, bond issues, power plant management, oil supply, airport deals, commemorative coins, even the renovation of the house he lived and died in, a pile of questionable deals, not criminal, not necessarily illegal, just . . . questionable. Now there were mutterings, not just among Palauans, that Salii had changed, that the idealist was now setting himself up as a businessman. Salii was getting in on the ground floor of a building that might never be built.

"Salii was a man for fast money," John Ngiraked says. "He did not like to earn money slowly." Actually, compared to a dozen other local promoters, men like Roman Tmetuchl, Polycarp Basilius, even Ngiraked himself, Salii's efforts seem paltry. There was a travel agency he sold to the Japanese, an office building in Koror, a tuna fishing venture whose two vessels rot among the Rock Islands, an embarrassing barge, the *Ark,* that he tried turning into a floating dinner restaurant. Salii came late and awkward to the dance of outside investors and local agents. But they knew he was there and maybe that was the point. He'd become like them.

▲ ▲ ▲

That last eighteen months, it was one thing after another, in courts, in newspapers, in Palau and Washington and New York, always something, and I can see Salii, sometimes planning carefully, sometimes improvising, finally succumbing.

His behavior grew erratic, as though he were in a bunker, under siege. Sometimes he'd snap at people. Other times, he'd welcome them, especially outsiders.

Government money was running out. Salii slashed work hours, cut salaries, issued warnings. Early in 1987 he furloughed government workers by the hundreds. In some ways, that was an adroit move, so adroit his opponents charge that he'd manipulated the fiscal crisis in order to force Palau to swallow the compact. The furloughed workers camped outside the O.E.K. That's for sure. There were angry letters, speeches, phone calls. That too is agreed. After that, accounts vary. You can believe that the workers were mainstream Palauans seeking relief from recalcitrant legislators. Or you can believe that they were a private army, a willing cadre of thugs who, with Salii's tacit consent, plunged the Republic into a breakdown of law and order.

"It was a summer of intense agitations," says one American I trust. "People were camped out around the O.E.K. They didn't look friendly but Palauans can look frightening anytime. You saw them and to some it would look like a picnic. To others everyone out there was carrying a concealed weapon, waiting for the enemy to come out. . . ."

In the middle of Palau's angriest summer, Salii pleaded for unity. "We have much to be proud of," he declared on Constitution Day, "because it was Palau that conceived the separation of Micronesia and the elimination of the Trust Territory . . . It was Palau that led the way from under foreign control. Yet there is much Palau needs to be forgiven for . . . We lost a great man, our first president, shamefully. We fight among ourselves, shamefully. We publically expose our differences, shamefully."

It was too late for eloquence, though. Palau's problems went deeper than words. Labor Day weekend made that tragically clear.

▲ ▲ ▲

But no. Pause a moment. Labor Day is a story Roman Bedor is entitled to tell. When we first met twenty years ago, he was a legal aide who was briefly celebrated for a plea he'd entered on behalf of a client whose auto muffler created a racket around Koror. His client couldn't be guilty of driving a car with a defective muffler, he reasoned, because the muffler, imported from California, had been *designed* to make noise and, ergo, was not defective. Anything but. "The Hollywood Muffler Defense," as it came to be known, was in vain, but I remember it, and him, with some affection. He's opposed the Compact of Free Association for almost as long as Salii advocated it. He's traveled to nuclear-free Pacific conferences, church group meetings and such all over the world. One night, watching cable TV in New York, I spotted Roman Bedor, warning viewers of the dark, nuclear future my friend Salii was determined to inflict on Palau. Some cast Bedor as the conscience of Palau. That, he's not. He's a lawyer. He's political. He's a relative of Roman Tmetuchl, named after him. Still, he's a man of courtesy and reason. And he owns what he claims is the fastest damn boat in Palau, which he takes me out in so we can relax and talk about the bloody past.

"That year, 1987, was the loneliest year of my life," he shouts over the roar of the 150 horsepower engines that propel us out into the Rock Islands. Once chunky, Bedor has now gotten huge. In his flowered shorts and shirt he looks like he could join a rap group. But there's a delicacy and refinement about him nonetheless, the way he steers his boat and picks his route. We find ourselves a quiet cove, pull the boat up to a white sand beach and sit in the shade, drinking soft drinks and eating some of those potato chips that snuggle up against each other in a tennis ball–type can. Every now and then another boat comes by, sees that we got there first, and moves off cheerfully. God knows what Palau would be like if Palauans didn't have these small, smaller, smallest islands to retreat to. Bedor spent lots of time out here when things in Koror weren't going well.

"Palau was a strange place to me," he continues, describing what led up to Labor Day 1987. "Your friends wouldn't even talk to you. I was torn and lost. Sometimes I went shopping, just to go into the store to have something to do."

On Labor Day, Palau went mad. In a last effort to save the compact, Salii had gone to the Ibedul, one of Palau's paramount chiefs. The Ibedul was a careful, diffident young man named Yutaka Gibbons. He'd been serving as a U.S. Army cook in Germany when his predecessor died. He was no friend of Salii's. Each man was what the other was not: the low-caste charismatic scholarship kid who'd been voted into power versus the wary, stolid fellow who'd inherited it. Salii induced the Ibedul to prevail on the people whose lawsuits challenged the compact's approval by just 50 percent. The suits were withdrawn for the time being, but the plaintiffs were not likely to be restrained for long. They sought the counsel of their informal adviser, Roman Bedor.

Night. Full moon. A sudden power failure. Police cars and fire trucks scrambled around town. Cars full of furloughed workers careened about, shooting weapons, shouting threats.

"They tried all the tricks in the book to get us to pass the compact," Roman Bedor reflects. "They wined us and dined us. That did not work. If they couldn't convince us, they tried to confuse us. But we opposed them in court and the courts decided we were right. Then they tried violence, intimidation, terrorism."

A bomb exploded outside the home of an anti-compact woman. Shots were fired at the house of an anti-Salii politician, O.E.K. speaker Santos Olikong. Roman Bedor had requested police protection, in vain. Now he sent his kids and wife away, secured his house, sent his father over to his office, a couple hundred feet away, to get a flashlight. A red car pulled into the parking lot. Someone knocked on the office door. His father answered. Shots were fired.

The old man was calm. Bedor Bings walked back from the office to the house. "I've been shot," he said. The people in the red car raced off, still firing. At first, the wound didn't seem bad, a shot in the side. But he died the next day. And—though Salii called at the hospital where the old man lay dying—Bedor blames Salii. "He may not have ordered them to go out and kill us," he concedes. "But he may have ordered them to go out and give us problems."

I don't believe—and Bedor avoids stipulating—that Salii ordered the murder. But it happened on his watch, in his presidency. Either things were under his control, which leads to one appalling conclusion, or they were out of control, which is bad too. Call Bedor Bings' death the work of hotheads and grant, too, that people die for political reasons in the most temperate and orderly of lands, that no nation is immaculately conceived, that Salii's opponents held him to standards that have not been met anywhere: in Japan, in the United States, hell, in Switzerland! Still, it's strange, sitting on a beach right out of a shipwreck cartoon, talking of arson, politics, murder. White beach, garden islands, pigeons flying from peak to peak and the nastiness trails after you or travels with you or maybe it's there, waiting for you to put it in your notebook.

"It should have been me," Roman Bedor says quietly. "At least they would have had the right person."

▲ ▲ ▲

Word got around. In the old days, Palauans settled things among themselves. Now, each faction had found allies in Washington and New York. "Different Palauans were accessing different groups," one American put it. "Salii was talking to people at the Departments of State and the Interior, people he'd negotiated the compact with. The people in the O.E.K.—Joshua Koshiba, Santos Olikong—were talking to people on the House Interior and Insular Affairs Committee. Roman Bedor had ties to Greenpeace. The women plaintiffs against the compact had lined themselves up with the Center for Constitutional Law in New York. The men arrested for Remeliik had brought the American Civil Liberties Union into the picture. A country of fourteen thousand people was totally fragmented. Everybody was talking to someone on the outside. Nobody was talking to each other. The place became quite frantic, quite hysterical. Everybody was using Palauans for their own purposes, and Palauans were using everyone for their own purposes."

Salii tried to patch things up, but when he went to Washington a few months later, testifying on behalf of the compact, he was trailed by opposing Palauans who charged that violence, intimidation, and anarchy had corrupted the whole compact-approval process. And then, Salii's Waterloo. Testifying before a House committee headed by Representative Stephen Solarz, he was confronted with newspaper reports that the now-bankrupt IPSECO firm had made payoffs to Palauan leaders. Salii's name was on the list, for $200,000.

He tried to explain. The payments—he admitted to $100,000—came before he was president when he was serving as an unpaid ambassador for Status Negotiations and Trade Relations. The money, he claimed, was for tourism consultation. The head of IPSECO was interested in starting up an airline. Besides, there were others who'd gotten payments: Carlos Salii for legal work, Hokkons Baules, a pro-Salii senator for boats and vehicles. Even the Ibedul, an early foe of the IPSECO project, received $100,000, he wasn't sure why, and businessman Polycarp Basilius was down for $175,000. Salii wasn't alone. But his reputation was damaged most, far more than, say, the Marshalls' Amata Kabua, who was reported to have gotten $200,000.

The evening of his Washington testimony, Salii retreated to his hotel and, according to a Palauan who accompanied him, drank wine, brooded, drank more wine. He was inconsolable. What had happened that day had been happening for a while, the transformation of a charismatic and idealistic campaigner into an American client. The man whom I'd seen, raising a call for island sovereignty, yesterday's dangerous radical, was now portrayed as America's deal-making darling, the Pentagon's genial host. And now, right in Washington, right where he'd never failed to dazzle—those deep eyes, that sudden grin, that sharp lawyerlike, more than lawyerlike, mind—he'd been brought down.

"Salii was really liked by the Americans," Dirk Ballendorf reflects. "The admiral on Guam liked him and the admiral before him really liked him. In Washington, it was the same way. They liked his looks, his sophistication, his take-charge-and-deliver. Lazarus was impressive. And I think Lazarus was impressed by his ability to impress. Then along came this fly-by-day whiz kid with some outmoded generators they couldn't sell in Africa, built to run on North Sea oil. They dumped them in the Marshalls and Palau. 'We'll build this power plant,' they said. 'You need power.' 'Yes we do,' they answered, 'but we've got no money.' 'We'll get you a loan . . . we'll use the compact money as collateral.' That was the mentality of the Palauans, of Palauan politicians. The Americans will give you anything as long as you're nice. But the Americans said, 'We won't pay your debts.' The Palauans didn't believe it. But the compact fails and they're screwed. And then the IPSECO payments really hurt Salii. He was too cool to be a crook. He had the image of a statesman. Opportunism got the better of him, though. He got involved and he just didn't see the way out. If he'd made a speech—an LBJ speech—he could have saved himself. He was a kind of fallen angel. He saw himself that way. . . ."

▲ ▲ ▲

No point, now, in lingering over Salii's final reverses. Reinstated lawsuits charged—and courts later agreed—that Salii's attempt to knock compact approval margin down to 50 percent was flawed. The Palau legislature, the O.E.K., had acted improperly in authorizing the vote. Though thirteen out of Palau's sixteen states, 73 percent of its voters, endorsed the compact, the vote was eventually nullified. In Washington, compact approval was now linked to the appointment of auditors and prosecutors who would probe Salii's administration. A commission of jurists investigated Palau and found that there'd been a "breakdown in the rule of law" during Salii's rule. Government Accounting Office auditors visited Koror, sifting through one contract after another. Everything was going wrong.

In public, Salii still played the part of the president who was guiding Palau into the American orbit on the best possible terms. He still believed he was right. Intellectually, nothing had changed. No one talked about independence anymore. And, though some erstwhile radicals were casting envious eyes at Saipan's commonwealth status, very few Palauans trusted outright assimilation into the United States. The middle course—free association—was still the way to go. But more and more players had crowded onto the field: politicians and lawyers; borers and barnacles on a ship that was foundering. It had gone on so long, this campaign, that it was hard to say what the issue was anymore. Was it military rights? The nuclear-free clause? Was it political status? Maybe not. Maybe people were the issue. Maybe Salii himself was the issue.

Toward the end he reached out for friendship. It wasn't easy. Palauan politicians don't have friends. They can't afford them. They have allies, cohorts, partners, people to hire, people to cut in, people to take with you on the campaign trail. But friends? I doubt it. That's the ultimate loneliness of islands, where closeness demands caution, partnership is always a deal away from betrayal.

Salii looked beyond Palau for company. He could be brusque when outsiders presumed too much. He could deliver the standard "you're not a Palauan" line as well as anyone. But more than one visitor from the old Trust Territory remembers how he welcomed them to Palau, seized on their presence, met them for early breakfasts, closed the door to his office and had the long, confiding chats that Palau denied him. And then there were the phone calls late at night, to friends he remembered from other times. Friends like me. He always had put on his best face for outsiders. Maybe he wanted to wear it more often.

▲ ▲ ▲

I come now to the day of his death. I find Haruo Willter in the Department of the Interior's Palau office, a remnant outpost of the old Trust Territory government. Haruo Willter is more than willing to talk about that last morning. Again and again, he's run through that last drive he and Salii took, searching for warnings of what was to come. What he said, what Salii replied, tones, moods, gestures, everything.

He described the impasse in Washington, where the House Interior and Insular Affairs Subcommittee was pressing for auditors and prosecutors, sending out the G.A.O. to poke around. More than once, in nightly phone calls, Salii had wondered if the House chairman, a Virgin Islands delegate named Ron de Lugo were not after him. Maybe the compact would stand a better chance if he took himself out of the picture. Willter relayed de Lugo's denial of any vendetta against Salii. Privately, he thought otherwise. "They were after Salii," he said.

From Washington, they turned to Palau and politics. Just one challenger so far, Moses Uludong, a shopworn radical, now pro-commonwealth, not a serious threat. But Roman Tmetuchl, John O. Ngiraked, Ibedul Gibbons, Vice President Thomas Remengesau were all expected to declare. Salii didn't seem worried. He reminded Willter of the campaign kickoff rally the next day. Then he went home to die.

There it ends, the filmstrip Willter has run a dozen times in his head. It stops abruptly, in midstory. As often as he replays it, he can find no reason for Salii to kill himself. Of course he had enemies in Washington. They were known to him. And enemies in Palau. So what? There was nothing new, he insists, nothing new. And that—I think—is precisely the point. Nothing new.

Some people in Palau still think Salii was murdered. Bonifacio Basilius, Salii's longtime aide, notes some confusion about where the gun was found, the direction of the shot. There's the chance that Lazarus, headed to his backyard, heard the front doorbell ring, turned back, admitted his killer. Carlos Salii is another skeptic. "Lazarus was not that kind of man," his brother insists. "There was no pressure on him that would have forced him to do that. The guy was going to be reelected."

Across the old Trust Territory, I've met people like this, old acquaintances from the Congress of Micronesia who think that there must be another explanation. They just can't picture it: the bright, sharp, tough Palauan putting a bullet through his head. The suicide frustrates them. It means that there was something they missed, some large imperfection in their knowledge. If knowledge is power, Salii's death weakens them. So they wonder about murder.

I cannot join them. The islands love conspiracies, and in the past there has been enough outside foulness to keep that passion alive. But when I picture Lazarus I see him alone, ending his life alone, and if this obliges to me to say why he killed himself—or why he killed himself *that day*—I must demur. I don't know. And I am not a Palauan. Not that the Palauans know.

Nothing new. That's the key, I think. The mistake is to think that suicides have single causes, to believe that something awful arrived on Salii's desk a day or two before he died. So people conjure mysterious meetings, secret letters—"flee, all is discovered"—fateful late-night phone calls. Failing that, he must not have killed himself. Not if there was nothing new. Couldn't he have gone on as the president of this not-quite republic? Sure he could have. Might he not have slugged out another presidential campaign? Granted, his reputation wasn't what it once had been, but it was no worse than his accusers'. Possibly, he could have run and won. But there was nothing new. For Salii, that was a death sentence.

What was special about him wasn't his brains—"Salii was smart, but—" and it wasn't his charm, which could come and go. It wasn't his drive. Lots of Palauans are ambitious. Nor was it his restlessness. There's a lot of that going around small islands. It was that he communicated—no, he embodied—the hope that America's accidental presence in the Pacific, the war, the trusteeship and all, would work out decently, would result in something that was splendid, that these small remote undeveloped islands—to describe them is to list their faults— could turn weakness into strength, that they could hold their own with the Americans, not just hold their own, but prevail, select, take the best, leave the rest, remain themselves and yet grow. It seemed like the longest possible shot, but Salii made it worth taking. On his good days, he made it feel like a sure thing.

A wonderful sense of possibility: that's what he had, especially when I first met him. Things seemed to be coming together then. The trusteeship was winding down, the islands stirring and straining. Salii had come back from Hawaii, the best and the brightest of an American-educated generation. And I was around, a Peace Corps volunteer, Salii's word man. A wonderful sense of possibility that deteriorated into opportunity and after that, opportunism. For that is what happened, all across the islands, that is what I've seen, traveling through, from the garbage empire that's a-building in the Marshalls to the garment factories and tourist hotels on Saipan, from the sullen shack settlements of Truk to the vacant green forests of Ponape. The islands could not hold their own, not with America, not with each other, not with themselves. That is what I heard in Amata Kabua's cheerful cynicism, in Tosiwo Nakayama's forlorn credo. That is what I saw in Luke Tman's eyes. That is what I see when I picture Lazarus at the end, his life's adventure turned tired and cynical, the Palau that was his base and strength now turned into a trap from which there was no escaping. Islands turned smaller and smaller, sinking under the weight of dreams they could not sustain. His enemies will say a sense of shame killed him. His friends—and I am one—will call it a sense of honor. No point arguing, honor versus shame. In the end, I believe they are the same.

◄ VI ►

"Salii should have come to me," Polycarp Basilius says. "I'm the only one he relaxed around. With me, there was no pretending. He should have come to me and I'd say, let's go drinking, let's go do something. When he got drunk his eyes would shine, they'd be bright, but he'd act so normal, you don't know he's drunk until you hear him singing. He should have come to me. I didn't realize things were so fucked up. Every time he comes to me, he laughs. I don't pretend he's president. That was his problem."

I find Polycarp Basilius in late afternoon, at the office where he runs a complex of businesses—shipping, construction, insurance, you name it—that have made him a king-maker, gray eminence, mystery man. I sit at his desk while he rummages through papers, signing checks. He's a dark, genial man, roguish and cunning, and it does me good to see him again.

Twenty-two years ago, when Lee Marvin and Toshiro Mifune were in Palau filming *Hell in the Pacific,* Basilius was the boss of the movie's locally hired labor, the boat operators, sand rakers, bamboo cutters. He'd just replaced someone who wasn't high ranking enough. Polycarp was kin to the Reklai, paramount chief of much of Babelthuap. Later, I ran into him on Saipan. He was a perennial in the Congress of Micronesia, though not as flashy as Salii. A watcher and waiter, I thought, a local-interests guy. He got to the U.N. a time or two—I remember sitting with him in a topless place off Times Square—but politics wasn't for him. Business was.

"I'm just like a shark," he likes to say. "If you hold a shark still, it dies. I can't relax. I want to do something." I know some of what the shark's been up to. Only some. He induced Japanese and Korean construction companies to build roads in Babelthuap, persuading them to wait for payment till the compact was passed. He cheerfully acknowledges bringing IPSECO to Palau. Someone would pay for the power plant sooner or later, he reckoned. And if not, so what? What are they going to do? Take back the power plant? Roll up the roads?

Very little happens in Palau, good or bad, that isn't traced to him, and he enjoys his shadowy reputation. On one of my earlier visits, he reproached me. We were sitting at the Cave Inn Bar, drinking. "How come," he asked me, "you're always writing about Salii?"

"The Castle" is Polycarp's place, a huge, nose-thumbing, king-of-the-hill palace high up on the slopes of Arakebesang Island. You can see it from the airport, when you fly in. Hell, you can probably see it from the moon. To get there you take the unmarked turn off the road, sweat out an amazingly bad drive uphill—he keeps the road that way on purpose he says, for protection, just as he drives a variety of cars, mostly junkers, and sleeps in a variety of places. The axle-busting road curls through a forest, passes a rusted-out Japanese tank and ends in back of The Castle. Polycarp, the Ludwig II of Palau, is waiting to give me a tour.

The ground floor is divided between servants' quarters and a gymnasium, with nine thousand dollars' worth of equipment, mostly used by his sons, although Polycarp is himself getting careful about his health. "I got tired of feeling fluffy," he says. "People here drink like it's work. They always finish a case of beer." The top three floors are all marble and Philippine narawood, empty bedrooms, house-size bathrooms, everything lightly furnished. Building places, not living in them, is Polycarp's strength. Repose escapes him.

There are two posters on the living-room wall. One, entitled "Ninety-Nine Bottles of Beer on the Wall," shows that many different brands. The other—"My First Million"—is a picture of a pile of money. I don't know how much Polycarp makes and I don't know how, but I've seen papers that credit him with as much as $5 million in recent years.

I can have a room here whenever I want, Polycarp says. I can come and write and no one will bother me. It's cool and quiet. The birds awaken you in the morning. The swimming pool will be finished next week. Anything I want to eat, just tell the girls, they'll cook it for me. We're sitting outside, savoring the view. And I am tempted. I see Malakal Harbor and the Rock Islands to the south, then the causeways and bridges of Koror, then the K-B Bridge that links Koror and Babelthuap, which was Polycarp's first big deal. There's a problem with the bridge, I hear. It's losing its arch; the main span is settling. Stay tuned for lawsuits. I can see the airport, cut into the red-clay hills of Airai. They're planning a new airport—Polycarp has something to do with that— inducing the Japanese to build and run it. I see the Grace Hotel, a Roman Tmetuchl deal that's limping along, knotted in litigation, and the airport terminal in court too. They can't use the terminal's second floor because of construction defects. The island landscape is littered with lawsuits. I can even see that womb of litigation, the IPSECO plant at Aimelik, halfway up the west coast of Babelthuap. Polycarp says he's offered to buy the place for $44 million. "I don't know where I'll get the money," he admits. "First you start, then you get the money." It's the same answer he gave me when I asked how he got money for this mansion. Well, how much did it cost? I press. A beaming smile, a prac- ticed shrug: "I don't know."

Late-afternoon sun slanting in from the west, flashing on rooftops, burnishing the islands with gold: it's that precious time of day again. The worst of the heat is gone, and right below us I see a woman working in a tapioca patch, a swatch of red clay scratched into hillside terraces that were built centuries ago. Beyond, there are banana trees, leaves stirring some in the breeze that kicks up around this time of day and birds, swiftlets, floating on cushions of humidity that the wind stirs up, like a nurse fluffing the pillows under a patient's sleeping head. Polycarp got to the emergency room while they were still working on Lazarus. He heard the air wheezing in and out of his chest as the doctor pumped up and down. He saw the blood from the head wound. He held his hand. And they weren't even friends.

The tide is coming in now and I can see fast boats racing in from the south, returning from picnics in the Rock Islands, where a few later afternoon showers have come to roost, and a few chunks of rainbow. Polycarp senses my enjoyment of the view.

"It's boring," he says. "I hate it." He gestures toward the shoreline, where the incoming tide is just starting to splash into the mangroves. "I'd like to do something down there."

"You want to pave the mangroves?" I ask. Our conversation is following a familiar pattern. I'm the outsider who enjoys what is. Polycarp is the scheming local.

"Every morning I look at it," he says, "and I think maybe I'll fill it in."

"And put up what? A hotel?"

"A hotel? I'd love it." He sounds gleeful. He loves twitting outsiders who come to Palau and discover paradise. He loves to shock them with his indifference, his enmity to things-as-they-are. He loves to kid. And I've never been able to decide whether he's only kidding. "People come here," he's told me, "and they say it's beautiful. They tell me you have to keep it as it is. I say, 'What for? I was born here. It's not beautiful to me.' I go to San Francisco. I see tall buildings. *That's* beautiful."

Maybe he's just kidding. Sure, he loves to kid. But maybe the man I'm sitting with embodies the final paradox. The greatest threat wasn't the Pentagon, wasn't in Washington or Tokyo. It was here, where the end of colonialism and trusteeship, the grant of free association, self-government, whatever meant the chance to rent, lease, sell off and sell out the gorgeous patrimony that survived two wars, four foreign administrations. And if you criticize, shake your head, even so much as wince, you're a reactionary who places reefs over people, mangroves over mankind, a neocolonialist Nature Boy who flies in, expresses concern, and leaves, conscience intact. Oh, I love these conversations with Polycarp Basilius. They serve me right. I had them coming to me.

"What do your parents think of this house?" I ask him. What I'm suspecting is that he didn't build this castle on a hill for the view it gave him of Palau, so much as the view it gave Palau of him.

"They hate it," he says. "They say, hey, you don't build a house like this in Palau."

"You get too high here," I say, "they try to take you down. One way or the other. Salii, Tmetuchl, it happens to all of them."

"But they don't know how to touch me," he shrugs.

"What do they think of you, though? The people down there."

"I know they despise me."

Dinner is ready: beef, fish and chicken, soft drink for him, beer for me. He'd like to leave Palau for a while, he confesses, just drop every-thing and go . . . where? Not Japan, that's for sure. The minute his arrival gets around, people will come after him, business-entertainers, profes-sional hosts. He hates that. Ditto, Manila. What he longs for, Polycarp says, is anonymity: the opposite of island living, a place without clan or family, business or politics, a place no one knows him. I vapor about New England in the autumn, the pine forests and high deserts of New Mexico. It's hard to tell a Palauan where to go. I guess he'll stay in Palau and cast menacing glances at the beauty that surrounds him. That's what draws me to him. All the way through the islands I've been dividing the people I meet into two basic types: the cut and the torn. The cut are the ones who are willing to cast off from the islands, take off, sell off, make out. They are the leasers of lands, the can't-stop-progress types, the deal makers and agents. The torn are the ones who are pulled in both directions, complicated and compromised. Polycarp talks a cut man's game—cut and run. But he's not running anywhere, not to New Mexico, not to New England, not anyplace but here. He's dangerous all right, more dangerous than he realizes, but he's a torn man after all.

"I'm looking for a market for mangroves," he muses, back to jerking me around. "I know they're good for charcoal. Manhattan exists without mangroves, doesn't it?"

That's right, I nod. No mangroves in Manhattan, east side or west.

"I like big buildings. Nightclubs. I've seen Singapore. I'd like Palau to be like Singapore. Big buildings, industry, commerce."

Now he homes in on the Rock Islands, which he knows I love. In the brightness of morning, they are Earth's perfect beginning. In the full heat of noon, their greens and blues are primary; after them, the whole rest of the world is drained and ashen. At dusk, they are all mellowness and gold, the colors you think of when you picture a day well spent, a life well lived. I love them. I love them on rainy days too, when they are silhouettes of charcoal gray, shark gray, and, at farthest distance, the gray of smoke.

"What a waste," he says. "I keep looking at the limestone and I wonder . . . how do you make cement? If I knew they were good for cement, if I could crush them, I'd have my machines out there tomorrow."

▲ ▲ ▲

We make an odd couple, Polycarp and I. We deserve each other, I'm the guy who remembers the time, the Salii time, when all things were possible. And Polycarp prospers in the era of anything goes. So we spend a lot of time together, my last weeks in Palau. Sometimes I check him in the late morning and I join the gang of people he takes for hot, heavy lunches at the Nikko Hotel. Once, I made the mistake of confessing that I've gotten just a little bored, charting Palau's endless wrangles. "You're bored and it hasn't been three weeks," he rejoinders. "Think how *I* feel."

He has his moods. Sometimes I find him buoyant, kidding. Other days, melancholy overtakes him. He's trying to resurrect the twenty-two-mile Babelthuap road project, which Salii tried and failed to push through. He grouses about problems in dealing with the government, its short work days, listless offices, indifferent people, endless paperwork. He derides Palau's preoccupation with the Compact of Free Association. Might as well declare independence and go on from there, he says, because negotiating with the Americans is like "fishing in a bowl of soup."

One Friday—a payday Friday—when the Palau government passes out checks, I find a ticked-off Polycarp. A newsmagazine has mentioned he got money from IPSECO. He doesn't deny it. What he resents is that the story identifies him as chairman of Palau's Development Bank. "I got the payment as a businessman," he protests.

It's a small island, I grant, wondering whether to mollify or divert him. He's already got one libel suit going against a Honolulu magazine that claimed that there were anonymous letters linking him to the Remeliik assassination. Now this. We've spent a lot of time talking about freedom of the press, *Times vs. Sullivan,* public figure, absence of malice, and my erudition has been about as convincing to him as my word-pictures of New England in the leaf-peeping season. So I decide to broaden the discussion. I wonder aloud what happened to Lazarus—all the talk about money, contracts, deals.

"We do business with Americans, we do it their way," he retorts. "No payments up front. We do business with the Japanese, we know there are advances and commissions. That's the way you do the deal or the deal doesn't get done. And IPSECO was English, so they pay travel, they put us up in hotels, feed us, entertain us. So you're telling me that's wrong? That's why the world is laughing at America. You only look at things your way."

He may be right. What brought Salii down, I guess, was the conflict between doing things the island way and playing by American rules. Both are imperfect systems, and when they overlap in a small place the results can be funny—Evelyn Waugh stuff, Paul Theroux stuff. Or it can shade into something sadder. The longer I'm here, the more I feel the irreconcilability of large places and small; it's hard for me to imagine how I ever convinced myself that things could work out. Do things the American way, do things island style, either way you risk damnation. Try the American way. Try a merit system in civil service or competitive bidding on contracts. Try to find an impartial jury, try to pass a zoning law, collect utility bills, give out a traffic ticket. You run up against families, alliances, customs, everything that makes the island what it is. I used to hope that Salii could find a balance in Palau, in his own divided self. I was wrong. I was wrong twenty years ago, I'm wrong now, I was wrong every day in between. But I was not wrong to hope.

▲ ▲ ▲

One night, Polycarp invites me to a party being given for some off-island businessmen, guys from Air Micronesia and its parent corporations, Continental Airlines and the United Micronesia Development Association. They've got plans for a hotel and golf course up on Melekeok, Polycarp's home territory, and this party is a get-together for grateful folk from Melekeok and nice people from outside who are planning to invest money. Now, one of the visitors gets up. Thanks for a wonderful visit, he says. Thanks for the fishing trip in the beautiful Rock Islands, for your food and hospitality. And—oh yes—one more thing. I've been to lots of places that were beautiful and they got ruined. I hope you don't make that mistake. I want you people to know how fortunate you are. Don't let this place change that way. Keep it unspoiled. You're living on paradise. . . .

I glance over at Polycarp, stare hard at him, hoping he'll turn toward me so I can see his face, which I suspect at this moment is trying to hide a look of utmost pain.

◄ VII ►

On my last night in Palau, I dream of Salii. It's not surprising that he should come to me. I've been turning his life and death over in my mind every day. His presence has been constant. In my dream, I see him in a room, lying in a bed, awake, looking up at me. And somehow I sense that our time together is short, that a clock is ticking somewhere, that the time of his death is an hour and a half away. As I speak to him, my voice breaks, the way it breaks in dreams, when you plead in futile protest, scream in desperation against what can't be changed. I urge him to pull back from the place he's come to. Take time off, go back to Angaur, off to New York. I'll write a speech. "I can get you out of this, man!" And he stays here, in bed—a hospital bed, a prison cell, I can't say—and shakes his head no, no, no. And I realize that I've come too late, that his life is over. And part of my life too.

I guess we failed. What I thought of as a gallant enterprise, bringing out the best in America and Micronesia, has turned tedious and corrupting. And the adroit, thoughtful fellow whom I hoped could confront a superpower on behalf of small islands has erased himself. The game will continue, to be sure, but without him and without me. I'm out of here.

▲ ▲ ▲

I awaken, troubled, to my last morning in Palau, rain filling the parking lot with puddles, linking up into streams that dribble into the mangroves in back of the hotel. I had the car washed yesterday. This morning I'll return it. I feel uneasy, packing as though I'm at a border post somewhere, crossing from one part of my life to another, crossing from time in Palau to time away from Palau, still uncertain what side I belong on, whether my exile is ending or only beginning. Torn.

At the Nikko Hotel, Lazarus's family is waiting for me. Tina flew in from Guam with Yvette, the Air Micronesia stewardess who's based there. Kate came home from Hawaii when her father died; she's been living here but not—I suspect—for much longer. Blanche is down from Saipan, and Scott, the fifteen-year-old son, is in from Hawaii, where he goes to Punahou School. It's a family reunion, I guess, and a homecoming, this brunch at the Nikko Hotel. And more, because it's also Father's Day; a day that passes quietly when I'm in New York, but here I'm surrounded by family.

I can see Lazarus in his kids. Not the trapped, wordless figure in my dream, but the dark man with the appraising eyes, the man with flair, life, confidence. He believed he could go anywhere, confront anybody, one on one, and not lose. Salii was smart, etcetera, etcetera. His kids are too. I sense that the ties that connected Lazarus to Palau—ties that bound and choked him—have loosened in this next generation, that the restlessness that propelled him will carry them even farther off and keep them there longer. And maybe—just maybe—bring them back someday. But that may be wishful. When you get right down to it, living on a small island these days is about the hardest thing in the world. I'm sure of that now.

After brunch, we separate. They return home, I go back to check out of my hotel. Even at modest rates, a month adds up and I reckon that this trip will have exhausted most of my publisher's advance. Dumb, dumb, dumb, Salii would say. Write a book like Sidney Sheldon writes. I drive down to Salii's house. The car I've been driving belongs to the family. I find them all sitting in the kitchen, absorbed in a game of win-lose-draw, a spin-off of a TV game show produced by Bert Convy and Burt Reynolds. Your partner draws a card, starts sketching, and you try to guess the name of the title or topic the drawing suggests. It's a silly game and of course I am sucked right into it. Scott draws a convoy of ships. The topic is TV shows. *"McHale's Navy!"* I shout out. A stick figure with musical notes pouring out from a goody-goody smile. "Marie Osmond!" The game gets heated. Nobody around this table likes to lose. When we win, we rub it in, cheer, high-five; when we lose we shake our heads at the way the other side gets all the easy questions. "Merry Christmas," we sarcastically congratulate. Caught up in this, I glance out to the office where Lazarus died, a quiet, still room with plans for his mortuary monument on the desk. From the back of the house—like a voice out of the past, the same past that has swallowed him—I hear the sound of chanting. Tina Salii's aged, bedridden grandmother spends her last days listening to taped chants, over and over again. "Don't you get tired of those chants?" they ask her. "I *never* get tired of them," she replies.

Damn! What now? It's time to leave for the airport and no one's gotten to twenty-one points. So we pile into a couple cars, cards and scoresheet in hand. I guess I regret that there's no time for an elegiac closure: a head-bowing moment in the office, a thoughtful pause in front of the pictures and crucifix that sit on a table in the hall. I hardly even have a chance for last reflections, as Koror passes in the rain. From the house Salii died in, past the house Remeliik died outside of, we drive on, playing Trivial Pursuit. Who recorded "You've Lost That Lovin' Feelin' "? And you better not say Hall and Oates! We take a table at a corner of the airport-terminal-they-can't-use-the-second-floor-of. Someone draws a book with a swastika on it, an arrow up and an arrow down. *"Rise and Fall of the Third Reich!"* People come over to watch; I sense rumors being born. What are they celebrating? What are those papers going back and forth? The plane lands and before I know it I'm gone. I could have found a better ending, Lazarus. Then again, we could have done worse.

▲ ▲ ▲

Now, heading toward Guam, then Hawaii, I wonder if I have exorcised myself of these islands. Certainly, they are not what they once were to me. So much has changed, and often for the worse. Time hasn't been kind: it's turned promises to deals. My friend is dead, others are dissipated, out of power, retired. The torn men are yielding to the cut.

I thought these islands were stable and stationary, could hold their own and a guest or two besides. But I missed what was happening right in front of me when these islands became something else, something more like ships, loose and drifting, small-feeling places to escape from, not to.

Even as I leave, though, I realize that I cannot quit completely. When you've lived in a place—knowing all along that there were bigger places out there, better ones too—you can't just walk away. Twenty-two years ago, when Lazarus drove me to the Saipan airport at the end of my Peace Corps hitch, I told him the only way I could face leaving the islands was by promising myself that I'd return. And return and return. I feel that way still, though I am less exhilarated by the prospect than before, suspecting that with each return, I risk finding less love in me for the islands, less in them to love. The promise I made to myself has become an obligation. Still, something will make Hawaii—when I get there—seem gross and inauthentic and New York—when I get there— costly and pointless. In Manhattan, on noisy horn-blowing phone-ringing days I will feel the wind blowing down the Tinian airstrips, look down through clear water on Truk's sunken fleet, wait for the rain to kick into the *nth* gear, like Ponape rain. And there will be nights when I'm in bed, eyes wide open, wondering if they're building casinos in the Marianas, opening the garment factory in Yap, wrangling with the compact in Palau.

The newspapers I subscribed to while I was out there pile up alarmingly. There's no time to read them through but I pick out headlines. Three out of six babies born in the Majuro hospital have syphilis. In Kusaic—Kosrae, now—someone dies of AIDS. In Ponape, the Federated States of Micronesia open their new capitol and—though they don't say why—the nation's first president, Tosiwo Nakayama doesn't attend the dedication ceremonies. In Truk, Governor Gideon Doone faces impeachment proceedings; on Guam former Governor Ricardo Bordallo, headed to prison, commits suicide. In Yap, two hundred Sri Lankan women start work in a new garment factory. And Palau schedules its seventh vote on a Compact of Free Association with the United States. The compact fails.

My story ends where it began, back at the college where the news of my old friend's death came to me. But there is no ending, I find. I follow the islands, they follow me. Smoking is forbidden in college buildings these days—say goodbye to the pipe-smoking professor—and I take my morning cigar out to the balcony I've made my roost. Once this was a professor's house, looking out at the brownstone dorms and classrooms that were Kenyon's ancient heart. The place has grown though—grow or die, they said—and the college spreads outward, transforming these old houses into offices, and it grows outward still, pushing suburban-looking streets into placid cornfields and orchards. The country yields, too tired to fight, doomed anyway, if not by Kenyon's minor progress then by Columbus, Ohio, exploding north in a wave of garden apartments, shopping malls, and "clean industry" that is lapping at the edge of this college hill. The world comes at us. Not we at it. My friend's death taught me that. My friend, my answer man, my off-and-on hero. The world comes at us. No man is an island? All right, I can hack it. No island is an island? That is harder to bear.

About the Author

A former correspondent for *The Wall Street Journal,* P. F. KLUGE has written for *Life, Smithsonian, Rolling Stone,* and many other national publications. His novels include *Eddie and the Cruisers* and *MacArthur's Ghost.* He teaches at Kenyon College, and lives in Evanston, Illinois.